D. J. Lawrence,

for Christmas. 1936.

AB

THE CHRISTIAN FAITH
ESSAYS IN EXPLANATION AND DEFENCE

THE CHRISTIAN FAITH

ESSAYS IN EXPLANATION AND DEFENCE

EDITED BY

W. R. MATTHEWS, K.C.V.O., D.D., D.Lit.

DEAN OF ST. PAUL'S

1936

EYRE AND SPOTTISWOODE

LONDON

MADE AND PRINTED IN GREAT BRITAIN FOR
EYRE AND SPOTTISWOODE (PUBLISHERS) LONDON

INTRODUCTION

THE reader who opens this book may be glad to know in advance what he should expect. He will find a series of essays on subjects fundamental in Christian belief by authors who have written with complete independence and have been free to express their own opinions. Thus no one, not even the Editor, is responsible for any views except those which are expounded in his own essay. This volume differs, therefore, in character and purpose from those composite works which from time to time have appeared as manifestos of a school of thought or an ecclesiastical party; it is not the statement of a controversial point of view, nor is it intended as propaganda for any movement. The scholars who have lent their aid to it have many different Church allegiances and no doubt would, on occasion, be found in opposite camps where the internal divisions of Christendom are concerned. They agree in being firmly convinced of the truth of the central affirmations of Christianity, and also in their belief that these affirmations can be presented in a manner which is not in contradiction with the best thought and scholarship of our time.

No complete harmony between the opinions and arguments of the various essays should be looked for, and doubtless a careful reader will discern disagreements. For example, there is a difference of emphasis, and perhaps of substance, between Dr. Dearmer's essay and that of Canon Barry, and again between the estimate of the value of " eschatology " suggested by Dr. Dearmer and Professor Duncan's view. These divergences are the necessary consequence of the scope and method of the book and, it

iii

may be claimed, do not affect the fundamental agreement of the writers. The mention of Dr. Dearmer's name reminds us of the severe loss which the Church, in the widest sense of the word, has sustained by his death, which occurred while this volume was in preparation. His essay on Christianity and Civilization was probably the last writing to come from his prolific pen, and he did not live long enough to revise it. Possibly he would have wished to modify some of his phrases on reconsideration, but there is no reason to suppose that he would have wished to alter any of the opinions and arguments. In these circumstances it seemed best to print it without revision, and it stands as he wrote it with one purely verbal amendment. Those who, like the present writer, were privileged to know him will not soon forget the stimulus and inspiration which they owe to him.

The plan of the book will be readily understood from an account of how it grew in the minds of those responsible for it. We felt sure that there are many intelligent men and women who are perplexed by what they hear and read about the position of Christianity in the intellectual world today. They are told that religion has been " undermined " by modern knowledge, and they can find no easy way of deciding for themselves whether this is true. What they need is a plain statement of the case from persons competent to give it; now this is what we hope we have here provided. The contributors have endeavoured to write in a style comprehensible to the man or woman who is accustomed to read leading articles in *The Times*. This does not mean that no intellectual effort is required on the part of the reader, for no honest writer on these subjects would pretend that he could make his meaning clear to those who want to be instructed without the labour of attention, and indeed the essays in some instances are necessarily too compressed to be light reading. We have eliminated, as far as possible, unusual or technical words, and in the few cases where they are employed it will be found that they are explained in the context.

No doubt a great deal of writing on theological questions seems to the layman to be about subjects which have no practical importance; this is often due to the layman's ignorance rather than to the theologian's incompetence; but we have tried to avoid even the appearance of irrelevance in this book by setting every author a definite question to answer. This volume might almost be regarded as an examination paper answered by experts. The reader will have little difficulty in discovering what question is being answered in each essay, and it is hoped that the questions asked cover the main topics on which the majority of potential readers would desire light. They are at least commonly on people's lips. Why Christianity in preference to all other religions of the world? What is the value of the Bible in the light of criticism? Can an educated man believe in the Christian God? What is the good of worship? What shall we think of Christ? Why do we need redemption? What is the use of the Church? Where is the place of Christianity in modern civilization? All these are questions which may be heard every day. But unfortunately the number of those who will ask intelligent questions is much greater than that of those who will "stay for an answer." It is astonishingly hard to induce some even among the "intellectuals" to listen to an exposition of what Christianity, as understood by modern and instructed believers, really means.

Thus an important part of the aim of each essay has been to explain what Christianity has to say on the chosen topic—elucidation is in fact the main element in defence. Dr. Edwyn Bevan has described one of the most exasperating aspects of contemporary religious controversy in terms which exactly hit the mark. "What strikes one about most contemporary attacks on Christian views of the world is how seldom they come to close quarters with any Christian view as set forth by its best exponents. They almost always attack Christianity as they have found it represented by some poorly educated clergyman in the next street, or some dull traditionalist who taught them at school. . . . By attacking Christianity in its most ignorant exponents, or even grossly caricaturing it after their own fancy, as a preparation for overthrowing it, they are able to arrive at the little chirrup of felt intellectual superiority far more easily than if they had to address themselves to a system of thought set forth by a competent and able contemporary thinker."[1] It has been our aim in this volume to collect brief statements by "competent and able contemporary thinkers."

The note of "crisis" which is sounded so strongly in Canon Barry's essay must find an echo in many minds. It becomes clearer that we are living in a creative moment of history. We see plainly enough in Berdyaev's phrase the "end of our times," but we cannot discern the new phase of human existence which is struggling to be born. The old civilization was partly built on the Christian faith and the Christian world-view; in so far as it had a soul it was a Christian soul. To many detached observers it seems that Christianity has spent its force and has no promise in it of further inspiration. The mind and spirit of the civilization of the future will be nourished from other founts. No one could deny that those who take this view have much evidence on their side, and it is a real possibility that the Church will become a diminishing section of the community living on memories of the past; but there is another possibility—that the Christian faith, cleared of some temporary elements and thought out

[1] E. Bevan, *Christianity*, p. 253.

afresh with sincerity and courage, will once again be the light by which men are guided to a nobler, juster, and more peaceful world.

The essays in this book are all written with the assumption that reason and thought have inalienable rights in the sphere of religion. There is at present a widespread revolt against reason, and it has invaded Christianity. Some distinguished theologians would tell us that we must rely upon some kind of "feeling," or upon a "Revelation" which produces no credentials capable of being examined by the intellect. It would be foolish indeed to ignore the importance, the fundamental importance, of religious experience, and certainly none of the contributors to this volume could be accused of doing so; to discourse about religion in the abstract without any reference to what religion means in human life is one of the most futile ways of wasting time; but the Christian religion, when it became a world-religion, necessarily formulated itself in a series of more or less coherent doctrines, which summed up the spiritual experience in which it consisted. The doctrines are not Christianity, but it cannot propagate itself from one generation to another without them. They are the symbols round which the Christian life is built. To labour, therefore, to explain and commend, and if necessary to revise, the great affirmations of the Faith is always an essential duty of the Church, and one which was never more obviously laid upon us than today. This labour of religious thinking is not the exclusive office of the expert theologian; it is a work in which all Christians have their part—for the mind of the Church is not that of the learned few but the corporate thinking of all believers.

W. R. MATTHEWS.

CONTENTS

CONTENTS

CONTENTS

WHY CHRISTIANITY?

By SYDNEY CAVE, D.D., Principal, New College, London

I

WHY CHRISTIANITY?

A BOOK concerned, as this is, with the affirmation of Christianity has at once to face the question, Why Christianity? Many who reject the special claims of Christianity are ready to admit the importance of religion. We know today how universal has been the influence of religion, and it is impossible even for the most prejudiced to assign its development to an interested "priestcraft." Everywhere and at all times men have sought to put themselves into relation with the power or powers of the unseen. The practical atheism of many in the West today is so incongruous with human needs that the vacuum thus created is beginning to be filled. Even where, as in Russia, religion is officially rejected, there have already arisen myths and symbols round which there gathers a devotion which serves as a temporary substitute for religious faith.

After the war there was, indeed, the attempt to substitute for religion the teachings of the so-called New Psychology. That attempt has already failed. Those who claimed that religion was thus discredited were fond of referring to Freud and Jung, though it would be an excess of charity to suppose that all who quoted the names of these most famous of Continental psychologists had read their writings. Now Jung himself emphasizes how indispensable is religion to mental health. He tells us that of the hundreds of patients who have come to him to be cured of their nervous disorders, of those over thirty-five years of age, "there has not been one whose problem in the last resort was not that of finding a religious outlook upon life," and "none of them has been really healed who did not regain his religious outlook."[1] The irreligion of many in the West is an abnormality, and to it this great psychologist assigns the neurotic restlessness of modern Europe.

But the recognition of the need of religion cannot in these days be regarded as identical with the acceptance of Christianity. It is the merest platitude to say that the earth has become a very small place, and that events in one country are now the concern of all. It is, and ought to be, no longer possible for any to speak as if Christianity were the only religion that claimed men's allegiance.

In this our age resembles that of the Græco-Oriental world in which the Church lived in close contact with pagan religions and had to face the criticism of its competitors. When Christianity became the nominal religion of the Empire it absorbed into itself many pagan cults, but, apart from the " heretic " Nestorians, Christians soon ceased to be in contact with paganism. One non-Christian religion was, indeed, known—Islam. But Islam was known only as men know an enemy whom they hate because they fear.

After the Reformation Roman Catholic missionaries spread far and wide their faith, and the Jesuits, especially, won in China and Japan a great, though transient, success. But Protestant Christians showed for long little interest in the non-Christian world. Protestant missions, as we now know them, derived their impulse from the Pietism of Germany and the Evangelical Revival in England. Their great pioneers were men of their age with a theology more deep than broad, and the conflict between Christianity and non-Christian religions seemed to them and to their supporters a conflict between truth and falsehood, light and darkness.

The intolerance of the early missionaries has often

[1] *Modern Man in Search of a Soul*, 1933, pp. 261 and 264.

been condemned. It ought in fairness to be remembered that they wrote of non-Christian religions as they knew them, not as they may be known today. Thus in India there are many today to whom Hinduism means the mysticism of the *Upanishads*, or devotion to the exalted Krishna of the *Bhagavadgita*. To the early Protestant missionaries, the mysticism of the *Upanishads* was little known, whilst the only Krishna of whom they heard was the lewd Krishna of the late *Puranas*; the *Bhagavadgita*, now familiar to every educated Hindu, was then but little known.[1] The Hinduism they saw was the Hinduism of crass idolatry, a religion which sanctioned the cruelties of widow-burning and infanticide, and which was used to perpetuate the degradation of the outcastes. Or again, to us the religion of the Parsis suggests at once the ethical monotheism of Zoroaster. But the first missionaries to Bombay cannot be blamed for their ignorance of Zoroaster's teaching, for the *Gathas* which contain that teaching were then known to the Parsis only as unintelligible charms. No great founder of a non-Christian religion has for us today so much fascination as Gautama the Buddha. But it ought to be remembered that it is only in comparatively recent years that the Pali books which record his life and teaching have been edited and translated, so that, in consequence, Buddhism, like Zoroastrianism and Hinduism, has undergone a notable transformation. Old customs and beliefs are still powerful, and " Higher " Hinduism and purified Buddhism are more restricted in their influence than many Western students of religion realize. And yet it is clear that it is impossible today to speak of the relation of Christianity

[1] For North India we have the evidence of Ram Mohan Rai; for South India that of Abbé Dubois. They refer hundreds of times to Krishna. Nowhere can I find in their writings any reference to the Krishna of the *Bhagavadgita*.

to non-Christian religions as if it were merely that of truth to falsehood.

An indiscriminate condemnation of non-Christian religions was excusable a century or more ago. It is inexcusable today. And yet that condemnation is still not unknown. When a few years ago the writer of this essay had to broadcast six talks on *The Living Religions of the East,* he anticipated that some Hindu or Muslim student studying in Great Britain would write to say that he had misrepresented his religion. He received no such complaint. What he did receive were indignant letters, signed or anonymous, from those who accused him of treachery to Christianity because he sought to speak of the religions of others with the same care and consideration as he would like others to speak of Christianity.

It is possible to recognize, as the writer to the Hebrews did, that God has spoken in divers times and in divers ways through the prophets and yet to confess that in Christianity He has spoken to men " in the Son." The history of religions shows that God has not left Himself without witness. Non-Christian lands have had their saints and seers. And those of us who have lived in a pagan land and been honoured by the friendship of men who, ignoring the base, have fed their souls on the highest elements of their religious heritage, can never speak as if in Christianity alone can be found men of spiritual insight and nobility. Religious men can understand each other, whatever be their religion, better than they can understand, or be understood by, men to whom the seen is the all.

One extreme leads to another. Clergy and ministers who speak as if there were no other religion in the world than Christianity have little right to complain if some of their hearers conclude that the representatives of Christianity are unfair to those of other faiths, and, in consequence, drift off to movements like Theosophy which assert that all religions teach the same truths. That they do not do.

Mrs. Besant claimed that "the secondary truths" of Theosophy "are the common teachings of all religions living or dead," and among these common teachings she included "the Unity of God, the triplicity of His nature; the descent of Spirit into matter, and hence the hierarchies of intelligences whereof humanity is one"; and "the law of causality—i.e., karma." Such a claim cannot be taken seriously. It is absurd to say that the religions of primitive peoples include her long list of doctrines, whilst among the higher religions, Christianity and Islam both reject the doctrine of karma, and Islam has no doctrine of the "triplicity" of the Divine nature.

The problem of the interrelation of religions cannot then be solved by saying that all teach the same thing. More attractive is the view expressed by that great leader of Neo-Hinduism, Professor Radhakrishnan of Calcutta University. Lecturing at Manchester College, Oxford, he compared the different religions to different colleges of the same University. "It is a matter of indifference what college we are in so long as all of them are steeped in the same atmosphere and train us to reach the same ideal. Of course there will be fanatics with narrow patriotism holding up Balliol as the best or Magdalen as modern, but to the impartial surveyor the different colleges do not seem to be horizontal levels one higher than the other, but only vertical pathways leading to the same summit."[1] We can agree with Professor Radhakrishnan that "there are good Christians and bad Christians even as there are good Hindus and bad Hindus." But his illustration assumes either that differences in religions, like differences of colleges, do not affect the truths we gain, or that, since

[1] *The Hindu View of Life*, pp. 47, 48.

truth lies beyond our reach, it is the quest and the goal that alone is of importance. If at Magdalen $2+2=4$ and at Balliol $2+2=5$, it would be a matter of considerable importance at which college we studied mathematics. Professor Radhakrishnan knows full well that the great religions of the world do not teach the same thing. But God is to him essentially unknown, and so he can be content to have God named by any name.

In his recent book *Counter-Attack from the East* Professor Joad has recommended to the West the philosophy of Dr. Radhakrishnan as the one best suited to enable the West to gain that " spiritual background without which its busy life lacks happiness and direction." This recommendation made by an avowed agnostic is less strange than at first sight it appears, for the Higher Hinduism of which Dr. Radhakrishnan is the distinguished representative is fundamentally agnostic. The final reality cannot be known; hence it matters little to what God men pray if only their worship aid them in their quest for the unseen.

But it is not only professors of philosophy who thus speak. In these days of popular cruises many have seen something of non-Christian lands, and are impressed by the manifest signs of devotion to religion. On a crowded liner going East, the lascars will turn to Mecca each evening, making obeisance and saying their prayers, with an unabashed piety which is in impressive contrast to the apparent irreligion of many of the passengers for whom even the Sunday morning service is too great an interruption to their pleasures. And in Muslim lands there is the unforgettable summons to prayer of the *muezzin* at the mosque, begun and ended with the cry *Allahu Akbar*, Great is Allah. And if the tourist is fortunate enough to go as far as Colombo, he will see there the Buddhist monks and temples, and, if he is wise, go on to Anuradhapura, once the capital of Ceylon, and there see the great *dagaba* which is said to enshrine a relic of the Buddha, and that most ancient of trees, sprung from a branch of that Bo-tree under which Gautama gained enlightenment. He will see, too, the ruins of vast monasteries and nearby a temple before whose serene image of the Buddha worshippers will be meditating and women bringing their offering of flowers. And if he be responsive to atmosphere, he will carry away from his visit the cherished memory of inviolable peace. There it might be well for the tourist to stop. If he go on to the mainland, he will see the vast temples of South India, the temple devoted to Siva at Madura and the Vaishnavite temple at Srirangam near Trichinopoly. Their immensity and wealth speak of the devotion that Hinduism has inspired, but the grotesque images and obscene frescoes are likely to lead the casual traveller to form an estimate of Hinduism far harsher than any that those of us who have known Hindus intimately would hold.

And many, who have not the opportunity of even gaining the hasty glimpse of other religions that a cold season trip affords, have friends who, in the army or in commerce, live in pagan lands, and may hold the common view that coloured peoples are best left to their own religion. That claim sounds tolerant. Often it is an expression of racial pride. It is easy for some of the West to forget that Christianity was in origin a religion of the East, and thus to speak as if its superiority to other religions were due to its being the religion of the "superior" so-called "Aryan race." We have an extreme and fantastic instance of this in the claim made by "German Christians" that they are Christians, but that in their Christianity Jews can have no full share. In our country those who speak as if every people had the religion best suited to it are generally less concerned with racial theories, but the same racial pride is there.

We need to look more carefully at the statement that we ought not to get any people to change its religion. Where the lower forms of religion are at issue, that statement seems an absurdity. We are reminded of a story which the bright wit of Oxford invented at the expense of Dr. Jowett. He is said to have admitted to Balliol a Hindu, a thug, whose caste duty it was to commit murder in honour of the goddess Kali. True to the requirements of his sect, the thug killed a man one day on the staircase leading to his rooms. The Master called him to him and said, " I should be the last to interfere with any man's honest convictions, but in the future do not, please, make a mess on the college stairs." Some time later the thug wished to become a convert to Christianity. The Master sought to dissuade him from this step. " I should be sorry," he said, " for you to abandon your picturesque beliefs, beliefs which moreover have the advantage of providing a convenient means of reducing the surplus population."

Absurd as is that story, it is not more absurd than is the view of those who hold that even the lower phases of religion are good enough for some. And such a view is usually advocated with more haste than thought. All who have to do with primitive peoples owe an immense debt to the researches of anthropologists. Some anthropologists are inclined to regret the curtailment of their field of study through the conversion to Christianity of simple peoples. But even an anthropologist if wrecked on a once savage island would have reason to be grateful if Christian missionaries had been there before him. Hinduism, in making of conquered peoples outcaste communities, showed a better way than that of the extermination which in the past has sometimes followed the invasion of European peoples. But it did not share with these its full religious heritage. Instead, it left them in ignorance and kept them in degradation. Planters who want docile coolies may prefer to have outcaste peoples left at the stage of animism, but no humane man, who understands the fear to which the belief in demons leads, can be content to say that the religion of the outcastes is sufficient and suitable.

This much many would admit. The real problem emerges as we consider the relation of Christianity to the higher religions of the non-Christian world. These all contain much truth. Is not the truth which they contain the truth best adapted to their adherents?

That was the considered and final view of one of the greatest of modern students of religion, Ernst Troeltsch. In an earlier book on *The Absoluteness of Christianity and the History of Religions*[1] he had sought to show that, whereas of the two types of higher religions the legal proclaim God's will but leave men still in subjection to the world, and the redemptive liberate from the seen by merging the world and men into God but in doing so empty God of all positive meaning, Christianity by its proclamation of a personal and living God who unites us to Himself meets the needs expressed by both types of religions, and is thus not only their climax but their converging point. Troeltsch even in this book refused to claim for Christianity that it was "unsurpassable." It can meet the deepest needs of men so far as they are at present known, but we do not know what new needs the future will reveal. It is enough that so far we can nowhere find God so well as in the life-world of the prophets and of Christianity, and of this whole life-world Jesus is at once the source and symbol.

To some of us who read his book it seemed impossible

[1] 1st edit., 1902; 2nd edit., 1912. This book and the discussion to which it led is described in the writer's *Christianity and Some Living Religions of the East*, pp. 27-33.

to stop where Troeltsch did. Unless in some sense or other we assert the finality of Christianity, we may not claim for it universal validity. Unless there be in Christ a revelation of God of such a kind that no new needs of any future age will show us God to be other than He be in Christ—so that in this sense the revelation is " unsurpassable "—then we may not claim that it is a revelation which all must accept. Conceptions of God found in other religions may, in that case, provide elements of the truth which Christianity lacks. And this Troeltsch came to realize. In a lecture written shortly before his death on *Christianity and World Religions*[1] Troeltsch reaffirmed our missionary duty to " heathen races " which " are being morally and spiritually disintegrated by the contact with European civilization." But we have no right to suppose that there will be any " conversion or transformation " from the great cultural religions to Christianity. For us of the West, " the only religion we can endure is Christianity, for Christianity has grown up with us and has become part of our being." But we can only claim "its validity for us. It is God's countenance as revealed to us; it is the way in which, being what we are, we receive and react to the revelation of God." " Other racial groups, living under entirely different cultural conditions, may experience their contact with the Divine Life in quite a different way." Thus all that can be hoped for is " a measure of agreement and of mutual understanding."

With this judgement very many would agree. But it is a judgement which involves not only the restriction of Christian missions to those lacking a high religious heritage, but also a radical reduction in the significance of Christianity.

Our Lord spoke to Jews who had for their most prized possession the noblest of all " Sacred Books of the East,"

[1] Published in *Christian Thought*, 1923.

24

the Old Testament. And yet He did not speak as if, having that, they had enough. He began His work with the proclamation of the Good News of God. The reign of God was at hand; let them repent and believe in the Good News. Unhesitatingly He revised that Jewish Law which to His hearers seemed the perfect expression of God's will. He bade men come to Him to find rest unto their souls, a yoke that was easy and a burden that was light. He spoke of His death as a "ransom," a means of deliverance for the many, and at the Last Supper connected His death with a new covenant of forgiveness. And His message lived, because His disciples were assured that God had raised up the Jesus who had been crucified.

The greatest of all Christian missionaries was a Jew who had been taught to prize his Jewish heritage. Since he was born at Tarsus he must have learnt something of the noble ethical teaching of those Stoic philosophers who were the glory of its University. Yet he felt compelled to preach the Good News of Jesus Christ to the Jews, and regarded himself as debtor not to "barbarians" only but to the "Greeks," to the "wise" as well as to the "foolish." In his time also there were "heathen races" which were "being morally and spiritually disintegrated" by the higher civilization of the Roman Empire. St. Paul did not confine his work to such. Instead, he proclaimed wherever he went that saving act of God in Christ which no wisdom of men—not even the noblest philosophy of his age—could have anticipated.

Later, as Christianity became better known, it was its exclusiveness that caused its offence. The Roman Empire was tolerant of new cults, and had no objection to the worship of alien gods. But Christians claimed for Christ a unique and sole supremacy. It was this "intolerance" of Christianity which led to the persecution of the Christians. Because of this "intolerance" many Christians had to die deaths of utter cruelty and shame. But without this "intolerance" Christianity would have been absorbed into the vast complex of contemporary religion. Thus the Christianity which Troeltsch prized as the only religion we of the West "can endure," would long since have passed away, and Europe would have lacked that religion which, in spite of all perversions and failures, has been, and still is, the hope and conscience of the Western world.

A great historian has pointed out that, in spite of all similarity of aspiration and expression, Christianity differed from all the cults of the Roman Empire in that it knew of a God who forgave the sinner, and had regard for the ordinary man in his guilt and sin.[1] It spoke of a God who seeks the lost until He find it, of a God who needed not to be appeased by bloody sacrifices but who had Himself taken the first step to remove estrangement; who was in Christ reconciling the world unto Himself. The glory of God could now be seen, not in the splendour of vindictive justice, but in the greater splendour of the face of Jesus Christ. To know the Son is to know the Father. In Christ's life and death and resurrection there was given to the world Good News of God which each man, be he Jew or Greek or barbarian, needed to hear and heed. Christianity would cease to be Christian were it only the religion of the West. It is either true or false. If true, it is a religion for the world. That claim to be absolute in its validity which Troeltsch called mere *naïveté* is integral to the very existence of Christianity. Without that claim Christianity would so have departed from its source and content that it would be better called by some other name.

Yet Troeltsch was right when he reminded us that

[1] Karl Holl, *Gesammelte Aufsätze zur Kirchengeschichte*, II., pp. 7-11.

Christianity has always existed in the world as a historical phenomenon, and as such conditioned by time and place. In this he was only saying what St. Paul expressed more concretely when he spoke of the treasure of the Gospel being in an earthen vessel. Its expression depends not only on the idiosyncrasy of its preachers, but on the idiosyncrasies of national characteristics. As Dr. Temple put it, " I am, as I hope, a Christian Englishman, but then I am only an English Christian, and my character is moulded not only by the spirit of Christ, but by the spirit of contemporary England, which are not the same."[1] Thus Hooker, Luther, Calvin were all great Christian teachers, but all had their national characteristics, and they could not be mistaken for other than they were, one English one German, and one French.

Our " unhappy divisions," now happily less acute, have their uses here. That Christianity exists in many forms is a reminder of the incompleteness of its interpretation, and may help to save us from the folly of supposing that in any of its empiric forms Christianity has found a final and so universal expression. We may not speak as if one particular interpretation of Christianity, or its corporate denominational embodiment, were final. Nor may we speak as if the economic individualism of the West were an inevitable accompaniment of the Christianity with which in our country it has been associated.[2] God's saving word to man in Christ remains, but our expression of it is inevitably influenced by our past traditions and present circumstances. It is not our " Christian civilization " that we are

---

[1] *Foundations*, 1914 imp., pp. 335 *f*.
[2] When I went to India in 1908, there were still being sold as Christian Apologetics books which pointed to the prosperity of Great Britain and America and spoke as if the acceptance of Christianity by India would mean the adoption of a competitive industrial system. Such Christian apologies naturally did not speak of the slums and unemployment of the West.

commissioned to proclaim, but that Good News of God in Christ of which the civilization of Christendom is as much a misrepresentation as an expression.

No theology is final, no social embodiment of Christianity is universal. And yet, as Christians, we believe that there has been given to the world in Jesus Christ a Gospel which alone can meet with adequacy the deepest needs of men of every race and clime. Such a belief cannot be " proved." Our judgements are judgements of value, and so an expression of what we chiefly prize. Thus to us, as Christians, personal communion with a personal God seems the highest experience of religion. A Vedantist, because of his acceptance of the doctrine of *karma* and transmigration, is compelled to think of the Divine as impersonal, and of the world of activity as illusion, and thus to seek not communion with God but identity with the attributeless Absolute of being of which nothing can be said but *neti, neti*, " He is not this, He is not that." But although the supreme significance of the Christian message cannot be proved, it yet is capable of confirmation. We do not believe in Christianity on the ground that it meets our human need, but, believing in it, we may expect that in it every human need will have its answer. And that is what we find.[1]

We will take as illustration the three most influential of non-Christian religions, Hinduism, Buddhism, and Islam. In each of these religions there are tendencies and aspirations which are at variance, and which find their unity and answer only in Christianity.

Of these three religions Hinduism is the hardest to describe, for it lacks a historic founder. Essential Hinduism

[1] The writer has dealt at length with Christianity as the answer to the deepest aspirations of Hinduism in his book *Redemption Hindu and Christian*, Oxford, 1919, and more briefly with others also of the great religions in *Christianity and Some Living Religions of the East*, Duckworth, 1929.

finds its first expression in the *Upanishads,* but behind
these ancient repositories of Hindu wisdom lies that long
course of religious development which is reflected in the
Rigveda and the *Brahmanas*. The hymns of the *Rigveda*
speak of a simple and, for the most part, cheerful worship
of the gods who were in general the personification of the
great objects of nature. One god there was comparable in
moral grandeur to the conception of God found in the Old
Testament—Varuna, the god of the encompassing sky.
Every hymn addressed to Varuna contains a prayer of forgiveness. But such hymns are very few, and in the *Rigveda*
the worship of Varuna was already in the background.
The quest of India's thought was not for one holy God,
but for a unitary principle of which the many gods were
the manifestation. In the dreary period reflected by the
Brahmanas that quest was continued, and to the unknown
God many names were given. At length, He, or rather It,
was named Brahman and Atman, and these two names
were identified. First in the *Upanishads* do we find the
explicit statement of that doctrine of *karma* and transmigration which has had decisive influence on all later
Hindu thought. That doctrine makes retribution the in-
exorable law of life, working on from birth to birth. In
consequence, the supreme quest of Indian thought and
piety has been the quest for liberation from the karmic
order. The *Upanishads* speak of many ways by which
that liberation could be sought. Most praised and trusted
was the mystic way. By knowing that the self was one
with the infinite Self, the Atman, which is identical with
Brahman, the final principle of the universe, redemption
could be obtained. It is impossible to read the musings of
these ancient seers without realizing that to some this
mystic sense of identity with the Infinite led to a glad sense
of liberation and of peace. But it was a solution which
took from life in the world all meaning, and made

God and the self alike unknowable, whilst the redemption which it proclaims makes meaningless our moral struggle.

The *Upanishads* are not works of philosophy, and their teaching is confused and self-contradictory. Since the doctrine of *karma* and transmigration had now become the axiom of Indian thought, it became impossible to think of God as active, and yet to regard Him as ultimately real, for, if He willed, He too would fall under the dreaded karmic law. The *Bhagavadgita* sought to evade this hard alternative by speaking of God as one who acted, and yet acted not, for He acted without thought of the reward of action. Today no Hindu book is so much prized in India as this *Song of the Lord*, but this aspect of its teaching has proved unsatisfying. It is in Sankara's massive exposition of the *Vedanta-sutras* that we find the most coherent expression of that philosophy which claims to be *the* Vedanta, the full expression of the philosophy implied in the *Upanishads*. Sankara secured unity by speaking of a higher and a lower knowledge, or, as he sometimes put it, of knowledge and of ignorance. To knowledge there is but one reality, Brahman, the ultimate principle of being. Since our self is one with Him, He, or rather It, can never be known and is Itself unknowing. Redemption consists in knowing the unity of the self with Brahman. Everything except Brahman belongs to the sphere of *maya*, to illusion. The gods, the karmic order, religion and morality, all alike belong to the sphere of unreality. Sankara's teaching is accepted by the large majority of Vedantins. It is significant that Sankara, who taught that the unknowable Brahman alone is real, is acclaimed as the writer of passionate hymns of devotion to the gods whom as a philosopher he held to be unreal.

We have here that conflict between head and heart which Hinduism has never succeeded in reconciling. Brahman alone is real, and yet the worship of the gods continues. There is an instructive story in the Hindi version of the *Ramayana* by Tulsi Das. A man goes to a seer to ask how God is to be worshipped. "The great saint, being himself a philosopher, began a sermon on Brahman, the unbegotten, the indivisible, the immaterial . . . identical with yourself, you and he being as absolutely one as wave and water; so the *Vedas* declare." But the man replied, "The worship of the impersonal laid no hold of my heart."

"The worship of the impersonal laid no hold of my heart"—these words express the inability of the classic Hindu view of the Divine to meet the religious needs of men. The acceptance of the doctrine of *karma* and transmigration has foiled all attempts to think of God as at once active and real. Piety has had to be content with devotion to some Divine figure who yet to thought is ultimately unreal. And these Divine figures are mythic, not historic. We have already seen how greatly prized today is the *Bhagavadgita*. In it Krishna is declared to be a living, loving God, and yet the claims of thought are met by identifying him with the Brahman of the *Upanishads*, so that he whose love has been extolled is described as "known to none," and "indifferent to all born beings," "loving none." The Krishna of the *Bhagavadgita* is the product of an imagination both pure and elevated. Modern Hindus often claim for Hinduism a superiority to Christianity in that Hinduism is not dependent as is Christianity on one historic figure. The history of the Krishna cult is the best answer to this plea. In Christianity imagination has been kept in check by the historic facts of Christ's life and death. In India there has been no such test of fact. The noble Krishna of the *Bhagavadgita* almost vanished from men's memory. It was the Krishna of the late *Puranas*, who was known and prized—a Krishna con-

31

ceived by an imagination puerile and impure. Hindus have worshipped the Divine under many forms, because the Divine has been regarded as the unknown. In Christianity there is no such distinction in character between God and His manifestation in Jesus Christ. God is for us the Father of our Lord Jesus Christ. When we think of God we think of Christ, for the holy love of Christ is the holy love of God, and, since God has revealed Himself to us in time, life in the world has meaning, for now in time we may share in that eternal life which death will not interrupt but consummate. The principle of retribution is recognized, not as a law working on with undeviating rigour, but as a means and not an end, and salvation is regarded not as severing from activity, but as showing itself in service. We are forgiven with a forgiveness which is at the same time an experience of the constraining of that love of Christ which is the love of God, and the content of the Christian ideal of character.

Buddhism, like Hinduism, can be understood only by reference to the doctrine of *karma* and transmigration. By the time of Gautama the Buddha (*c.* 560-480 B.C.) that doctrine had already become an axiom of Indian thought. And Gautama left wife and child and home that he might find a way of deliverance from *karma*. He sought that way by speculation and by asceticism, but failed to win the peace he sought. At length, as he meditated, he realized that there was one link in the chain of existence which could be broken—the link of "thirst," desire. Thus he became the Buddha, the Enlightened One, and felt himself free from any further birth. The early Pali books depict him as refusing to answer the questions which agitated men's minds. He would not say whether the man who has won deliverance would be existent or non-existent after death. The *Nirvana* he had won and preached meant the bliss of emancipation from rebirth. That was enough.

It was useless to ask whether it meant extinction or a life of future bliss. The famous Four Noble Truths express his diagnosis of men's disease and point the way to its cure. These Noble Truths express the fact of suffering; its cause, the " thirst," desire, that leads to rebirth; the cessation of suffering consequent on the complete cessation of this " thirst," the destruction of desire; and the path that leads to the cessation of suffering, the holy eightfold path of right belief, aspiration, speech, conduct, means of liveli-hood, endeavour, memory and meditation.

This way of deliverance was open only to those who could abandon every human tie and join the Order of monks. Serene himself the Buddha brought to others serenity. His was a way of deliverance for the few. The supreme God he ignored or denied, and as one who had reached illumination he was superior to the gods, for they were still enchained in the cycle of *karma* and trans-migration.

How the Buddha thought of himself we do not know. In reading the Pali texts it is difficult to tell whether words assigned to him are his, or whether they represent the later Buddhist teaching. The famous *Sutta of the Great Decease*, which tells the story of the gracious end of his gracious life, speaks of him on the eve of his death bidding his dis-ciples to be a refuge unto themselves; the truths and the rules of the Order would be their teacher, and gives as his last words: " Behold now, brethren, I exhort you, saying, Decay is inherent in all component things. Work out your salvation with diligence." But even this *Sutta* narrates the marvels which accompanied his death, and tells us that he bade his friend treat his remains as men " treat the remains of a king of kings."

Even the Pali texts later speak of him as " the god of gods," and in the " full " Mahayana of the Sanskrit *Lotus of the Good Law* he is for all the purposes of religion the

33   c

supreme God,[1] and with him are associated a vast number of other divine beings on whose help men are bidden to rely.

Early Buddhism lacked the apparatus of a popular religion, and exists commonly in association with other cults. Even in its so-called Hinayana form, it has been associated in Ceylon and Burma with demon-worship. In the " full " Mahayana, it has a polytheism as prolix as that of Hinduism. In the form most active in Japan today the True Pure Land Sect, the historic Buddha recedes into the background. Even monasticism is abandoned, and salvation is sought by simple trust in Amida, the mythic Lord of the Western sky. In this form, Japanese Buddhism has shown extraordinary power of assimilating to its use Christian modes of worship and ways of propaganda.

Of Islam we can speak very briefly, for of these three religions it is the best known to the West. No one can read the *Quran*, and especially its shorter and earlier *Surahs*, without realizing Muhammad's intense zeal for the sole supremacy of Allah. Allah is revealed not in a person but in His messages to Muhammad, from which later the *Quran* was compiled. In the *Quran* Muhammad is not depicted as sinless; to one prophet only no sin is ascribed, but that prophet is not Muhammad but Jesus. When Islam came into close contact with Christianity, incidents were introduced into the *Traditions* designed to make him the worthy rival of the Christians' Lord. In the *Quran* Muhammad is not said to have wrought miracles. Now, in imitation of the Gospel story, miracles were assigned to him, and the infallibility of his character strongly asserted. Later, from the Sufis, the mystics of

[1] Just as in the *Bhagavadgita*, the Krishna, the supreme God of his worshippers, is identified with the attributeless Absolute of the Vedanta, so the full Mahayana holds that ultimately all is " emptiness."

Islam, there came a doctrine of Muhammad's person which owed much to Christianity. To him was assigned the saying, "He that has seen me has seen Allah." He is the Perfect Man, and adored as God's perfect image. Such teaching has in recent times gained fresh influence. It would be a painful task to speak of the defects of the Prophet's character. We would prefer to speak of his greatness. But it is instructive to compare the simple acceptance by early Muslim biographies of his sexual excesses with the elaborate explanation of them made by modern Muslims, anxious to present a picture of Muhammad consonant with modern and Christian ideals. Such are not content to see in Muhammad a great leader of men whose excesses can be explained by the circumstances of his age and place. Instead, he is depicted as a Prince of Peace and the one perfect saint the world has known.

It is significant how great has been the realized or unrealized influence of Christianity, so that those of other religions have been driven to assimilate the objects of their devotion to the character of Jesus. That for the time has blurred the difference between Christianity and non-Christian religions, for it has led to a revaluation of the heritage of the past. The best is now prized and prominent, and this process of purification and transformation has brought new life to religions that seemed moribund.

But from the West has come to the East not only Christianity but also modern industrialism and science. Rightly used, industrial science could do much to rid the East of its extreme poverty. Instead, it is tending to destroy ancient modes of life without providing anything better in their place, and to lead to a hard materialism for which wealth and power seem the only objects worth man's quest. In the East, as in the West, secularism is proving the deadly enemy of all religion.

In that conflict with secularism all religions are now implicated. Natural science has so far had more influence in the East than that other product of the intellectual activity of the West, historical criticism. Christian teachers have learned with whatever difficulty to submit the documents of the Christian faith to the scrutiny of historical criticism, and their meaning and value have thereby become more clear. But the Krishna whom men through Christian influence now idealize is a mythic figure. The Muhammad praised as the perfect saint is not the Muhammad of the *Quran* and the early Arab lives. Sooner or later, the dissolvent effect of criticism will be felt. It will be a tragedy, indeed, if the impact of the West upon the East should merely effect the destruction of its religious heritage. And yet only the true can stand the test of fact.

The examination of other religions does not lead to the conclusion that all religions are equally true or that any non-Christian religion can be a substitute for Christianity. Instead, it shows the unique significance of Christianity not for the West alone but for the world. The realization of that significance should create in us not arrogance but humility. We are the trustees of a Gospel which is all the world's concern, and have kept ill our trust. We proclaim a message which the civilization of the West has hidden and obscured. As we remember the fervent devotion which even ugly idols and unworthy myths have evoked, we may well be ashamed of the coldness of our own zeal. But the lack lies in ourselves, not in Christianity.

The full significance of Christianity will be shown when it is interpreted from the standpoint of the needs of all peoples. Men like Aggrey of Africa, Kagawa of Japan, N. V. Tilak and Sadhu Sundar Singh of India are already an indication of how congenial Christianity can be to men of varying types and races. And there are today in non-Christian lands multitudes of people who, approaching Christianity from the standpoint of their own needs, have found in it what they sought and for whom Christianity is their own religion, and not merely the religion of the West. It is impossible to " prove " that Christianity is of universal validity. But the judgement of faith finds confirmation in fact. The future of Christianity is the future of religion, for the Christian message is of One whom God has given to be the Saviour of the world, and He can meet the needs of men of every race and clime.

THE BIBLE: ITS UNITY, INSPIRATION, AND AUTHORITY

By J. K. MOZLEY, D.D., CANON OF ST. PAUL'S

II

THE BIBLE: ITS UNITY, INSPIRATION, AND AUTHORITY

WITH the possible exception of the Darwinian theory of evolution, the critical view of the Bible (to give it a title well known if not very happily chosen) has involved more change of religious outlook during the last seventy years than any other single fact. That becomes clear in the light of a simple contrast. On the one hand, the Bible was regarded in the pre-critical era as able to give an inerrant and conclusive answer to whatever question might be asked on any subject relevant to the essentials of Christian faith. This inerrancy was, moreover, not confined to such vital subjects: Biblical inerrancy at that point was bound up with an inerrancy that belonged to the Bible in its own right. The Bible could give infallible answers because of its own intrinsic infallibility. Thus the Bible did not belong to the region of uncertainty or doubtfulness in any way whatever. As compared with any other Christian truth, the truth of the authority of the Bible was primary, whereas all other truths were dependent upon it, in so far as appeal had always to be made to the Bible as the source of the knowledge of them and the seal of their validity. The all-important questions were, "Is it in the Bible?" and "What is in the Bible?" The Bible, which could answer all questions that could be asked in relation to essential Christian dogma, so much so, indeed, that it was thought of as settling the primary question as to what is essential dogma, raised no question with regard to itself. Christians who were divided from one another on various points of doctrine and ecclesiastical

order, were at one on the Bible. The fact of sharp differences as to the right use of the Bible (the place of private
judgment), as to the nature of its authority (along with
the authority of tradition and of the Church, or quite
independently of any such thing), even as to the content of
the Bible (only the Hebrew Old Testament or, in addition, the books of the Apocrypha existing in Greek), involved no real dogmatic disunity as to the Bible. It would,
for example, be most misleading to say that the appeal of
Protestants in matters of Christian doctrine was to the
Bible, and that of Roman Catholics to the Church. The
results of the Reformation were of great importance in
connexion with the appeal to the Bible, and questions of
a highly controversial character necessarily arose around
the Bible; but any idea that Roman Catholic theologians
were not much concerned with the Bible because they
did not rest their teaching upon it would be ludicrously
wrong. Of the Bible, if it is the right account of its
nature which is under consideration, and not the way in
which it should be used, the Roman Catholic estimate was
no less exalted, no less an essential piece of Christian
dogmatic, than was the Protestant.

The other term of the contrast reveals at once this great
difference: the Bible, from being simply an answer, has
become a question, so momentous a question that in it all
other questions about Christianity are involved. Instead
of being an unchallenged court of appeal its right to be
more than a witness is put in doubt. The *one* Christian
view of the Bible, carrying with it various consequences
for faith and life, ceases to exist, and for it there is obviously no one single substitute. The post-critical era sees
very different reactions within the Christian tradition,
with some of which we shall soon be concerned. Outside
the Christian tradition the view of the Bible which had
been generally accepted in that area of thought was con-

firmed—that the Bible was one of a number of sacred books, interesting in the light it threw upon human beliefs, but possessing no authority for religious thought or life, a library of great archæological, but of no present and vital, moment.

If the cause of this change, which has introduced a question mark into the Christian attitude to the Bible, be sought, it lies in the results which are supposed to follow from the methods of criticism, largely but not exclusively literary, which have been applied to the Bible. It is, of course, a quite unscientific simplification of the issue when it is supposed that before the rise of the "Higher Criticism" there was no such thing as Biblical criticism. For some of the problems, both in the textual and in the literary sphere, were patent, and some examination of them, with a result following thereon, was unavoidable. Origen in the third century was well acquainted with problems as to the true text of Scripture—that is, as to what the author of a particular book had actually written. Augustine a century and more later knew that an explanation was needed of the close resemblances often to be found in the texts of St. Matthew and of St. Mark. His solution, that Mark was follower and abbreviator of Matthew, is one that a great number of scholars today would find it necessary to reject, but it is a critical solution. No one could think of Colet and Erasmus as other than " critics " in their attitude to Scripture, while Luther, as is well known, did not hesitate to bring to the evaluation of the various books in the Bible the criterion of whether or no he found Christ preached therein. Why then, it may be asked, did the "Higher Criticism" give rise to such an outcry and to such protests, more especially as the "Higher Critics" were not, at least in their own judgment, entering into the dogmatic region and making either affirmations or denials with regard to Biblical inspiration? The answer shows how impossible, in fact, it was to isolate the Bible from the rest of the Christian tradition. According to that tradition the Bible was to be regarded as infallible, whatever, precisely, infallibility might mean in relation to the particular form of literature which was under consideration. Obviously, such a book as Proverbs cannot be infallible in just the same way as such a book as Judges, and neither can be infallible after the manner in which the word may be applied to Revelation. The connecting-link was to be found in the thought of the perfect adequacy of the individual medium, whatever it might be. In every case the mind of the Holy Spirit, who uses, while not suppressing, the mind of the particular writer, finds perfect expression in respect of that which the Spirit desires to teach.

This is not a sheer portent as it would be if, for instance, the level of moral excellence and spiritual truth, of which the Incarnation was the presupposition, were found already present in the Old Testament before the Son of God was incarnate. But (so ran the main tradition) the book is entirely trustworthy in respect of the teaching which it is giving. Therefore the idea that Proverbs could at some point suggest an unworthy ethic or that Judges could give incorrect history, or that Revelation could be in error in its outlook upon the final issues of human life, would have seemed to involve a less than Christian conception of inspiration. That was not the case necessarily with Colet's notion of the " accommodation " to the minds of his readers which Moses employed in writing the account of creation. But it was necessarily the case with the view that Moses had made definite mistakes in his record of creation—and had not known that they were mistakes. The Victorian controversy as to the accuracy of the Genesis record of creation, in which such men as Gladstone, Huxley, and Wace took part, is most instructive in this context. Very few of the combatants on either side would have claimed that it made the smallest difference, from the religious standpoint, as to what was the true order of creation. But Moses, or rather the Bible, gave one order, and some sciences, which could easily, if not quite fairly, be described as " science," indicated another. To many Christian people it appeared that, if this latter view were correct, the Bible would have lost its authority; where it ought to have been right—that is, in a statement of fact, which either is so or is not so—it would have been proved wrong; in which case, at no point could it any longer be assumed to be right.

Clearly, in the whole of this way of thinking, immense weight falls on what is supposed to be the one true Christian way of thinking about the Bible. There is no understanding of the controversy about the Bible apart from reference to the main Christian tradition as to the way in which the Bible shall be valued—which is not the same thing as saying, the way in which the Bible shall be interpreted or used. And that bears notably upon questions of authorship. Some of the Biblical books have definite names of authors attached in the text; the letters of St. Paul are an obvious instance. But some of the books do not, so far as their text goes, involve any claim to authorship. In the Old Testament no such claim is made in respect of the Pentateuch, or of the historical books which follow on the Pentateuch, or of the Wisdom literature, with the exception of Ecclesiastes. The Prophetic books are neither histories nor moral treatises nor devotional meditations, but, taken as a whole, accounts of the coming of the word of the Lord to the particular prophet, as a result of which he uttered a message to king or people; there is a constant interpenetration of book and prophet, but it does not amount to an assertion that the prophet was the author of the book. Someone, but not necessarily

45

the prophet, put together these various utterances. In the New Testament the Gospels lack distinct statement in the text as to who was the author. We come nearest to it in the Fourth Gospel (xix. 35, xxi. 24), but there no name is mentioned. The Epistle to the Hebrews begins with singular abruptness without any indication of the writer's name. It is worth while pointing this out, because part of the real pain and sense of crisis which the progress of the "Higher Criticism" brought was due to the break with tradition in this matter of authorship. It might have seemed as though on the theory of Biblical inspiration, which had long been a theory of Biblical inerrancy, it did not matter at all who wrote the books, except when the book claimed to be the work of a named author. But, in truth, this sense of loss, if a book were not to be assigned to him whose name it had long borne, was a sign that the old theory was much more than a hard-and-fast piece of theological mechanics. After all, no one thought that the documents had fallen from heaven, and it was perfectly natural and intelligible that it should appear to make a difference if "author unknown" was the verdict upon a number of writings to which honoured and beloved names had been attached.

It is the kind of method used, with its literary and historical consequences, which has distinguished the "Higher Criticism" from anything that went before it. The analysis of documents, the discrimination between the sources which the writer or the final editor employed, the attempt to determine by a variety of considerations the probable date of a document, the recognition of special interests, religious and others, which may have influenced the writer in the ordering of his work and in the nature of his emphases—such methods as these have been the tools which scholars have brought to their task. There is nothing in them which is, as such, inconsistent with a rigid doctrine of Biblical inspiration and even of inerrancy; but in fact such methods and the old ideas as to the Bible do not easily live together. With the methods results follow which only a dogma binding upon Christian faith could prevent. If the authority of the Bible is really bound up with the notion of Biblical inerrancy and with the kind of statement about the Bible to which any Christian communion would have been willing to commit itself, it must appear to anyone who is prepared, broadly speaking, to affirm the conclusions to which the critics have come, very difficult to give much substance to faith in the authority of the Bible.

The word "results" is one that should be used with great care. There is not one that has not been challenged from what I may call the conservative side and by men who use the weapons of scholarship. So far as the Old Testament is concerned, arguments drawn from the work of archæologists and Assyriologists are directed against the arguments which have depended mainly on methods of literary analysis in connexion with the books of the Old Testament. But it cannot be said that there is any sign of a withdrawal from the main positions which have been occupied in the course of the development of the "Higher Criticism." And among the positions to which I have referred, one of the most important is the conviction that the relation of the literature of the Old Testament to the time in which the events recorded happened varies immensely. R. H. Malden, the Dean of Wells, has stated the results, in this connexion, of the work of a great number of Old Testament scholars, and I cannot do better than quote his words, taken from his recent book, *The Inspiration of the Bible*. "The Old Testament," he says, "as it stands now is the work of the returned exiles from about the year 500 onwards. That does not mean that none of it is older than that. They collected such older writings as they could take with them or as could be found in what remained of Jerusalem. Some of them they edited very freely. Others were added as time went on. In this way a canon (*i.e.*, a collection of books which was regarded as of indisputable authority) was formed. Its exact limits were not settled finally until after the beginning of the Christian era."

With the New Testament the case stands very differently. There is no such gap between events and record as is a feature, according to the critical view, of the older literature. The traditional view of dates and authorships is much easier to maintain. Nevertheless, it cannot fairly be said that the course of discussion has secured the historic belief that the first and the fourth Gospels, as we have them, are the work of, respectively, the Apostles St. Matthew and St. John. There is also, at least, doubt as to the authorship of those epistles which do not belong to the Pauline collection, while within that collection the two letters to Timothy and the one to Titus, generally known as the Pastorals, raise questions as to their derivation which have caused many New Testament scholars to deny that these letters, anyhow in respect of all their contents, should be ascribed to the Apostle.

All this to which I have drawn attention is the background of what has been called " the modern view of the Bible." In that view there is a definite break with tradition both on the literary and on the historical side. That is true of the attitude which Dr. Gore adopted equally with that which is associated with Dr. Fosdick. The latter would follow the more advanced higher critics to an extent which would never have been true of the former; but so far as the old dogma of Biblical infallibility involved an assertion of complete inerrancy, and, by close though not essential association, of the correctness of those ascriptions of authorship which had been habitual in the Church, the tradition was decisively abandoned by both these teachers. Now, in the face of the results which have been set forward as following upon the investigations and analyses of the documents, more than one attitude can be taken and has been taken. Thus, in the first place, it may be said that the results must be accepted as true; that they are fatal to the Biblical outlook in religion; that the whole idea of revelation must be surrendered as bound up with the supposed supernatural character and infallible testimony of the documents; that the Bible cannot be scientifically henceforth regarded as anything more than a collection of man-made writings about religion; and, finally, that owing to the dependence of Christianity upon the Bible the results of the " Higher Criticism " are a refutation of the claim of Christianity to be the true religion. Secondly, the results may be held to be wrong at every point, where they involve the conclusion that the Bible is in error. This does not in itself mean a rejection of the whole critical procedure nor a re-establishment of the traditional position as to dates and authorships; but in effect it is likely to amount to a thoroughgoing reassertion of that position. Thirdly, there may be a frank acceptance not only of critical methods, but also of a number of what are claimed to be the true results,[1] with the consequential abandonment of the traditional position. But from this there is, so it is argued, no valid decision either that Christianity is not the true religion or that the Bible possesses no authority of a unique character.

It is this acceptance of some of the conclusions which have followed upon the new methods of Biblical study,

[1] It is to be noted that a comprehensive phrase such as " the results of the Higher Criticism " is absurd. There is no fixed table of results. Immense differences show themselves as between particular scholars. Where they are at one is in the denial of Biblical inerrancy: for this, they would say, is shown at one point or another to be untenable.

coupled with a firm assurance that the truth of Christianity is in no way imperilled thereby, to which many Christian teachers find no difficulty in committing themselves. Some of them may take a view of the question of miracle or of the nature of dogma, which, broadly speaking, is a mark of a modernistic Christianity, but numbers of them would not do so. It is quite incorrect to suppose that the theologians and scholars who were specially responsible for making higher critical methods and results familiar within their various Christian communions were, for the most part, men of a radical or modernistic outlook in theology. That was not true of S. R. Driver, or H. E. Ryle, or A. F. Kirkpatrick, or W. Sanday—at least, for the greater part of his life—in England; or of A. B. Davidson, or G. A. Smith, or James Moffatt in Scotland. Robertson Smith himself was, in the stage of the great controversy which rose around his name, no theological revolutionary. Certainly the great majority of those who have been in the forefront of the investigations and discussions concerning the Bible, ever since these began to raise problems which were the concern of the ordinary Christian and not simply of the expert scholar, have been able without any sense of strain to combine an attitude to the Bible, which in its denial of Biblical inerrancy would have deeply shocked their predecessors in learned research, with an attitude to Christian theology in no striking or essential manner different from that which the same predecessors adopted.

But, while this fact may point to the practicability of the famous advice, whether actually offered or symbolic of a point of view, which Westcott is said to have given to the Harrow boys, that they should combine a firm faith in criticism with a firm faith in God, it does not mean that there is no outstanding question to be answered as to the true theological estimate of the Bible. On the contrary, no statement of Christian truth can be adequate which does not find a place for a description of, first, the relation between Christianity and the Bible, and, secondly, of the nature of Biblical inspiration and authority.

It is likely that a large number of Christians, if asked about the foundation of Christianity, would reply that the foundation was the Bible. At no point in Christian history would that answer have been true. The Bible is not the foundation but the expositor and witness. The Bible to Christianity is not as the Quran is to Islam or as the Book of Joseph Smith is to the Church of the Latter-Day Saints. Christianity is not the religion of a book in any sense that could imply that the book is itelf the revelation. The Bible is not the revelation any more than it is the Gospel or the foundation. It is the record of that revelation through which God made Himself known to man in the reality of His righteousness and holiness and judgment and mercy, enabling men to whom He spoke to find the true meaning of human history in the light of His purposes. This revelation reached its final stage in the revelation of Christ the Son of God; but when it is thus described one must beware of thinking of a process whose end could have been anticipated from the first. In that sense the Incarnation is not a climax, and the Barthian protest against any view of it which suggests that it is the highest point attained in an evolutionary scheme is well justified. It is of the nature of the Bible to present the revelation which God has made, whereof the supreme fact is certainly the fact of Christ, in a form which neither owes itself to any general philosophical notion of the relation in which God stands to man nor can be treated as an illustration of any such relation. The attempt has indeed been made, but the Bible is too intractable as material for it ever to be made successfully.

But when the Bible is defined as the " record " of a revelation it is important that the word " record " should not be misunderstood. The Bible is not a record as the term is used when we speak of a gramophone record. That record is good, when it is good, simply as a re-embodiment of the original. All we ask for is that the original should be reproduced with as much accuracy as possible. The gramophone is not there to be an interpreter. But the Bible is constantly exercising the function of an interpreter: its purpose is to enable, and indeed to challenge, men to look on life in a particular way, and that is the way of the Bible's own interpretation. This office of an interpreter runs through the Bible: it is one of the reasons why we rightly do not substitute some such phrase as " the Biblical writers" for "the Bible." The former phrase makes it hard not to think of the Bible as the volume which is composed of a number of individual contributions. And while that is, from one angle, a quite true account of the Bible, from another, and that an angle which allows of the nature of the Bible being apprehended, it is profoundly unsatisfactory. For it obscures both the unity of the Bible and the fact that unity is one which is a divine endowment. It is the unity which results from the fact that the Bible is the word of God. And of that more must now be said.

The Bible contains a great many words of men about God. They come in very different contexts and are of strikingly varied content. When taken in detail through the particular books they produce almost as great an effect by their unlikenesses as by their resemblances. Leviticus and Amos, Joshua and St. Luke, Ecclesiastes and St. John suggest contrasts rather than comparisons. One may wonder, if one can escape from the idea of the one Bible with which one was brought up, how books so different in quality and outlook, which must reflect authors of vastly dissimilar experiences and thoughts about life, came to be united in a single volume. And so long as one is convinced that the Bible is no more than a library of men's thoughts and words and judgments, that is a natural and proper conclusion at which to arrive. Well might one write over it the first four words of the famous Greek hexameter:

Πολλαὶ μὲν θνητοῖς γλῶσσαι : mortals, indeed, have many voices.

Yet to regard this as the conclusion of the whole matter, to end on the note not of unity but of variety, would be to lose the key to the Bible. The Bible is not a jumble of incoherent elements, a collection of literary and religious *disjecta membra*. Obviously there is much outside the Bible showing a religious elevation, which, if that were the criterion for inclusion, would give a title for a place. Sometimes enquiry is made as to why in our Church services there should not be readings of other books besides those which are included within the Bible. Passages in the *Phædo of Plato* would come easily to mind. The suggestion may in itself be quite harmless; but it would cease to be so the moment the idea was started that because of the amount of religious edification to be found in writings that are not part of the Bible, the distinction between the Biblical and the non-Biblical is a merely conventional piece of piety, void of real value. Such a verdict would be far removed from the truth. It would ignore the distinguishing note of the Bible that in it God is the Subject of revelation in word and action, in such a way that the characteristic movement of the Bible is not from man to God but from God to man. That movement is set forth in different ways in the books of the Bible: in Job and Ecclesiastes, for instance, it is set forth negatively; the problem is as to the apparent lack of movement from God to man, when it is just that movement which is most urgently needed. But it is here that the unity of the Bible is to be discerned. We must, if we are to understand what the Bible would tell us about itself, complete the above-mentioned hexameter:

μία δ' ἀθανάτοισι : but immortals only one.

People who want to try to escape from the difficulties which are presented to them in the Bible sometimes think that they can cut themselves free of them by saying not that the Bible is the Word of God but that it contains the Word of God. Neither from the apologetic nor from the dogmatic side is this distinction of any value. Not from the side of apologetics, since the sceptic or doubter can quite fairly point out that even if there could be any agreement as to what sections of the Biblical content may be rightly described as the Word of God, the unity of the Bible would have been sacrificed, and the question as to its origin could be answered only by the utterly feeble reply that the Bible was partly from heaven and partly from men. Nor does this well-intentioned formula fare any better if it is examined from the dogmatic side. Whatever place belongs to the Bible in Christian theology belongs to it as a whole. If in any sense at all the thought of the Word of God may be brought in in connexion with the Bible it will be fatal to the maintenance of that wholeness, if in the course of the development of the dogmatic scheme it were necessary to enquire whether allowance were being made for the possibility that at such and such a point reference to the Bible might be illegitimate, since in that particular context there was no certainty that the Bible was containing the Word of God.

The Bible is a unity through its testimony to the revelation of God which it both records and interprets. That this testimony is itself God's Word, whereby what God has done is made clear by God's witness to its character and its relation to Himself, is certainly not something that can be proved. We cannot ask for the Bible more than

54

we can ask for that revelation of God which is the theme of the Bible. The truth of that revelation cannot be proved in such a manner that henceforth faith becomes otiose since all is knowledge. That the meaning of the life and death of Jesus is that " God was in Christ reconciling the world to himself " is an assurance of faith, and remains so, when all that can quite rightly be said in favour of its truth from an examination of the relevant facts has been said. So it is with the Bible; its nature as the word of God, as the book in which the deeper tone of the one divine voice is heard through the many changing tones of the human voices, is not open to demonstration; but, in the Christian view of the Bible, it is finally true that it is the Word of God, just as it is finally true about Christ that He is the Word of God. In neither case would the substitution of the expression " contains " or some similar term be an adequate embodiment of Christian faith. On this subject of the unity of the Bible and of the relation of itself as witness to that of which it is the witness there is a passage in Dr. Marcus Dods' book *The Bible, its Origin and Nature* to which I would draw attention, not only for its own sake, but because the book, though now more than thirty years old, is adorned by that wisdom which is characteristic only of those who through patient and humble learning have become masters with a right to speak on some great subject. The passage comes at the end of the first chapter on " The Bible and Other Sacred Books." " The key to the secret of the unifying element," he says, "is . . . the essential characteristic, the very meaning and substance of the books. Prior to Scripture, and underlying it, is God's revelation of Himself in and to Israel. The Bible gives us an inspired utterance, record, and interpretation of this revelation. It is primarily the record of God's manifestation of Himself in history as winning and ruling men. Its unity is to be found in the unity of God's purpose. Or it may be said that its unity is to be found in its centre, Jesus Christ. In Him is the supreme manifestation of God, and in Him the Bible finds its unity."

The affirmation of the unity of the Bible necessarily raises the question of the exhibition of that unity in the relations of the Old and the New Testaments. That in any particular way the Old Testament writers had the events of the New Testament and the nature of the Gospel before them would not easily be held except by those who started with a fixed view of the character of prophecy, especially in its predictive aspect. Yet, without doubt the belief that the Old Testament is fulfilled in Christ and that in Christ God has said "Yea" and "Amen" (2 Cor. i. 20) to His promises has been a vital element in Christian faith from the first, and is integral to the Christian philosophy of history. Frederick Robertson put his conviction in a direct and simple way when he said that "Scripture is full of Christ." This may be expanded in the thought that whereas the dominant religious idea of the Old Testament in respect of the relations between God and Israel is the idea of salvation, which remains constant through all the variations of the idea—e.g., physical or spiritual, present or future—the dominant religious idea of the New Testament in the same context, but with an inevitable widening of the concept of Israel, is the coming of Jesus, the Christ and Son of God, who is the bearer of salvation. The Christian contention is that the Old Testament converges upon the coming of the Messianic salvation and the Bearer thereof,[1]

[1] Dr. Wheeler Robinson thus states the relation in his book, *The Religious Ideas of the Old Testament*, " Israel, holding fast to its belief in the presence of Yahweh with His people, projected the same faith into the future, and created the Messianic hope, the light of Israel's dark days, the inspiration of its later history, its immediate point of contact with its greater successor."

but that the nature of that advent, and the manner in which that salvation would be revealed as something which had actually been brought to pass, could not be known with any exactness until it had come to pass. Two passages from the Old Testament relevant to this relation of salvation hoped for to salvation in which hope becomes assurance may be briefly discussed. The first is the account of the intended offering of Isaac by Abraham in Genesis xxii. As it stands it has nothing to do with any general principle of atonement or salvation. Dr. Peake commenting on the story in his own *Commentary on the Bible* will not allow that the writer wished to suggest that human sacrifice was repugnant to God; "the point is that Abraham accepts, with unfaltering obedience, the demand for the costliest offering, recognizing God's right to make it." Why, it may be asked, should this story, which must certainly present difficulties to some minds, be read on Good Friday in church, and, therefore, clearly be regarded as providing a type of Calvary? Not by any detailed application of the narrative; we do not think that Abraham to Isaac is as the Father to Christ; and the substitution of the ram in the final issue for Isaac brings in the notion of the worth of animal sacrifice which it was part of the effect of Calvary to destroy (see the Epistle to the Hebrews). But the point where the story of Mount Moriah and the story of Mount Calvary do come together is in the absolute readiness of will which the narrative suggests as the attitude of Abraham and Isaac, whereof Christ's perfect obedience to the will of the Father is the antitype. So in Hebrews, in the great tenth chapter of comparison between the sacrifices of the Law and the sacrifice of Christ, the writer puts into the forefront of his exposition of the work of Christ the word of the fortieth psalm, "Lo, I come to do thy will, O God." The atonement of Christ is to be seen in the obedience of Christ, even to the death of the Cross. The second passage is the fifty-third of Isaiah, the chapter of the Suffering Servant. That is directly concerned with the problem of salvation and atonement; as to the immediate significance of it there is no agreement among scholars. But what the Christian Church saw at a very early date, and what there is good reason for believing to have been in the mind of our Lord Himself, was that a fulfilment, or, perhaps it would be better to say, an embodiment of the figure there delineated, in such a way that the picture came to life, was the one way by which salvation could be brought. The "Messianic" salvation must come through the redemptive and vicarious work of One who could *be* the Suffering Servant.

In the quotation from Marcus Dods' book occurs the phrase "inspired utterance"; and from the notion of the unity of the Bible we pass to a consideration of the inspiration of the Bible. Clearly the two notions must be in close relation, for if the unity of the Bible cannot be truly understood apart from the affirmation that it is the Word of God, then that unity represents a divine activity present throughout the Bible, of which the term "inspiration" is an adequate symbol. That the Bible is inspired is, indeed, a primary Christian conviction; it is from this that certain consequences have been drawn, such as infallibility and inerrancy, which retain their place in Christian thought because they are held to be bound up with the affirmation of inspiration. But the deductions can be rejected without any ambiguity as to the fact of inspiration. Neither "fundamentalists" nor sceptics are to be followed at this point. Nor, on the other hand, is there any gain in substituting the conception of inspired men for that of the inspired book. Our concern with the Bible is with its content, not with its authors. That is the truth in Luther's characteristic outburst that any teaching which fails to proclaim Christ is not apostolic though St. Peter or St. Paul were its author, while whatever preaches Christ is apostolic, though its author were Judas or Annas or Pilate or Herod. Moreover, the writers of the Biblical books differ in all sorts of ways, while it is in that which belongs to or even constitutes the essence of each particular book that they are at one. Thus the Bible is inspired because it is the adequate and indispensable vehicle of revelation; but inspiration does not amount to dictation by God.

It appears to be supposed that the *problem* of inspiration, in so far as with it is involved the question of inerrancy, is one that is really confined to the Old Testament, and much is made of the re-establishment of Old Testament history through the labours of archæologists. But if anyone wished to see how difficult it is to equate inspiration with inerrancy he could hardly do better than secure a synopsis of the first three Gospels and study the text of the three accounts of our Lord's ministry. He need assume nothing as to the inter-relations of the synoptic accounts; but if he goes through the material he will find numbers of small differences which in themselves are usually of no importance and certainly do not impair in any way the trustworthiness of the narratives, while yet they make any doctrine of verbal inerrancy at least exceedingly difficult. Let anyone consider the problem which arises in the Marcan narrative as compared with that of St. Matthew and St. Luke as to the relation of the cock-crowing to Peter's denial of our Lord. The inspiration of the Bible cannot be demonstrated as a result that follows upon an examination of a particular set of facts. If that were the truth of the matter it would be possible for anyone to recognize and affirm the inspiration of the Bible, which would mean that it had ceased to be a distinctive Christian belief. Any such attitude to inspiration would not only conflict with the

Roman Catholic acceptance of the Scriptures as the inspired Word of God on the authority of the Church, but would be inconsistent with the Reformers' doctrine that the Scripture is verified as the Word of God by the internal witness of the Holy Spirit within the soul of the believer.

Inspiration does not involve inerrancy. On the other hand, inspiration, if interpreted as an eye for spiritual reality, which it is assumed that the Biblical writers had in a high degree, leaves out the one thing which really matters—namely, the objective fact of inspiration in its relation to the objective fact of revelation. An exact definition of inspiration that will not say either too much or too little is not easily found. In his essay, " The Holy Spirit and Inspiration," in *Lux Mundi*, which, both for its own importance and because of the results which flowed from it, is one of the documents to which reference should always be made in any discussion of modern developments on the Biblical question, Dr. Gore wrote, " The Church is not tied then by any existing definitions. We cannot make any exact claim upon any one's belief in regard to inspiration, simply because we have no authoritative definition to bring to bear upon him." This would, of course, not be accepted by a Roman Catholic theologian as a valid statement; yet even the definition of the Vatican Council of 1870, that the Church holds certain books as sacred and canonical, "quod Spiritu Sancto inspirante conscripti Deum habent auctorem " ("because written through the inspiration of the Holy Spirit they have God as their author "), is of the nature of a statement of a fact rather than of a theory.[1]

[1] There is a statement—it can hardly be called a definition—of inspiration in *Inspiration and the Old Testament*, by T. H. Sprott, afterwards Bishop of Wellington, N.Z., which seems to me to come near to the heart of the matter. " This inspiration, then, is strictly correlative to revelation, as interpretation to the thing interpreted. It does not immediately communicate knowledge, much

The doctrine of inspiration is the assertion of the divine character of the Bible: the adjective "God-breathed" comes from 2 Tim. iii. 16. The problem of inspiration arises out of the recognition that along with the divine there is the human. It is the sense of the necessity for the human factor being recognized as really contributing to the formation of the books, and as not being simply an instrument which can be used in this way or that by the force that employs it, which has been specially influential in protest against the deductions which were drawn from the fact of inspiration. Coleridge objecting to the idea that the Bible was dictated by an Infallible Intelligence; Westcott contending that inspiration acts not on man but through man, in such a way that the personality of the teacher is preserved; P. T. Forsyth continually distinguishing between the Bible and the Gospel in the Bible, and expressing himself in such terms as "There was a Bible within the Bible which the dissector's knife could not reach. Criticism of the Book might be free, so far as faith in the Gospel was concerned"; Barth and Brunner rejecting with the utmost clearness the old doctrine, as it had been held in the theology of Protestant scholasticism, and declaring, as a passage of Brunner's, which would be accepted by Barth, puts it, that "Biblical criticism is nothing but the act by which we recognize that the crib is not Christ,[1] that the ground is not the gold, that God's Word is only indirectly identical with the Bible's word, although we have the one only through the other"; all

---

less knowledge upon all conceivable subjects. It is concerned with one factor in experience—the Divine." And, further on, "This limitation of interest to the Divine is, as we have seen, the Bible's own account of itself. It is meant to 'make us wise' indeed, but 'wise unto salvation'" (pp. 59-61). The whole book is one of value for the study of the Bible.

[1] A reference to Luther's saying that "The Scriptures are the crib wherein Christ is laid."

these and other attitudes to the Bible are ways of asserting that in the Bible both the divine and the human are present, that they do not exclude one another and that the fullest recognition of the human ought not to lead to any hesitation in the affirmation of the divine. And the Christian verdict as to the outcome of that process of criticism which assumes that the Bible on its human side is open to all the research which is applied in connexion with ancient documents and ancient history could hardly be better expressed than in the words of Benjamin Jowett in his contribution to *Essays and Reviews*, "When interpreted like any other book, by the same rules of evidence and the same canons of criticism, the Bible will still remain unlike any other book."

So we come finally to the nature of the authority of the Bible. It is an authority which has application only to Christians, and in the case of Christians its authority will depend, in respect of its character and extent, on the doctrine about the Bible which is accepted.

That authority may be understood along either of two lines; but both lines are necessary for its full appreciation. In the first place the authority of the Bible is the authority of the Word of God—that is, of the Gospel of which God is both Subject and Object: the Bible exists to maintain and express the Gospel in one way, as the Church in another. This Gospel is itself both supreme authority and supreme gift; and the accepting of it as gift and yielding to it as authority is in essence a single act. The idea of " having this man to reign over us " can be the more distasteful because of the association of the blessings which man most needs with the confession that this man and no other has an absolute claim upon man's loyalty and service. Thus the authority of the Bible is related not to its form but to its substance—that is, to Christ, whom the Bible presents as the King in that very act which made

Him the Redeemer. The writing of the New Testament added nothing to the authority over the Christian which already existed in the fact of Christ and the Gospel, while the authority of the Old Testament was of continued indispensable meaning to the Christian because the Old Testament had its summing up in Christ. So much for the one line. The other derives from the thought not of the substance of the Bible but of Him who is the source of that inspiration whereby the Biblical writers became in their different ways witnesses to and exponents of the Gospel. The phrase in the Nicene Creed as to the Holy Spirit, that He " spake by the prophets " may be extended to cover the relation of the Spirit to the Biblical writings. And here there may be a place for the distinction which some desire to draw between the Scriptures and the writers themselves. Forsyth, who was far more concerned with the Gospel in the Bible than with the men who wrote the Bible, nevertheless can say, " What made the inspiration of the book? It was the prior inspiration of the people and of the men by the revelation. . . . Inspiration is the state of a soul, not of a book—of a book only in so far as the book is a transcript of a soul inspired."[1] We cannot hold that the revelation is God's and leave no place for an activity of God in the record which answers to the revelation. That would be a kind of queer Pelagianism, in which man would appear as an adequate interpreter of God, without it being necessary to bring in the thought of a divine activity in the process. Nor can this difficulty be surmounted by a suggestion that what we have in the Bible is the authority of religious experience. Man's religious experiences are, as such, no more authoritative than his religious ideas. Apart from the fact that there is need of great discrimination within so varied a phenomenon as that of religious experience, it is not the experience which

[1] *Positive Preaching and the Modern Mind*, p. 16.

is the authoritative thing but that which lies behind it and has created it. The Bible, as human religious experience, has no special authority, though it has many lessons to teach; it is when behind the human form of the experience there is discerned something which the Spirit was saying to the men of the Bible and the writers of the Bible that we pass beyond the human and find ourselves in the presence not of the word of man but of the Word of God.

Thus in the Bible there is the unity of authority which proceeds from the presence in the Bible of the Word or Gospel of God, which is the revelation of God's grace calling for the obedience of faith, and of the Holy Spirit through whom the Bible is both a unity and an inspired record.

The form of the Bible is human; we can never be free from the limitations of human records and recorders. But the substance of the whole Biblical material is not a human message but a divine one, the Gospel. From it the authority of God is no more to be detached than the true divinity of the Son of God is to be separated from the true and complete human nature which the Son took in the Incarnation. It is in that which God says to us in the Bible, which also He enables us to hear, that the Christian confesses the authority of the Bible.

THE CHRISTIAN BELIEF IN GOD

By W. R. MATTHEWS, K.C.V.O., D.D., D.Lit., Dean
of St. Paul's

E

III

THE CHRISTIAN BELIEF IN GOD

I

THE Christian teaching about the nature of God did not come into the world as a wholly new and original message. It is a continuation and development of the idea which Hebrew religious teachers had expressed. Jesus and His Apostles were Jews and were nurtured in the piety of the Old Testament. The Christian revelation of God has always been regarded by the Church as the completion of the partial revelation given " at sundry times and in divers manners " through the Prophets. For this reason the Old Testament is a part of the Christian Bible.

It would be impossible here to trace the development of the religious thought of the Hebrews from its obscure beginning in nature worship to the sublime conceptions of the later chapters of Isaiah, but the reader may be urged to pursue this, surely the most fascinating of all studies, in such a book as *The Religion of the Hebrews*, by Oesterley and Robinson. Only a knowledge in some detail of the stages through which the evolution of religion passed can give us a real notion of what is meant by " progressive revelation." For our purpose, however, it will be sufficient to give a brief account of the final phase of the process and to sum up the ideas about God which were adopted and expanded by Christ.

The Hebrew Prophets were the great reformers of Hebrew religion, and it is to them that all the most distinctive and valuable elements of the Jewish belief in God

67

are due. Amos, Hosea, Isaiah, Micah, the "unknown prophet" whose writings are the second part of the so-called Book of Isaiah, Jeremiah, Ezekiel, form a continuous series of great teachers who asserted with compelling earnestness, not only the reality of God, but His righteousness. To those who have been born in Christian lands the conception of God is bound up with that of goodness, and they find it hard to realize that morality and religion are not necessarily allied with one another, but may even be enemies. We owe this to the success of the work of the Prophets. Their supreme achievement was to impress the identity of God with goodness on the mind and imagination of the Hebrews by their unwearied insistence that God is at least as good as the best human being. Another contribution which they made to religious thought and experience was closely connected with the first—the establishment of Monotheism, the belief that there is and can be only one God.

These two great truths were not attained without struggle, and we can see a development of insight in the prophetic mind as we pass from Amos to Jeremiah, but the earliest writing Prophet[1] strikes the note of moral faith which resounds throughout, growing in depth as it passes from one to the other of the great revealers of God. Amos denounces the religion of his day because it supposes that sacrifice can please Jahveh and does not understand that justice is required in those who would approach Him. Jahveh[2] is a moral person, and there can be no knowledge of Him in those who are morally corrupt. Another great Prophet of the eighth century B.C., Hosea, has a similar point of view; for him, too, moral purity is the only quality which can recommend the nation to God. He has,

[1] Amos, B.C. 765-750.
[2] Probably the correct form of the word given in our Bibles as "Jehovah."

however, one addition to make. In his mind Jahveh is not only the vindicator of the moral law against transgressors, He is merciful and loving and requires mercy from His worshippers. " I desire mercy and not sacrifice and the knowledge of God more than burnt offerings."[1] The standpoint of the Prophets, of the earliest as well as the latest, is summed up in the words of the Psalm, " The Lord is righteous; he loveth righteousness; the upright shall behold his face."[2]

In Isaiah, who also belongs to the eighth century B.C., we find the same moral standpoint, which here leads to an ethical conception of the holiness of God. Holiness means literally " separateness " and need not have any moral implications. In the lower religion " holiness " signifies simply the gulf which divides the divine beings from all others, and the danger of attempting to cross it without proper ritual safeguards. In Isaiah holiness connotes the absolute distinction between God and moral evil. This is a conception whch is central both for the Hebrew and Christian belief in God.

Though these earlier Prophets speak of the government of the nations by Jahveh and His supreme power, they do not explicitly assert that the gods of the heathen are non-entities and that Jahveh is the only God. When we come to the Prophets who lived during and after the Exile we find an explicit and memorable statement of Monotheism. The author of the second part of Isaiah (B.C. 546-538) asserts in majestic language the great truth of the unique-ness of God. Jahveh is the transcendent Creator and Governor of the world, which is small and almost negligible compared with His greatness. The nations are to Him as "a drop in a bucket." But this remote and wonderful God, of whose understanding there can be no searching by man,

---

[1] Hos. v. 6.   [2] Ps. xi. 7.

is also near. It is He who will " feed his flock like a shepherd,"[1] and not only His chosen people, but all nations, for this great religious teacher has reached a truly universal outlook.[2] His faith is that Jahveh is the God of the whole earth and will be the Saviour of all nations, using Israel as the instrument of their conversion.[3] No more sublime thought of God was attained by the Hebrew Prophets, but Jeremiah and Ezekiel have their own contribution to make. Jeremiah takes up the old idea of the " Covenant " between Jahveh and His people and gives this old notion of a bargain between God and the nation a deeply spiritual interpretation, by speaking of the " New Covenant " which shall be written in the hearts of men, not on tables of stone, but upon " their inward parts." Both Jeremiah and Ezekiel bring out an aspect of the action of God in the world which had been obscured in earlier Hebrew thought—His concern with the individual. To them, more clearly than to any other Prophet, it was revealed that God deals not only with nations but with persons—nay, chiefly with them.

Hebrew religion was not philosophical in temper, though the " Wisdom " literature, represented by such books as Proverbs and Ecclesiasticus, remains to show that this element was not entirely absent; but, on the whole, the Hebrew belief in God was purified and elevated, not by the work of thinkers, but by men of profound moral insight and heroic virtue. To the Hebrew, God was not primarily the explanation of the world, nor did he conceive of the Deity as the " eternal Thinker." To the Jew, God is first of all creative and righteous Personality whose will is revealed in nature and history, but pre-eminently in the Law and the Prophets. The contribution of the Greek mind to the development of Monotheistic belief was of a different character. Here the chief agents were philoso-

[1] Isa. xlv. 11.   [2] Isa. xlv. 22-23.   [3] Isa. xlv. 1-4.

phers, who were concerned with understanding the world and rejected the Polytheism of traditional religion on the ground of its inherent absurdity. We must not, of course, suppose that thinkers such as Socrates and Plato were indifferent to the problems of conduct and the nature of the good life; on the contrary, they have much to say on these topics, and the conclusions to which they came when their insight was most impassioned were not far from the revelations of Deutero-Isaiah. In Christian thought these two streams were destined to flow together, and the body of Christian doctrine was to be built up by the aid of Greek philosophy. Already in the New Testament itself there are traces of the influence of pagan philosophy. St. Paul, for example, uses conceptions and terms derived from the Stoics, and, in the opinion of most scholars, the Gospel of St. John, in representing Christ as the Word or Reason of God, has adapted an idea from Platonism. But in spite of this, it remains true that the belief in God which is presupposed throughout the New Testament is essentially that of the great Hebrew Prophets.

Jesus was nurtured from childhood in the piety and faith of the Jewish people. There can be no doubt that He accepted the belief in God which was current in His time and among His people. He did more than " accept." To Him the God of the greatest Prophets was the supreme reality—so much so that He seems never to have felt the need to argue on the matter. There were no doubts to be laid to rest. If we ask what was original in Jesus' belief about God, we must answer, first, that He presents the spectacle of one, unique so far as we know, for whom God was always the most real of all beings and to whose consciousness God was always present. It is sometimes alleged that the new belief about God which Jesus taught was the divine Fatherhood, but this cannot be truly asserted without qualification. As we have seen, the Jewish belief

71

included that of the loving-kindness of God, and Jewish piety could conceive that He pitied His children like a father.[1]

There is, however, a new note in Jesus' teaching on the love of God. He introduces the idea of a seeking and adventurous love. The Father is not content to wait for the sinner to turn to Him in penitence; He goes forth to meet the transgressor; He seeks the lost sheep until He finds it. This thought, which is expressed in more than one parable, goes beyond any theory which we can find explicitly stated in the Prophets.

The teaching of Jesus centres upon the Kingdom of God, and we may learn what He thought of God from what He tells us about God's reign. That the rule of God would be manifested had long been a subject of Jewish expectation. More than one Prophet had looked forward to the " Day of the Lord," which would be the beginning of His Kingdom, and at the time when Jesus was born the so-called "Apocalyptic" writers had given this hope a vividness and a definition which affected the minds of many Jews who were " waiting for the consolation of Israel." The teaching of Jesus on the character of God, particularly His emphasis on His Fatherhood and loving-kindness and His seeking love for the lost, brings with it a new conception of the manner in which the righteousness of God is to be shown. There can be little doubt (though some have doubted it) that Jesus regarded Himself as the Messiah, the inaugurator of the Kingdom, and hence as, in a unique sense, the agent and the representative of God. That the Kingdom would be preceded by wars and tribulations and that the Day of the Lord was a time of judgement was a commonly accepted belief. The originality of Jesus' thought about the nature and activity of God is seen most of all in the conviction that God's representative, the Messiah, must

[1] Ps. ciii. 13.

suffer for the sins of men, and that, in this sacrificial self-devotion, the glory and the righteousness of God would be supremely manifested.[1] The idea which had been expressed in the " Servant Songs," which now form part of the Book of Isaiah, was combined in Jesus' thought with the office and work of the Messiah, and self-sacrificing love was shown to be, in deed as well as in word, the highest revelation of God.

The Christian belief about God is governed not only by the teaching of Jesus, but by the belief of the Apostles that He was the supreme and final revelation of God. The Incarnation is at the centre of all Christian theology and must determine for it the idea of the divine nature. In its simplest form this belief is summed up by St. Paul, " God was in Christ reconciling the world to Himself." There is little in the New Testament which could be described as philosophical speculation about the divine Being. The existence of God is taken for granted, and the character of God is that of the Father of the Lord Jesus Christ. The love of God is revealed in Christ who " came down from heaven " for us. It seems that in the wonder of that saving act of God all doubts about the love of God were swallowed up. For those who had seen God " in the face of Jesus Christ " the questions were answered, or rather were irrelevant.

The belief in the love of God does not, however, remove all elements of sternness from the thought of God's relation with man. St. Paul can still speak of the " wrath of God " and the need to escape from it. We notice here that the prophetic tradition is still potent. The holiness of God is not abolished by His love. His reaction against evil is, for the New Testament as well as the Old, that of condemnation. It is thus most misleading to say that the New Testament proclaims the love of God, unless we go

[1] *Cf.* C. H. Dodd, *The Parables*, pp. 79, 80.

73

on to define that love as holy. It is not a complacent acceptance of all human beings as they are, but a will for their highest good, and is, therefore, compatible with anger against their sinfulness.

It is sometimes said that the doctrine of the Trinity is the distinctive feature of the Christian conception of God. There is a sense in which this is true, but it would be a mistake to suppose that the developed doctrine can be found in the New Testament. What we find there is the religious experience out of which the Church dogma grew. The worship which the Christian community, apparently from the earliest times, gave to Christ was bound, sooner or later, to raise the question of the relation of Christ to the Father; further, the members of the primitive Christian fellowship were conscious of the presence of the Spirit of God in the common life of the Church in a degree which had no exact parallel in the Hebrew religious experience. How far the Church had gone in the first generation towards the full doctrine of the Trinity may be seen in St. Paul's mode of benediction, " the grace of the Lord Jesus Christ, and the love of God and the fellowship of the Holy Spirit."[1] The later developments which are summed up in the " Nicene Creed " were contained already, potentially, in the earliest Christian thought and experience.

II

The statement of the Christian conception of God even when joined to an account of how it came, its antecedents, and its full emergence in the New Testament, is not, of course, by itself conclusive evidence that it is true. It is possible to admit that the belief in God which sustained and inspired the Prophets and Jesus is sublime and attractive, but to entertain grave doubts whether it is not one of the pathetic illusions which have from time to time com-

[1] 2 Cor. xiii. 14.

forted men in their shadowed passage from birth to death. Nevertheless the reader may be invited to pause and consider whether the story of what was felt by those who received it to be a revelation of the Eternal does not carry its truth in its face. Though we do not question the rights of the critical intellect to sift and weigh and enquire, we must beware of handing over to it tasks which it cannot perform. Reason is not so much the instrument for the discovery of truth as the faculty by which we test alleged truth. Thus it is notorious that we cannot give any quite conclusive reason for the belief that other persons besides ourselves really exist. We cannot demonstrate beyond all possible cavil that they are not mere appearances in our dream. We firmly believe that our fellows exist in the same way as we do long before our reason raises the question. We know it, as we say, "by experience," and to the present writer it seems the most probable hypothesis that we have, in fact, a direct experience of the being of other selves. The point which this example is intended to illustrate is that all our most fundamental beliefs come from experience. When we reason about them we are surprised to find that they are less certain than we had supposed, and in most cases cannot be called more than extremely probable hypotheses.

The belief in God depends, in the last resort, on experience, on what has been called "revelation"; but it is, in this respect, in the same position as the other beliefs on which we act with complete confidence every day.

The witness of religious experience to the reality of God has genuine weight, even though we may have difficulty in deciding precisely what importance should be given to it. There is no logical absurdity involved in the view that the whole of so-called religious experience is nothing but illusion, and this opinion has been defended, from the standpoint of psychology, by distinguished authorities, among whom the best known is Dr. Freud. The technical arguments on which this verdict of some psychologists has been based have been severely criticized and are found, on analysis, to assume the very question which is at issue.[1] To a mind which is not determined to be sceptical at all costs the development of religion as a whole, its persistence and its progress from crudity to sublimity, must convey the impression of a growing apprehension of Reality. It is difficult to understand the type of mind which can dismiss the whole process of religious development as a mass of puerile error. If we attach any importance at all to the religious consciousness, then the great succession of Hebrew Prophets and their culmination in Jesus must be regarded as the most significant of all the phenomena which are presented to us. The Christian belief in God has no interest in denying that there has been a revelation in other religions; when it is intelligent, it gladly recognizes the fact; but it maintains that the revelation from which it takes its rise is more continuous, more impressive, and more worthy to be regarded as final, than any other.

The belief in God, then, comes to us not primarily as a result of difficult reasoning but out of the life of humanity. But have we exhausted the subject of experience as a foundation of belief when we have drawn attention to the revelation which has been given through Prophets? There is, in the opinion of the present writer, an immediate experience of God in every human life. We are so constituted that we have a dim perception of the Reality of God, though it may, in many cases, be dormant and unrecognized. We may argue ourselves into Atheism, but by nature we are believers.

We have to account for the fact that we recognize reve-

[1] For an explanation and justification of this statement I must refer to my essay on " The Future of Religion " in *Psychology and Modern Problems*, University of London Press.

lation, that the Bible, or some part of it, "finds us," in Seeley's famous phrase. The revelation which is in us responds to, and enables us to recognize, the revelation which comes to us from history. Here once more we must confess that the determined sceptic may refuse to be persuaded, for he can allege that this response in us is only one more illusion. He may, in fact, adapt Charles II.'s explanation of the vogue of a popular preacher to this case, "His nonsense answers to their nonsense." We may, however, urge that the determined sceptic should be logical enough to criticize all experience, and beliefs which arise out of experience, in the same drastic manner —beliefs, for example, such as that in a real external world and in the existence of other persons.

Though belief in God does not originate from philosophical or scientific reasoning, it can be both defended and clarified by thought. It is the opinion of some distinguished thinkers that the existence of God can be demonstrated, and some also of His fundamental attributes. We cannot here enter into the discussion of this question, which would require a careful consideration of the so-called "proofs." Perhaps it will be enough for our purpose to point out that they have not been found conclusive by all competent thinkers. This does not, of course, prove that they are not in fact conclusive, because those who fail to be convinced by them may be, in this respect, incompetent thinkers. But we have first to reckon with that plausible attitude which goes under the name of "Agnosticism." At first sight it seems reasonable enough to say, "There is so much difference of opinion and the questions raised are so complex that I am led to think we cannot know whether God exists or not. We must resign ourselves to ignorance, and, while not denying that possibly there is a God, refuse to commit ourselves to the belief." The discussion of Agnosticism often becomes confused, because it is easy either to overlook the partial truth which it contains or to mistake that partial truth for the whole truth. There is a sense in which every intelligent Christian must be agnostic. Clearly we should be excessively self-confident if we supposed that our minds could comprehend the nature of God completely and adequately. The intellect of the creature cannot enter fully into the thought of the Creator. But there are a great many intermediate stages between knowing everything and knowing nothing. It is true that we cannot know all about God, but we can know all that is necessary for our lives. The attitude of thoroughgoing Agnosticism is really impossible. We may say that we will dismiss the problem of God from our minds, but it is not so simple a matter to dismiss the problem of the universe. What kind of world is it in which we find ourselves? That is a question which forces itself upon our attention, often against our will. And it is a question of vast practical moment, for it would seem obvious that the kind of world we suppose ourselves to be in must have some close connexion with the kind of life we suppose it to be most reasonable to live. When we have asked that question we are confronted with the problem of the existence of God. Nor can we say that we will leave it unanswered. We must act on one hypothesis or the other. To leave the question open means that, for practical purposes, we have answered it in the negative, for belief in God will play no part among the motives of our actions, and it makes little difference whether we call ourselves agnostics or atheists —except perhaps that in the former case our feeling will be wistful and in the latter contemptuous. The question, Does God exist? cannot be evaded.

There are many ways by which the mind can come to an assurance of the reality of God, and if this were an exhaustive treatise we should have to consider them all.

Since this is out of question in an essay, the best way will be to state the line of thought which most commends itself to the writer.

The idea of God, as we have seen, is not one which we have thought out for ourselves or which springs up as a bright conjecture in our minds; it comes to us from the life-experience of the human race and is, in some profound manner, consonant with our own nature. Thus the belief does not stand, as it were, on an equality with rival beliefs. It is not unreasonable to start with a prejudice in its favour. We need not be ashamed of hoping and expecting to find that the belief is true, for only the shallow and unwise delight in contradicting the instincts of the race. But we rightly submit this belief to the criticism of reason, and we should be prepared to abandon it if we conclude, after the best consideration, that it is condemned at reason's tribunal. We may perhaps think of belief in God as one of the hypotheses which have been suggested for solving a part of the riddle of the universe. This does not mean that God must remain for us a *mere* hypothesis. He may become for us the one luminous reality; but it may help us to think clearly if we regard belief in God as one among other possible answers to our " riddle."

Belief in God means essentially that we hold Mind to be the creative power behind phenomena and that the most Real, because the originating, Being is also the highest and best—the Source of all good. The direct opposite of this belief is Materialism in all its many forms. Under " Materialism " may be included any theory which would find the clue to the meaning of the universe not in mind but in mechanism, and it matters little in principle whether the machine is conceived as an old-fashioned type of stresses and strains, or as an electrical machine. The essential feature of all philosophies which are opposed

79

to belief in God is that they seek to account for the higher types of existence—such as mind—solely by reference to lower, such as atoms. The general objections to every kind of Materialism are overwhelming, and consist largely of a demonstration of the absurd conclusions to which the theory must lead when thought out. Thus, to take one example, if mind is the complex arrangement of non-mental elements which have been assembled in a fortuitous, that is in an unguided, manner, it is impossible to suppose that the mind should be capable of discovering truth, since all its thoughts must be the outcome of non-mental causes. Hence we are reduced at once to complete scepticism. Every theory, including the materialist theory, is ground out by the unthinking machine. It is becoming evident that Materialism has not the support of natural science, which formerly it was supposed to enjoy. Many eminent modern physicists, in view of the recent developments of the study of the structure of matter and of astronomy, have concluded that science suggests rather an "idealistic" philosophy—i.e., one which regards reality as mental rather than material.

The belief in creative mind has no serious opposition to encounter from science, and it may be observed that those eminent scientists who still maintain that it has belong, on the whole, to the older generation, which has not emancipated itself from the habit of thought of the nineteenth century, or else are Russians, who, for obvious reasons, are bound to be respectful to the Victorian materialism of Karl Marx. We are, therefore, at liberty to consider without any prejudice the grounds for belief in God other than the evidence of religious experience. As we have already noticed, there are certain "proofs" of the existence of God which have been and are considered by eminent thinkers to be conclusive. Probably this is too large a claim for them, but they suggest at least aspects of the world which, when carefully scrutinized, lend support to the belief in God and endow it with a very high degree of probability. A full discussion of these arguments must not be looked for in an essay, for each one of them has been the subject of a vast literature. We can only indicate briefly their nature and refer the reader to works which have discussed them for further information. Anyone who thinks that the argument for Theism can be written on half a sheet of notepaper has not begun to understand the difficulties of philosophical enquiry.

An argument which is still the centre of controversy starts from the existence of the idea of God in the mind and seeks to infer the reality of God. The so-called "ontological argument," when stated thus baldly, sounds singularly unconvincing, but we must observe, before we dismiss it summarily, that it has been accepted by some of the greatest philosophers, many of whom, such as Spinoza, had no religious allegiance. Of course, it would be absurd to contend that any idea which came into our heads must be the idea of something which really existed, but the point of the argument is that the idea of God is quite different from any other idea. It is the conception of the Most Real and Most Perfect Being, and it is alleged that we cannot think of this Being as not existing. It is the idea of a Being which necessarily exists. There is also another way of putting the same kind of argument. We have the idea of the Infinite and Perfect. If we did not have the idea we could not recognize that we ourselves and all other objects of our daily experience are finite and imperfect. But whence did this idea come? It cannot have been derived from the objects which present themselves to our attention in space and time, for they are all imperfect. We must suppose, therefore, that our minds are in contact with the Perfection of which we have, though confusedly, the idea.

The argument which has been of most account in the history of thought on the subject is the cosmological, which again can be presented in several forms. The most fundamental expression of it draws the distinction between "contingent" and "necessary" being. All the things and events which enter into our ordinary experience are contingent, that is they might have been different, and they depend on other things and other events for their existence. The mind, in its search for explanation, cannot rest satisfied with the contingent, for however great a heap we make of merely contingent being we never get any nearer to an explanation of being, since there is always the same need for explanation. A is explained by B and B by C, and so on without end. To reach an end, to satisfy the quest of the reason, we must postulate the reality of a necessary Being, one which needs no further explanation and depends for its existence on nothing outside itself. Thus we arrive at the idea of an eternal Ground of the universe, and we have further a rational method of determining the nature of that Ground. It must be adequate to support and account for the universe of our experience. The qualities which we find here must be based upon the nature of the Creator. Thus we cannot suppose that the character of God is lower than the highest values of created being. It must, indeed, since God is infinite, be infinitely higher. The reader is invited to remember that this is a crude and imperfect summary of an argument which lies at the root of all constructive thought. Every sentence of it requires amplification and defence. All kinds of critical questions can be raised concerning its every step, but in essence it is not abstruse or alien to the thoughts of the plain man. It is simply the development of what we all experience when, perhaps looking at the starry heavens, we ask, Who or what is behind all this?

Closely allied with the foregoing argument is the

familiar "argument from design," called by the learned the "teleological argument." Though this again has given rise to the most abstruse discussions, it is in its essentials simple enough. From the appearance of purpose in the world it infers the existence of Creative Mind. For some time after the general acceptance of the Darwinian theory of evolution this argument was under a cloud, as it was widely thought that the way was open to explain by natural causes all the phenomena which had formerly been regarded as evidence of intelligent contrivance in nature. Of late, however, it has become more evident that what was required was a wider sweep in the search for signs of purposiveness. Science itself has never been able wholly to dispense with what Aristotle called "final causes"— *i.e.*, those which explain the means by the end—and it becomes clearer as reflection goes deeper that the " emergence" of mind in the course of evolution requires for its full understanding the idea of " guidance " or " direction" in evolution. Professor Stout's great book on " Mind and Matter" reviews all the possible theories of the generation of mind and concludes that none will meet the situation or give any plausible account of the phenomena except one which holds that mind—that is, purpose—is present throughout the process. Professor Whitehead again, whose approach to philosophy is through mathematics and physics, leads us away from the conception of the universe as a machine and towards a conception of it as an organism, in which ends and purposes are fulfilled, and which cannot be understood without the idea of final causes. The old argument from design is reappearing in a new and stronger form.[1]

In modern thought on the problem of the existence of God much weight has been given to the moral argument

[1] I must refer the reader to my book *The Purpose of God* for a full explanation and defence of this statement.

and to the implications of "values" in general. Clearly the fact that the universe appears to be a sphere in which we have duties to fulfil and in which we may attain various forms of good is of great importance. It cannot be a negligible or unmeaning circumstance. Many are the ways in which the moral life has been employed as a starting point for a train of reasoning which supports the belief in God. In the end they all turn upon two thoughts, (*a*) that when we reflect upon our moral experience, we are led to ask, What is the basis of this sense of being under an absolute obligation, which seems to be an essential element of the good life? (*b*) that, when we reflect upon the meaning of " good " in its various aspects, we are led to form a conception of an Absolute Good which would include them all and from which they derive their value. No doubt, there are other systems of belief which strive to do justice to the facts of our moral experience, but it may be urged that none of them so fully and intelligibly meets the conditions as the belief in Creative Mind, which is the norm and source of all values.

When we are dealing with those life-interests which go beyond our own personal and individual desires, when, that is, we are concerned with truth, goodness and beauty, we are in contact with something absolute. Though our interpretation and our experience are relative and conditioned by circumstances, though, for example, every philosopher or artist has his own individual life, tastes and fortunes, yet the activity of the search for truth or the creation of beauty implies that there is an absolute truth or beauty. Without that implication all our higher life, the life of the spirit in the widest sense, would fall into ruins and we should be driven back, if we were consistent, on the foolish scepticism which is implied in the proverbial phrases, " there's no disputing about tastes " and " everyone has a right to his own opinion." No one really believes these proverbs, for we all in fact dispute about beauty in art and we assume that a foolish man has no right to his opinion every time we try to argue him out of it.

The assertion is often heard that the tendency of "modern thought" is against religion. If by that is meant against belief in God the statement is certainly untrue. On the contrary, the most remarkable feature of post-war philosophy is the emergence of Theism as one of the two or three "live hypotheses." Indeed we might go further and say that there has been an impressive convergence upon Theism from many widely separated points of view. Nearly all the constructive theories at present current are types of Theism. Nothing like this could have been said twenty years ago. Then, apart from Materialism and scepticism, there was the theory of Absolute Idealism, which was the predominant view in the Universities of Great Britain and America. Though the adherents of this philosophy, for the most part, were respectful to religion, they were mainly opposed to belief in God, except in the sense that God might be regarded as a popular and mythological picture of the "Absolute." Today that rather superior philosophy is almost entirely abandoned. As examples of the way in which thought is coming to the idea of God from many angles of approach we may mention a few distinguished thinkers and schools of thought. M. Bergson, one of the most original philosophers of our time, began by a brilliant development of the theory of the "Life Force" and Creative Evolution. It seemed as if he was substituting a blind tendency for the divine Mind. In his last book, however, *Morals and Religion*, his thought has moved on, and we find him speaking a language with which no believer in God could have any serious quarrel. A. N. Whitehead, the thinker who began by profound researches along with Bertrand Russell in the philosophy of mathematics and logic, passed on to the study of the philosophy of nature in the light of modern physics, and then to a critical survey of the causes and nature of civilization. In the final result Whitehead has reached a general conception of the universe in which God is the central Reality. Among those who follow the idealist tradition we may note that the most prominent representatives both in England and Germany are Theists. Nor must we omit to mention the vigorous revival of the Scholastic philosophy in the Roman Catholic schools and elsewhere, which has forced the philosophical world to take seriously once more the " proofs " of the existence of God which Kant was formerly supposed to have refuted. We seem to be approaching the position in which there will be only three serious rivals in the intellectual field—the scepticism which asserts that the problem of the universe is utterly insoluble, a discredited but still practically active Materialism, and some form of Theism. The reader who has no expert knowledge of philosophy may therefore be assured that, when he allows the various considerations to which we have referred above to move his mind to belief, he is supported and confirmed in his resolution by a considerable weight of contemporary thought.

III

The Christian view of the nature of God is determined by the belief that Jesus Christ is the unique Son of God and the Incarnate Word or Thought of God. The meaning and basis of that belief are discussed in another essay. It is impossible here to do more than refer very briefly to two topics which are specially relevant to the Christian conception—the belief in the love of God and the doctrine of the Holy Trinity. On neither subject will the reader expect more than a summary statement.

86

THE CHRISTIAN BELIEF IN GOD

That God is love has been called " the hardest part " of
the Christian faith to believe. It is perhaps also the hardest
part to understand. The word " love " is one of the most
ambiguous terms in the language, and it is important to
know what sense is intended when assertions are made
about the divine love. The New Testament does not use
the common Greek word, but has brought into prominence another " agapē," which is relatively little used elsewhere in Greek literature. Probably this is deliberate and
was the result of a desire to dissociate Christian love from
some elements which were deeply seated in pagan ideas.
The word " agapē " does not convey the thought, which is
inherent in the other word ("erōs"), of the search for some
satisfaction of desire, whether sensual or spiritual. Love
in the New Testament is more closely connected with the
will than with the emotions. Love is set forth as the principle on which all conduct should be based, as the " fulfilling of the law " and the sum of all virtue. Plainly this
would be an absurdity if " love " meant a condition of
warm affection, because the emotional attraction and re-
pulsion which we feel with regard to other persons are
largely instinctive and beyond the control of our will.
" Love " here means, first of all, a disposition of the will
to seek and promote the highest good and well-being of
all our " neighbours." There is no absurdity but rather
the plainest truth in saying that such a disposition can be
cultivated and that it is the root of all good in so far as
we are social beings.

The love of God is to be conceived then as, in the same
way, a settled will for the true welfare and good of His
creatures. God's love is perfect because His will is un-
wavering and His insight, both into the nature of good
and the possibilities of His creatures, complete. In fact
the noblest and wisest human love is a reflection of the
divine love. Obviously such a love can rightly be called

"holy," for it is bound up with good, and has no meaning apart from the thought of the will to produce the highest values of personal life. Such a love has nothing in common with that easy-going, indulgent affection which does not look beyond the immediate pleasure or comfort of the loved object. "Agapē" in human beings is quite consistent with a salutary sternness towards the loved person and with the acquiescence in hardship for him when that is the upward path. The love of a good man may be felt as terrible as well as comfortable by one who is living in accordance with evil principles. In the same way, the love of God does not mean that He wills for all His creatures at every moment an easy and pleasurable experience. Quite the contrary; He may will that they should undergo the discipline which will be the means of their ascent to new levels of moral and spiritual life. To the sinner His " love " may appear as " wrath."

Belief in the love of God can be supported by the kind of reasoning which argues that God cannot be lower than the best man. If we agree that God exists and that He is not only the Supreme Reality but the Supreme Good, and if we also agree that love, in the sense indicated above, is the principle of good, then we have a ground for belief that God is love which cannot be shaken by appearances to the contrary. We may readily admit that the belief would remain a probable conjecture, or even only a possible theory, apart from the revelation of the love of God in Christ, but when we accept that " good news of God " we find that it has corroboration from the conclusions to which thought points us. Though the assurance of the love of God could never come to us in full measure through reason alone, when we have it through revelation it appears not contrary to reason.

The problem of evil is, of course, the source from which the most constant doubts about the truth of the love of

God originate. The prevalence of suffering and of sin seems to contradict our faith. We have already observed, however, that the love of God is in no sense incompatible with the existence of hardship, and we must add now that it is not inconsistent with the existence of moral evil. The word "omnipotent" as applied to God cannot be taken as meaning that He can will contradictory and mutually discordant things. If it be a limitation that He cannot contravene His own nature of wisdom, then God is, in this sense, limited. He could not create beings with the possibility of freedom and, at the same time, leave them free to do only what was good. He could not will freedom and un-freedom for one and the same being. The creation of beings with freedom and with responsibility involves that they should have the power to misuse freedom and to choose wrongly. That evil should have an opportunity of entering creation was, if the phrase may be pardoned, one of the necessary risks of a real creation. The alternative was to make, not men, but puppets. Though the power and the persistence of evil remain a dark mystery, we can see that the existence of evil is not in itself an argument against the love of God.

Here again the Christian revelation helps us to hold more firmly and with deeper insight to a truth which reason would suggest. The Gospel is the proclamation that the Creator has not left the world to struggle unaided against the evil which has so disastrously corrupted it. He has taken the initiative to rescue and redeem. The Incarnation and the Passion of the Son of God are the sign that God, with a cost to Himself which we cannot understand, has taken the burden of evil and is overcoming evil with good.

That pain is also a dark mystery few would deny. To the human view at least, much suffering seems to be purposeless and to have no connexion with merit or demerit.

Though more of the suffering of men is due to evil doing and evil thinking than is generally admitted, we cannot claim that all human pain is of this nature, still less that of the other animals. We have already observed that the love of God is not inconsistent with the existence of a world in which struggle against difficulties is demanded, but clearly this does not cover all the problem. We have to confess that we have no satisfactory answer to give to the question, Why is there so much suffering, and so much moreover which has no apparent good effect? The Christian belief in God, however, has two affirmations to make which relieve the practical pressure of the enigma of pain. First, it asserts the reality of a life beyond and the promise of a " glory which shall be revealed in us " to which " the sufferings of this present time " are not worthy to be compared. When we look at this present order we see only a small part of the " great design." Secondly, the Christian doctrine of God assures us that He is not aloof from suffering. The Passion of the Son is a revelation of the life of the Eternal God, and hence we may learn that He bears not only the sin but the pain of the world, and from this gain confidence in the mystical experience that pain, endured in the spirit of Christ and in union with Him, may be a creative power for good and a partaking in the work of redemption.

The doctrine of the Trinity has sometimes been called the distinctive feature of Christianity. There is truth in this, though the first triumphs of the Church were gained before the doctrine was clearly formulated and expressed. Into the subtleties of the theological questions which arise in connexion with this dogma we shall not here enter, nor do they affect in any serious degree the faith of the ordinary Christian. It is, however, important to observe that the doctrine is not a piece of gratuitous speculation which theologians who had nothing better to do have tacked on to the Gospel. A practical purpose is behind it; nothing less than to guard the essentials of the Christian faith. It is intended to preserve the right to offer worship to Jesus Christ and to the Holy Spirit as divine, while at the same time retaining unimpaired the belief that there is only one God, which the Church inherited from the Jews. The doctrine of the Trinity was the way by which the Church avoided Polytheism. The adoration of Christ, which was the centre of the Church's life, might have issued in a belief that He was a second God beside the Father; that it did not do so is due to the fact that the leaders of the Church, under the guidance as Christians believe of the Holy Spirit, stated and thought out the doctrine of the Trinity which they believed, and with justice, could be found in germ in the New Testament. The dogma was not an addition to Scripture but an explanation of what Scripture implied.

Though the doctrine of the Trinity is the proclamation of a mystery into which our minds cannot penetrate far, it is quite untrue to say that it is the proclamation of a self-contradictory idea. Much perplexity has been caused by an elementary mistake. People have asked how can one be also three, as if the question were one of arithmetic. They fail to distinguish between unity and units. A unit is anything which we agree to count as one, and obviously, while we keep to the agreement, we cannot also call it three. But a unity is something real, not something adopted for convenience like a unit. It is a whole made up of parts or elements. What is asserted is that there are three Persons in the unity of the Godhead. St. Augustine and many other Christian thinkers have pointed to suggestive analogies in our own personal experience and in the life of a society. We have intellect, memory, and will, for example, united in one personal life; or again when we are knowing ourselves in a moment of self-consciousness we consist of knower, known, and knowing. The latter analogy would take us far if we pondered upon it, but here we must leave the subject with the bare suggestion that any deep reflection on our own nature will convince us that the doctrine of the Trinity is not theological nonsense but consonant with the nature of the highest and fullest type of existence known to us in experience—personality.

The subject which has been briefly surveyed in this essay is not only the most important which the mind can contemplate but of urgent practical interest. Religion in some form will certainly not vanish from the earth, nor are there any signs of the decay of the religious motive. Many secular and political movements, for example Communism and National Socialism, have enlisted an emotion which is in its nature religious. The question is not whether men in the future will be religious, but whether they will direct their worship and aspirations towards some object of the present, some imagined Utopia it may be, or to an eternal and invisible God. Immense issues for society and civilization turn upon the answer to this question. Men whose hopes are solely centred upon a " good time coming " in the present world and who have shut out from their thoughts all belief in a " Beyond this world " tend of necessity to be ruthless in pursuit of their aims. The dazzling prospect of the earthly paradise justifies all means which are necessary to attain it. When men believe in God they know that there is a good beyond all earthly satisfactions—to be in the presence of God, who is both the Author and the Home of their spirits. The Christian who finds God revealed in Christ has a foundation to stand on from which he can see that mercy and purity of heart are good quite apart from their social usefulness at any given time, and he will have a motive to be merciful even when expediency cries out for cruelty.

The question, Does God exist? and the closely related question, What is God like? have been the central theme of human thought ever since it began to leave childhood behind. When we reflect that God is Creator and we creatures it should not surprise us that the subject is inexhaustible and that the problems of belief are always reappearing in new forms. The present essay is offered to the reader as some guide to his own meditations and with the purpose of helping him to see, amid the modern confusion, where the questions on which he must make up his mind really lie.

THE HISTORICAL VALUE OF THE GOSPELS

By G. S. DUNCAN, D.D., St. Mary's College,
St. Andrews

IV

THE HISTORICAL VALUE OF THE GOSPELS

How far can we accept the Gospels as records of historical facts? The importance of this question is obvious, for how can Christianity as a religion continue to be accepted as true if its historical basis is discredited? And the frequency and insistence with which the question is asked is an indication of deep and widespread interest, not unmixed at times with uneasiness and scepticism. It is common knowledge that criticism has been at work on the Gospels, giving rise to new views on the problems of their origin and their historical trustworthiness. Accompanying this knowledge there is often the suspicion that the credibility of the Gospels has been seriously undermined; because doubt is recognized to be legitimate regarding certain episodes, some people are disposed to disbelieve all. Apart from the suspicions current among the ill-informed we have to reckon with a readiness among intelligent readers to dismiss much in the Gospel stories as wholly incompatible with the historical and scientific outlook of the twentieth century. Whereas the Gospels were once studied largely because of the religious and theological issues to which they gave rise, a matter of more primary concern today would seem to be their historical truth.

I. DOUBTS AND DENIALS

No book in the world has in the last one hundred years been subjected to so rigorous investigation as the Bible; and however seriously criticism might be occupied with peripheral questions like the composition of the Pentateuch or the interpretation of the Apocalypse, it is only natural that it should devote itself with especial vigour and concern to the central issues raised by the Gospels. Here progress has in the main been sought along the two-fold path of historical and literary criticism. To those who have no first-hand acquaintance with the matter it would be hard to convey an adequate idea of the wide range of learning and the patient care with which the task has been pursued; every episode, every saying has been studied, so to speak, under the microscope, and each fresh ray of light appearing in any one department of study has been made to yield its contribution to the elucidation of the central problem of the truth about Jesus Christ. No matter what conclusions these enquiries may yield, whether they contribute to the establishment or the over-throw of the traditional position, scholars are agreed in recognizing their legitimacy and their value. But we need not be surprised if at times their contribution has seemed to be mainly of a negative character. And as an introduction to what follows it may be well at this point to state some of those more negative views.

(1) With regard to the Fourth Gospel, traditionally regarded as written by St. John " the beloved disciple," it is asserted that St. John can have had no share whatsoever in its composition, and that its late date and its wide divergences from the other three canonical Gospels deprive it of any substantial claim to historical value. (2) Even the other three Gospels, commonly called the Synoptic Gospels because of their general agreement, have their unreliability exposed by the serious disagreements which exist in their accounts of matters of first-rate importance—e.g., the Infancy narratives and the Resurrection appearances, the Lord's Prayer, and the Sermon on the Mount. (3) The earliest of the Gospels, that of St. Mark, on which those of St. Matthew and St. Luke are

dependent, dates (it is generally held) from a period of approximately forty years after the Crucifixion of Jesus, so that there is a sufficiently long interval to allow for a radical distortion of the original tradition and for the growth of unhistorical accretions. (4) A special form of this last criticism is that associated with the Form-Criticism School, whose contention is that, while the Gospels afford good evidence of what the early Christians believed about Jesus, the very "form" in which the stories are told is a proof that they have only a secondary and perhaps a negligible value as evidence for what Jesus actually said and did. (5) In some cases negative criticism, stressing the paucity of references to Jesus outside the sacred writings, and claiming that as a religious or social movement Christianity can be explained without reference to a historical Founder, goes to the extreme position of asserting that Jesus never lived.

II. GOSPEL ORIGINS

In face of these various doubts and denials, what has criticism today to say regarding the origins of the Gospels and their general claim to historical truth? Precise answers to such a question are impossible, for Biblical Criticism is not an "exact" science. Certain positions are more or less surely established, but in regard to most problems we must be content to indicate the general direction along which advance is proceeding.

The Need for Gospels in the Early Church. The way in which we today speak of "the Gospels" might suggest that the term "Gospel" meant originally a written account of the earthly life of Jesus. This is very far from being the case. Originally "the Gospel" was a message, a piece of news—it told men something which otherwise they could not know about God, His character and His purposes; and from the nature of things it was first of all a spoken message, and only later did it assume written form. What gave the early Christians the assurance that they had a gospel to proclaim was the revelation which they claimed to have received through Jesus Christ, the Son of God; and by this revelation they meant, not that Jesus before He died had taught them certain truths about God, but rather that by His life (which, of course, included teaching), His violent and shameful death at the hands of men, and His victorious rising from the dead, they had learned something quite definite about the ultimate triumph of God's purposes and about the methods by which these purposes were now being worked out. They looked forward to the time when Jesus, who by His Resurrection was obviously marked out to be Lord and Christ, should appear in glory as the world's Judge and the Inaugurator of a new kingdom of righteousness; they rejoiced even now in His continued spiritual presence with His people; but in so far as they looked back to His earthly life it was to secure confirmation for the faith which sustained them amid present trials and the confident hope with which they looked out on the future.

Thus the early Christians never had that biographical interest which with us today demands that after a great man's death his "life" should be written, with a record of his ancestry, birth and home-training, and a chronological and documented account of his career. Nevertheless there were certain aspects of the earthly life of Jesus which they could not help recalling, and ere long these recollections were committed to writing. First in importance and perhaps in time was the record of how Jesus had been condemned and crucified by the powers of this world, and how God had raised Him from the dead. Other stories, notably His "miracles," were recalled as evidence that even when He walked on earth the blessing of God was with Him (cf. Acts ii. 22). Many other tales which in themselves might have appeared trifling came to be preserved and recorded because they were seen to possess a religious significance; they could be appealed to for the upbuilding of spiritual life within the Christian community or the combating of doubts and difficulties raised by unbelievers. At a quite early date a record was also made of some of Jesus' sayings and discourses, for the words of the Lord deserved to be invested with no less authority than the revelation given in the Law and the Prophets. It is probable, too, that an early compilation consisted of selected texts and passages from the Old Testament which were claimed (especially in mission preaching to the Jews) as having now received their fulfilment in Jesus.

The Synoptic Gospels. The writer of the Third Gospel tells in his preface (Luke i. 1-4) that at the time when he began to write there were already in existence various written records of the Gospel story. Even Mark, the earliest of the canonical Gospels, may be dependent on earlier written sources, but if this is so we have no certain means today of disentangling them. Both Matthew and Luke make use of Mark and of a collection of sayings, now no longer extant as a separate document, which critics refer to as Q. A very special importance attaches to Q in view of its early date and the character of its contents—it includes, *e.g.*, the material (distributed by Luke over various parts of his Gospel) which Matthew has collected in the Sermon on the Mount; and as shedding light on the self-consciousness of Jesus it may be noted that it contains the remarkable saying on the mutual understanding of the Father and the Son in Matthew xi. 25-27, Luke x. 21, 22. In addition Matthew preserves for us some material which he alone has—he is interested in showing how Old Testament prophecies have been fulfilled in Jesus, and in some of his additions we may trace the influence of legend (*e.g.*, xxvii. 51-53). Luke too has a special source (we may call it L) of considerable interest and importance—it contains *inter alia* some of the best-known parables like the Good Samaritan and the Lost Son, and special material relating to the Passion and Resurrection *e.g.*, the story of Christ before King Herod and His appearance to the disciples on the way to Emmaus. An attractive theory, first propounded by Dr. B. H. Streeter, is that Luke's first attempt at Gospel writing was based on this special source (L) and Q, and this original Gospel of his (Proto-Luke) was amplified at a later date by additions from Mark to give us our present Gospel. If this theory be accepted (and there is much to commend it) Mark is only a secondary source for Luke; and in Proto-Luke, which within limits we may claim to be able to recover by separating the Markan material, we have a new Gospel-source, independent of Mark and in some respects perhaps not inferior to it in value.

Probably tradition is correct when it assigns the Second Gospel to John Mark, the young man whose mother's house in Jerusalem provided a meeting-place for members of the early Church (Acts xii. 12), and the Third Gospel to Luke, "the beloved physician," who accompanied St. Paul on his travels. If Matthew, one of the Twelve, has anything to do with the First Gospel, we ought probably to attribute to him the authorship of one of the sources (Q, or the collection of Old Testament prophecies) rather than of the Gospel as a whole. According to tradition (and criticism on the whole endorses this) Mark derived his material largely from St. Peter, for whom he acted as interpreter. On that score alone his Gospel has a strong claim to historical value, and it ought to be especially revealing (as indeed it is) in the light which it sheds on the attitude to Jesus of St. Peter and his fellow-disciples. Luke, who accompanied St. Paul to Jerusalem (Acts xxi.

17) and subsequently spent two years at Cæsarea during St. Paul's detention there, would know how to turn to account the opportunities he would frequently have of gathering information regarding the life-story and teaching of Jesus.

There is considerable dispute regarding the dates of the Gospels. Mark is generally placed within the years 65-70; for Matthew and Luke various dates are suggested between 75 and 95. There are signs, however, that a reaction is setting in against such late datings. We may dismiss the contention that Luke is dependent on the *Antiquities* of Josephus (93 A.D.), and his language in xxi. 20-24 (to which there are Old Testament parallels, *cf.* Zechariah xiv. 1-11) need not imply that Jerusalem had already fallen (70 A.D.). The ending of Acts suggests for that book a date in the sixties when the issue of St. Paul's appeal to Cæsar is still being awaited, and this points to a still earlier date for Luke and Mark. Q need not be later than 50 A.D., and may be earlier. A remarkable contribution to the subject is the recent volume entitled *The Four Gospels*, by Professor C. C. Torrey of Yale, one of the foremost Semitic scholars of our time, who argues that all our four Gospels are translated from Aramaic or Hebrew originals, and are all to be dated early—Mark, he holds, was written in the year 40, Matthew shortly afterwards, and Luke and John about the year 60. New Testament scholars will not readily admit the translation hypothesis in the form in which Professor Torrey presents it; but in forcing us to recognize that Aramaic documents play an unquestionable part in the formation of the Gospel tradition, he has greatly strengthened the case for an early dating of our Gospels or at least of their sources. And the earlier we are able to date them, the stronger is their claim to historical trustworthiness.

The Fourth Gospel. The origin of the Fourth Gospel

is one of the obscurest of literary riddles. Even today there is no agreement as to its authorship; its date is usually placed towards the end of the first century; and there is general readiness to admit that it is concerned less with historical fact (in the narrow sense of the term) than with spiritual interpretation.

Yet to anyone familiar with the negations of a generation ago the outstanding fact about Fourth Gospel criticism today is the positive reaction which has now set in. If the Gospel in its present form is not the work of the son of Zebedee, a strong case can be made out for regarding it as based upon his testimony and reminiscences. We no longer set aside its evidence as valueless where it happens to differ from the Synoptics. In some cases it may be taken as supplementing the Synoptic tradition; *e.g.*, Jesus and the Baptist must have carried on parallel ministries previous to the death of the latter and the inauguration by Jesus of His Galilean ministry, and Jesus must have visited Jerusalem, perhaps on several occasions, before the final visit which is the only one recorded in the Synoptics. Thus it is possible that the Fourth Gospel, which tells of three Passovers, gives a truer idea of the length of the ministry than the Synoptics, which refer only to one. In other cases we may regard it as correcting the Synoptic tradition; *e.g.*, in placing the Last Supper on an earlier evening than the Passover it avoids the impossible situation created by the Synoptic account according to which the crucifixion took place after the feast had begun. Even more remarkable is the growing recognition of genuine historical elements in the distinctively Johannine traditions of the teaching of Jesus. There are indeed wide differences between the Synoptic teaching, simple and gracious and illustrated by numerous parables, regarding the Fatherhood of God and the coming of His Kingdom, and the long Johannine discourses, records of controversies with the Jews or intimate talks with the disciples, in which attention is focussed rather on the authority of the Son. But such a contrast ignores vital elements in the Synoptic presentation of Jesus and His teaching which only require the strong light of the Fourth Gospel to show them up in clear outline.

As further enhancing the historical value of this Gospel we may note that topographical and geographical details, together with many subtle references to Jewish customs and ways of thought, indicate that embedded in it are genuine Palestinian traditions derived from someone who had companied with Jesus. Further, the researches of trained Semitic scholars like Professor Burney of Oxford and Professor Torrey of Yale constrain us to recognize that in some parts at least of the Gospel there is traceable behind the Greek the influence of an original Aramaic, and for that reason both these scholars plead for a much earlier date than that which has been popular until quite recently in critical circles. Corroboration for this earlier dating comes also from two quite recent papyrus discoveries; the first, *Fragments of an Unknown Gospel* (published in 1935 by the Trustees of the British Museum), shows that the Fourth Gospel was in some quarter (Egypt?) sufficiently known and used to be accepted as an authoritative source before 150 A.D., perhaps even between 100 and 125 A.D.; the second, *An Unpublished Fragment of the Fourth Gospel* in the John Rylands Library, Manchester, dates from about the year 130, proving that by this time copies of the Fourth Gospel were already in circulation in Egypt.

There remains, however, considerable difficulty in interpreting aright the evidence of the Fourth Gospel. We shall refer later to its treatment of the miraculous. It is noteworthy that the stories of the Feeding of the Multitudes and of the Raising of Lazarus are followed by dis-

courses in which Jesus claims to be the Bread of Life
(vi. 35) and the Resurrection and the Life (xi. 25), which
seems to indicate that it is the spiritual truth embodied in
the episode that means most to the evangelist. The religious insight of the writer is such that he does not seem
to have drawn a clear distinction (and he certainly makes
it difficult for the twentieth-century reader to do so)
between historical happenings of a bygone generation
and the spiritual meanings which he now draws out of
these facts. Nevertheless, the time is past when we may
lightly dismiss this Gospel as one which has little or no
concern for historical truth; and in any attempt to trace
the development of Jesus' ministry or the character and
substance of His teaching criticism is today disposed to
attach increasing value to its evidence.

III. PROBLEMS OF INTERPRETATION

Does Christianity require a Historical Basis? Hand in
hand with the analysis of our literary sources goes the
task of interpretation. Here an important issue confronts
us at the outset. How far is it true to say that the Christian
religion stands or falls with the truth of the Gospel story?
There are devout believers, of the type frequently called
mystical, whose sense of the Presence and Power and Love
of God, just as it is not greatly nourished by the narratives of a past revelation, would not suffer any appreciable
loss if these narratives were entirely withdrawn. There
are speculative thinkers who assert that a truly spiritual
religion should, by its very nature, be independent of the
trammels of history; in this respect, they tell us, Christianity stands on a lower plane than the religion of the
Hindu, and every disproof of its so-called historical evidences is welcomed as bringing nearer the blessed day
when (in the words of Huxley[1]) " no longer in contact

[1] *Nineteenth Century*, July, 1899, p. 22.

with fact of any kind, Faith stands for ever proudly inaccessible to the attacks of the infidel." Here we come face to face with serious questions, not merely regarding the place which there may be in history for a divine "revelation," but even regarding the meaning of history itself. Suffice it to say that, whatever difficulties may be occasioned by its historical foundations, Christianity will never consent to their abandonment or admit indifference with regard to their truth. Why is it, we may ask, that so large a part of the Christian Scriptures (Old Testament and New Testament), which might reasonably be expected to deal with religious *ideas* and *sentiments*, should be given over to *narratives*? In seeking an answer we remember that these narratives preserve for us something more than the story of Israel among the nations, to be set alongside the story of Babylonia and Greece and Rome, something more than the life-story of one great religious teacher, Jesus of Nazareth, to be paralleled by the stories of Buddha, Confucius and Mohammed; they are told because they witness to *the developing purpose of God*, a purpose which, as is made apparent in the narratives of Genesis and the Acts of the Apostles and in the messages of the prophets, is never limited in its scope, but from first to last concerns humanity, or indeed the universe, as a whole. It is an essential element in the Christian Gospel and in the Christian philosophy of history that, following a long preparation in a particular nation, there ultimately appeared on the plane of human history One in whom God Himself is revealed to man, and through whom something full and final is accomplished for the turning of the tide of human history and the ultimate triumph of the righteous purpose of God. This does not mean that acceptance of the Christian Gospel, or of the Christian view of history, implies the literal truth of everything that is related in the Gospel story: if recognition of myth or allegory in the Genesis stories of Creation has not altogether robbed them of their value, may not the same be true within measure regarding the Gospel stories of the Redeemer? With some of the more disputable of these stories we shall deal in the subsequent pages; but whatever concessions may be made in details, "the *whole* point of the Christian story is" (to quote the words of Professor A. E. Taylor[1]) "that it claims to be a story of an *opus operatum*, an act which has, in fact and not in fiction, been achieved by God through man and for man."

The Mythical Interpretation of the Gospels: Just one hundred years ago, in 1835 and 1836, there appeared in two volumes the epoch-making *Life of Jesus* by David Frederick Strauss. Strauss, for whom as a convinced Hegelian facts had meaning primarily as the embodiment of ideas, was willing to accept the idea of the God-man as realized in the historical Jesus; but a ruthless examination of the Gospel narratives led him to believe that in practically every case we could see at work the pious imagination of the early Christians investing their Lord with all the wonderful associations of Old Testament patriarchs and prophets and the heroes of popular belief. Whatever truth there was in the Gospel story was thus for Strauss inextricably intertwined with myth and legend. Scholarship today, though it may still learn much from Strauss' sustained thought and critical insight, recognizes fatal weaknesses in his method of approach to the Gospels; but while the main body of responsible opinion has sought a truer line of advance, there have not been wanting those (notable among whom is the French Liberal Catholic scholar Loisy) who have carried the mythical interpretation still further. Among critics of this type the vision of Jesus "fades in ancient shades," a sharp distinction has to

[1] *The Faith of a Moralist*, ii., p. 117.

be drawn between the Christ of faith on the one hand, and on the other the Jesus of history of whom little is known that can be regarded as established fact; and only a step separates this position from the extreme negation according to which the very existence of Jesus is not fact but fancy.

The Thesis that Jesus Never Lived. Early in the present century a number of scholars, working along a variety of lines, began to demonstrate that Jesus never lived. Their views have received so much attention in certain quarters that some reference must be made to them here; but among responsible scholars they are entirely discredited, and it is worth recalling that one of the weightiest refutations of them comes from a source by no means biassed in favour of traditional theology, in a volume entitled *The Historical Christ*, by Dr. F. C. Conybeare, and published by the Rationalist Press. Jensen, a distinguished German Assyriologist, put forward the wild idea that Jesus, like various other Scripture characters, was a literary fiction, derivable ultimately from the Babylonian saga of the God-man Gilgamesch. Kalthoff, a Social Democrat, interested mainly in sociological theories, explained Christianity as a mass-movement in which the proletariat of the Roman Empire adopted certain Jewish Messianic conceptions, and Jesus was nothing more than a personification of its ideals. The Christ-myth thesis was taken up and developed in Britain by a well-known journalist and Member of Parliament, J. M. Robertson, in America by an erudite Professor of Mathematics, W. Benjamin Smith, and on the Continent by Dr. Arthur Drews; and more recently it has been revived in France by P.-L. Couchoud, whose views have received an undeserved prominence in the pages of the *Hibbert Journal*. Stated generally, the contention of these writers is that the distinctive features of Christian faith and worship are older than Christianity, that their revival and development in the first century A.D. is due to a strong current of religious syncretism working in certain Jewish sects, and that such names as "Jesus" and "the Nazarene," so far from having anything to do with a historical Jesus of Nazareth, are religious names traditionally associated with the expected Jewish Messiah.

Most of the arguments of these critics, when they have facts at all to support them, are based on a misreading of the evidence; and it can be said of them, as of the arguments of Kalthoff mentioned above, that by such reasoning it would not be difficult to explain the Reformation without Luther or Marxian Socialism apart from Marx. Much is made of the paucity of references to Jesus outside the Christian Scriptures. But when we consider the peaceful character of the ministry of Jesus, and how few points of contact He established with the world beyond Palestine, what was there, we may ask, in His life-story which must necessarily have arrested the attention of pagan writers? Moreover their silence is not complete. Among Roman historians there is at least one reference which cannot be explained away: this is where Tacitus (*Annals*, xv. 44), writing early in the second century with regard to the Neronian Persecution, says that "Christ, from whom the Christians received their name, had while Tiberius was Emperor been condemned and punished by Pontius Pilate." There is a still more remarkable testimony in the Jewish historian Josephus, but its authenticity is not beyond question. The suggestion that in pre-Christian times the name "Jesus" was in use as the name of a God is unsupported by evidence. We may say without hesitation that the whole story of the rise of the Christian movement and the Christian Church—supported as that story is by the evidence of St. Paul, writing about the middle of the first century—becomes meaningless unless we can connect it with the life and death of a historical personage, Jesus of Nazareth.

The Liberal Interpretation. When the twentieth century began, the dominating influence in Gospel criticism was that of the Liberal Protestant School on the Continent. Much of the work of this School was made familiar to English readers through translations, such as Harnack's *What is Christianity?* Bousset's *Jesus,* and Weinel's *Jesus in the Nineteenth Century*; and there was also Schmiedel's much-discussed article on Gospels in the *Encyclopædia Biblica*. It was a presupposition with those writers that the miraculous elements in the Gospels are unhistorical; the evidence of the Fourth Gospel was largely set aside; and within the Synoptic records there was a tendency to limit the kernel of historical truth to what is found in the earliest sources, Mark and Q.

The zeal with which all the forces of scholarship were marshalled in this resolute attempt to get back to "the Jesus of history" was attended with certain well-marked, and on the whole beneficial, results: despite some serious aberrations it seemed as if the fog in which the Gospels had been enveloped was at last dispersed, critical issues had become clearer, and many for whom the Christ of the Creeds had lost His appeal rediscovered a Master whom they could follow and even adore. An immense stimulus was given to the popular study of the Gospels. Many helpful studies began to appear, some (like Dr. T. R. Glover's well-known lectures on *The Jesus of History*) showing the influence of the Liberal School while by no means accepting its presuppositions or conclusions. With less happy results "amateur" critics were moved to reinterpret the Gospel story. A beautiful but unconvincing study by Mr. Middleton Murry represented Jesus primarily as "a man of genius." In more than one recent novel He has been enveloped in an atmosphere of

romance. Thus to many in our day, learned and un-
learned alike, Jesus is an inspired teacher, a heroic martyr,
a peasant-saint, a dauntless reformer, humanity's best
leader and guide in its quest for fuller life. But the question remains: Is this the Jesus of the Gospels?

The Eschatological Interpretation. Just when it was
being confidently claimed that the Liberal School had
restored to us the human figure of the Man of Nazareth,
the challenge was raised (first by Johannes Weiss, the
foremost New Testament critic of this century, and
himself a product of the Liberal School, and then by
Albert Schweitzer, the great scholar who is now a missionary on the Congo) that there were other elements in the
Gospels the neglect of which rendered the liberal interpretation not merely inadequate but completely false.
" The kingdom of God is at hand " (Mark i. 15). " There
be some of them which stand here which shall not taste of
death till they have seen the kingdom of God come with
power " (Mark ix. 1). " Ye shall see the Son of man sitting
on the right hand of power, and coming in the clouds of
heaven " (Mark xiv. 62). The Jesus represented by these
sayings, so far from being the man of clear vision and
well-balanced mind whom each successive generation
ought to take as its spiritual leader in the onward march,
seems to stand on the brink of eternity, calling on men to
prepare for a new and imminent World-order and for the
Judgment which must precede it. Attempts, such as that
of Emmet and Dougal in *The Lord of Life,* to dismiss the
apocalyptic elements in the Gospels as unhistorical or un-
essential have not been successful. Jesus, we must now
acknowledge, is not to be understood apart from His
eschatology. But the question remains: are there not
other vital elements in His outlook and teaching of which
the eschatologists take too little notice?

Form-Criticism. In quite recent years the traditional

interpretation of the Gospels has been challenged from still another angle. As we have already shown, the task of the evangelists was subtly different from that of a modern biographer or historian. They were members of a living religious Society: their aim, therefore, was to collect isolated traditions current in the Society and to present these in some kind of unity. There is certainly truth in this, even if it may not be the whole truth. But now two questions arise. The first concerns the order and arrangement of the narratives: may it not be that the order given in Mark (which is followed for the most part in Matthew and Luke) is in no sense chronological, and therefore gives us no clue to the course of development during the ministry? The second is still more serious; on this view is not the historical truth of the separate narratives undermined? Arguing, on very plausible grounds, that one strong reason why certain stories of Jesus were preserved in the early Church was that they were felt to have a bearing on the Church's life and problems, Form-Criticism goes on, still with some plausibility, to say that the use which the Christians made of these traditions (in their meetings for worship, for example, or in missionary preaching and apologetic) helped to determine the "form" which the traditions assumed; we may illustrate this from the various "miracle stories," or from the episodes in Mark iii. 6, where five stories of conflicts with the Jews provide settings for memorable sayings of Jesus. From this many form-critics proceed to the wholly unwarranted conclusion that, as we today have these traditions only in the form and setting which appealed to the needs of the early Church, they may shed light for us on the life of the Church, but they shed none or next to none on the life of Jesus.

Two of the leading representatives of Form-Criticism in Germany, Martin Dibelius and Rudolf Bultmann, have recently had works translated into English; but a more significant fact for English readers is the appearance of Professor R. H. Lightfoot's Bampton Lectures for 1934, entitled *History and Interpretation in the Gospels*. Bultmann is thoroughly sceptical regarding the historicity of the Gospel traditions. "I do indeed think," he writes, "that we can now know almost nothing concerning the life and personality of Jesus." In his case, however, the scepticism of a Strauss is strangely combined with the ringing prophetic notes of a Karl Barth: Jesus is the Bearer of the Word, and the Word would stand even though it could be shown that Jesus never existed. Lightfoot's criticism is likewise full of negations, and at heart he seems more sad. "The form of the earthly no less than of the heavenly Christ is for the most part hidden from us. For all the inestimable value of the gospels, they yield us little more than a whisper of his voice; we trace in them but the outskirts of his ways."

Verdicts such as these from scholars of repute may well occasion alarm; but among critics in this country the predominant reaction has been amazement, followed by emphatic dissent. A fixed idea may limit the vision and distort the judgment. Are we to assume that, when the early Christians were "forming" the Gospel traditions, there were no eye-witnesses left who could supply authentic versions, or that the personality of Jesus had been so unimpressive that no clear recollection survived of what He said and did, or of the background and historical development of His ministry? The analysis of "forms" has indeed something to contribute to Gospel criticism. It may, for example, suggest that certain stories are too closely modelled on Old Testament parallels to be entirely free from suspicion as historical records. It may remind us that something more is needed to explain the general structure of Mark than the simple testimony of St. Peter.

But only in rare instances can the form in which a story is told be made to yield evidence against its truth. Though the way in which Mark groups his incidents shows that his aim is not always to be strictly chronological, yet there is strong reason to believe, as the late Professor Burkitt so tirelessly emphasized, that we have in his Gospel a reliable outline of the development of opposition to Jesus during the ministry and of the way in which Jesus reacted to the changing situation in thought and deed. And when we recall the early dates that must be assigned to the sources of our present Gospels and the faithful part which oral tradition played before the narratives were written down, must we not conclude that, if the Gospels witness primarily to what the early Church believed about Jesus, they must also be accepted with the utmost respect as evidence about Jesus Himself?

General Conclusions. Our study so far as it has gone suggests certain general conclusions.

(i.) The Gospels do not pretend to be " lives " of Jesus. The early Christians felt no need for a biography of Him whom they called Lord and Christ. The modern emphasis on "the Jesus of history," however natural and indeed necessary it may be for a later generation, would have seemed in their day misplaced. A " Life " of Jesus, as we today understand the term, can thus never be written : the Gospels do not provide us with the material for such a work.

(ii.) But scepticism can be carried too far. In the first place, there is more connected material in the Gospels than some modern criticism is wont to allow, and Mark's outline enables us to trace in a general way the development both of external events and of Jesus' thoughts and plans during the ministry. In the second place, the Gospels do provide us with material, if not for a biography, at least for a portrait of Jesus—a portrait which has the best claim to be accepted as in all essentials reliable because it is derived ultimately from the witness of men who themselves knew Him in the flesh and who had entered, as mere " outsiders " could not do, into the secrets of His mind and spirit. The candour with which the Gospels depict the weaknesses of the disciples—their lack of understanding, their bickerings and ambitions, their failures at times of crisis—and the simplicity with which they describe certain human traits in Jesus—His indignation, His weariness, His " agony " in the Garden—ought in themselves to remind us that the early Christians were for the most part men and women whose aim was not to present the world with creative literary masterpieces, but simply to tell of things which they had seen and heard and to witness to the truth as they knew it.

(iii.) We have surveyed certain critical interpretations of the Gospel story, no one of which can be regarded as dealing adequately with the evidence of our sources. It has been said that criticism is like a sieve, and the results vary according to the size of the mesh. The Jesus of some critics is simply a modern hero in an ancient dress; and they discard as unauthentic whatever in His life or teaching seems to accord ill with the ideals and ways of thought of their own day. Other critics mistake half of the truth for the whole, and reject everything, however well-authenticated, which would blur the clear outline of their own theory. The result is that there are in vogue today many reconstructions of the Gospel story which on critical grounds have far less claim to historical reality than the one which generally accompanies devout acceptance of the Christian faith.

The question of the historical value of the Gospels demands that an attempt be made to reconstruct the Gospel story as a whole; and to such a reconstruction we now turn.

IV. RECONSTRUCTION

"*Whom say ye that I am?*" All earnest discussion of the Gospels comes ultimately to a focus on this question which Jesus Himself addressed to His disciples. Our concern in this chapter will not be to justify any particular interpretation of Jesus, but to arrive if we may at the historical facts on which all interpretations must be based. We cannot forget that the draperies of a traditional theology seem to many earnest men and women to obscure the sublimely human features of Jesus; and instead of the Christ of the orthodox faith they would prefer, so they tell us, to see again the Man of Nazareth standing as of old in the midst of a toiling, suffering world and calling on His brethren to follow Him in the way that alone will lead to victory and peace. With such a plea, when it is made in good faith, we may indeed have the fullest sympathy, even though, as a religious issue, we may question whether any merely human master can give his fellows such victory and peace as is here desired. But, confining ourselves strictly to the historical issue, there are two relevant considerations for us to keep steadily before ourselves. The first, which will emerge for treatment in the two essays which follow this, is that even to the historian no account of Jesus can be completely satisfactory which leaves unexplained the faith and convictions of the first believers and of the Church throughout the ages. The second is that it is seriously open to question whether the Jesus of the Gospels is adequately described by the terms Teacher or Leader or Hero or Saint. Critical study of the Gospels rather supports the view that He is one who claims for Himself an authority that is unique, and who as regards the Kingdom (or Rule) of God which He proclaims speaks and acts as if in Himself that Kingdom has already come and only through Him can other men enter into it.

General Outline of the Ministry. Great uncertainty
attends all efforts to establish the precise chronology of the
Gospel story. Unless the reference to Archelaus in Matt.
ii. 22 is a blunder, the birth of Jesus must be placed before
the death of King Herod the Great in 4 B.C. We know
that a census was held by Quirinius in 6 A.D.; and it has
been computed that there may have been a previous one
(Luke ii. 2) fourteen years before, which would give 8 B.C.
as a possible year for the Nativity. The crucifixion is
generally dated as in 29, 30, or 33.

We shall deal later with the story of the birth of Jesus.
There is no evidence to displace the familiar tradition
according to which He worked, perhaps as a carpenter,
in His native Galilee until about the age of thirty, when
He was caught up in the revival mission of John the
Baptist from which His own public ministry took its rise.
In submitting to baptism by water at the hands of John,
He received also, we are told, the baptism of the Spirit,
and He who was accustomed to call God Father was then
acknowledged by God as His beloved Son. From that
time Jesus never doubted that He stood in a unique relation to God (" beloved Son " is equivalent to " only son "),
and that He had in consequence a unique vocation in
connection with the fulfilling of God's purposes for the
world and the establishment of God's Kingdom. Such a
vocation might be described as Messiahship, though Jesus
resolutely kept clear of conventional and, as He felt, per-
verse conceptions of what Messiahship involved. The
pictorial stories of His temptations in the wilderness,
which possibly formed part of His self-revelation to His
intimate disciples, show with what clearness of vision and
strength of purpose He set aside all conceptions of duty
which were merely selfish, nationalistic, or worldly.
Every line of action had to be judged by the question : is it
what the Father expects of the Son? Only by helping men

to see the Father whose face the mists of life had obscured and by bringing them back into that intimate relation of Sonship from which they had allowed themselves to be severed could He fulfil His ultimate task with regard to the establishment of God's Kingdom.

The Kingdom of God—this is the vision which was ever before Him. For that hope He lived, and in the end He died for it. So real was it to Him that He began His ministry declaring that the Kingdom of God had dawned. Men listened, not merely because in the religious history of Israel the Kingdom of God was a familiar and a glowing hope, but because of the authority with which He spoke and acted. But they had not yet learned to mean by it all that Jesus meant, for they had not yet learned to mean by "God" all that He meant. So in addition to assuring them of the present reality and ultimate triumph of God's Kingdom, He devoted Himself, by word and act, to helping them to know God as Father, and to see the whole of life, with all its varied individual and social duties, in the light of that revelation.

There were implications in His teaching which inevitably provoked opposition. To the earnest but legalistic Pharisee He seemed to be setting up His own authority as higher than that of the Law; to the Sadducees and the Herodians and all who were interested in the maintenance of the *status quo* He seemed a dangerous " radical " whose doctrines and whose influence with the people might be attended with undesirable repercussions. But if the synagogues were closed to Him He could proclaim His message in the open. If the nation would not respond to Him he could, like Isaiah, seek to win a remnant of it. He gathered around Him a band of disciples. Out of these He selected an inner band of Twelve, to provide, as He believed, the beginning of a true family of God the Father.

At one period of the ministry Jesus and His disciples

retired to the far north—there are references to the coast-
land near Tyre and Sidon (Mark vii. 31) and to the
villages around Cæsarea Philippi (Mark viii. 27). In this
half-pagan territory beyond the jurisdiction of King Herod
He was free from the curiosity and superficial enthusiasm
of the Galilean crowds, free also from the danger of
premature arrest and death, and, above all, free to devote
Himself to the training of the Twelve. A turning-point
was the confession of Peter (Mark viii. 27-29), evidencing
as it did that in the minds of the disciples their Master
had a Messianic authority greater than that of even the
greatest of the prophets.

Assured by this confession that the time was now ripe
for the final conflict, Jesus turned His steps to Jerusalem,
determined there to challenge His nation to accept or
reject Him. His repeated references to death in His teaching of the disciples show that He clearly realized what the
issue must be; nevertheless He goes to Jerusalem, not as a
lamb to the slaughter, but as a warrior to the fray. He
arrived in Jerusalem in time to keep the Passover. By a
hurried manœuvre, however, on the part of His enemies
He was secretly arrested before the Feast began. At once
He was arraigned before the high-priest and accused of
blasphemy, then dragged before the Roman Governor,
Pontius Pilate, and denounced as a dangerous traitor.
Lack of evidence moves the Governor to dismiss the case;
but the ecclesiastical leaders are insistent, and Pilate fore-
sees trouble if he refuses to let them have their way. Thus
within a few hours of His arrest Jesus is condemned to be
crucified, and the verdict is carried out without delay.
The Gospel story, however, goes on to relate that He was
raised from the dead, and that He appeared to the disciples
who were disposed to scatter or had already done so.
And rallying from their confusion and despair the Twelve
with other believers assembled in Jerusalem as a corporate

fellowship, and from such beginnings there arises the Christian Church.

Jesus and the Kingdom of God. In any estimate of the teaching of Jesus emphasis ought firstly to be laid on its deeply spiritual and ethical character. Jesus has brought to the world a conception of the divine nature and of human duty which, though verbal parallels may be quoted from earlier religious teachers, is so full of life and power that it may truly be called new. But Christ's teaching is not, as is all too frequently assumed in some quarters, to be summed up under the two heads of a spiritual outlook and a code of morals. As we have already pointed out, there is in His teaching an eschatological element which is not to be ignored. Sayings such as those about the coming of the Son of Man have as authentic a place in the Gospel tradition as "love your enemies" and "with God all things are possible"; and they are not to be explained as the mere reflection of the eager expectations of the early Christians or as the adoption by Jesus of popular apocalyptic imagery for the embellishment of simple spiritual teaching. Schweitzer has undoubtedly gone too far when he finds in Christ's eschatology the one key to His teaching, and regards His ethic as an *Interims-ethik,* adapted to the needs of an age which is doomed soon to pass away. Nevertheless we err if we forget that, like all great seers and prophets, Jesus had constantly in His mind's eye a vision of "the End," when God's purposes should be fulfilled and when, as a prelude, men should be brought face to face with their Saviour and their Judge. Hence the Kingdom which He proclaimed was not "a far-off divine event," the inevitable consummation of a long, slow process of moral advancement; it was God's Kingdom, and God Himself would bring it in by His own redeeming and renewing activity. It is, moreover, a fundamental element in Christ's teaching that the

Rule of God has already begun in Himself, and manifests itself here and now wherever men are willing to "receive" it; but its final consummation, just because it entails not an improvement in the present world order, but the introduction of a new order in which God is the acknowledged King, will be accomplished not on earth but (as we say) in heaven.

The Miracles of Jesus. This is not the place for a discussion on the general question of miracle. The words normally used in the Gospels to describe the "miracles" of Jesus mean literally "works" (*erga*) or "powers" ("mighty works," *dynameis*); in the Fourth Gospel there is also the description of them as "signs" (*sēmeia*). And in the Gospels a miracle is always regarded, not as a wonder (in the modern sense of a violation of the uniformity of nature), but rather as a manifestation of unseen Power, an indication that God Himself is at work in His world. Naturally the performance of such works of power did excite wonder, and it may reasonably be conjectured that in some of the narratives amazement has led to misconceptions—the real significance has perhaps been misunderstood, minor accompaniments have been invested with an importance which did not originally belong to them, supernatural agencies have been traced behind events for which today a natural explanation would be accepted as satisfactory. A recognition of these and other possible factors, together with a perverted conception of what is meant by "natural law," has frequently served (though in some previous generations perhaps more than in our own) to encourage the belief that the miraculous elements in the Gospels, whose development in a wonder-loving age could easily be understood, are wholly incompatible with our own more scientific outlook and may safely be discarded as accretions. But however natural it may be to sympathize with this contention, there are serious objections to it which must be faced. It is not scientific criticism to set aside the evidence of our sources merely because that evidence conflicts with certain presuppositions of "modern thought." If we cut out the miraculous from even the earliest of our Gospels we are left with a narrative which has ceased to be intelligible. The Gospels, if they are to be trusted at all, represent Jesus doing mighty works, or enabling God to do them through Him; and He does them in virtue of His perfect faith in God, sometimes also because the recipients of His blessings have the receptive spirit which accompanies faith. Modern enquiries into the power of mind over matter may help us towards a sympathetic understanding of the situation. Jesus seems to have encouraged the belief that, with a similar faith in God, other men might do similar works of power; and Church history provides evidence, both in the first decades and in later periods, that the followers of Jesus, claiming to act in His Name, have at times been enabled to perform such works. Nevertheless the fact that Jesus normally, as it appears, was able to perform mighty works which to ordinary men (including even those who profess to believe in God through Him) are normally impossible, is an indication that a complete harmony of mind and spirit characterized His relations with God, such as does not characterize the relations of other men—that harmony which in Scripture is expressed by the unique relationship between Father and Son; and it was from this perfect communion with God that Jesus' faith proceeded, and with it His power to work miracles.

Though some such general view seems forced on us by the evidence of our sources, the miracles of Jesus will never cease to raise serious questions for the student of history, and many of these questions must remain unanswered. In any particular case allowance must be made for the possibility of misinterpretation. The so-called "Feeding of the

Multitude" (Mark vi. 35 *ff.*, viii. 1 *ff.*) may have been a
symbolic or sacramental act by which Jesus emphasized
the unity of the Christian Fellowship—the episode of the
foot-washing (John xiii. 4 *ff.*), and the ritual of the bread
and the wine at the Last Supper are a reminder that Jesus
could teach by acted as well as by spoken parables. It is
open to belief, in accordance with a literal interpretation
of Jesus' own words in Mark v. 39, that the daughter of
Jairus whom Jesus brought back to life was "not dead,
but asleep," though it is clear that this is not how the
Evangelist meant the story to be interpreted. It has often
been remarked that the treatment of miracle in the Fourth
Gospel differs from that in the Synoptics; there is sometimes a notable heightening of effect—*e.g.*, Lazarus has
been dead for four days (John xi. 39)—and Jesus exercises
His power less in response to an attitude of "faith" than
in order to stimulate "belief" in Himself and His mission.
The narrative of the raising of Lazarus, it is true, is characterized by a quite remarkable realism—for Jesus displays
throughout intense human sympathy, and is not a mere
impassive medium for the operation of supernatural power
—and on that account it ought not to be too readily dismissed as apocryphal; nevertheless there are grave difficulties in the account which we have in the Fourth Gospel,
and there is the further objection that in the Synoptics
there is no hint, direct or indirect, that an event of such
far-reaching interest and significance had been a prelude to
Jesus' final visit to Jerusalem. The difficulties connected
with the story of Water turned into Wine (John ii. 1-11)
are thus summed up by a recent commentator (Professor
G. H. C. Macgregor, in the *Moffatt Commentary*): "It is
recorded by none of the Synoptics; unlike the better
attested miracles it is performed in the realm of inorganic
matter by a process which it is hardly possible to conceive;
finally, and this is of chief importance, from the ethical

point of view it is unintelligible and purposeless "; and the theme is expounded as " the transmuting of the water of the old Jewish ceremonial into the wine of the new Christian Gospel." It is altogether probable that the story had a basis in fact; but it may well be that it had meaning for the Evangelist, just as it has had meaning for Christian preachers ever since, primarily because of some great religious truth which it seemed to prefigure.

Today, owing to advances in the study of psychology and to accumulating evidences of faith-healing, many who are sceptical about the Gospel miracles in general are prepared to believe that Jesus worked marvellous cures. A special feature of His healing ministry was the expulsion of " demons " or " unclean spirits." It was a popular belief that bodily ailments often proceeded from demon-possession, and that many of the distresses, including death itself, to which humanity as a whole was subject came from the domination of the world by evil spirits. Jesus Himself shared that belief, and it is the clear evidence of the Gospels that when He came to grips with those powers of evil He did so as a " strong man " armed with the power of God and commissioned to overthrow them. And just because the mission of Jesus is not that of the medical man or the wonder-worker, but of the divinely commissioned Son of God, we are debarred from accepting as altogether beyond dispute the widely prevalent conclusion that while He may have healed the sick He never brought men back from the grave or triumphed over the forces of nature. The Gospels represent Jesus, not merely as working miracles, but also as refraining from working them—the mere suggestion of turning stones into bread, of using His power solely to change earthly conditions, was indignantly rejected as a temptation of the devil; and we may therefore say with confidence that every miracle which He performed was inspired somehow by the free creative Spirit of God working for the establishment of good and the dethronement of evil. Apologists of a bygone age appealed to the miracles as constituting in themselves a proof of the divine character of Jesus. Today our practice is to reverse the reasoning, and from what we know of the inner life of Jesus we believe that such a One may have been able to do what the Gospels represent Him as doing. Nevertheless what Jesus *was* and what He *did* are not to be separated; and when we take a conjunct view of the evidence of the Gospels we see that His mighty " works of power," according to which blind men received sight, lepers were cleansed, and the dead raised (Matt. xi. 5), were regarded by Him as an evidence that in Him the Kingdom of God had begun.

The Self-Consciousness of Jesus. How did Jesus interpret His own Person and mission? For various reasons the question here raised is not easily answered. In the first place, " our Gospels are very far from being a sort of psychological novel with Jesus Christ for the Hero."[1] In the second, though He continually challenged men by the authority by which He spoke and acted, Jesus felt it inconsistent with His mission to proclaim to all and sundry the grounds on which that authority rested.

For a right understanding of Jesus' self-consciousness we must learn to look at Him, as it is evident He looked at Himself, in the context of the Old Testament revelation. Throughout all that revelation there rings the promise of God : " I shall be your God, and ye shall be my people." The implication is, not that God already *possesses*, but that He is seeking to *secure*, such a people—a people that are His in the sense that they reflect His character and are fit to be used as a channel for His revelation to the world and an instrument of His advancing purposes. It was the sublime conviction of Jesus that, following on the long

[1] Burkitt, *The Gospel History and its Transmission*, p. 77.

centuries of preparation in Israel, God had now commissioned Him to bring this people into being. And this
commission He could only fulfil if He led men into the
same intimate relationship with God the Father as at
present was His and His alone.

(*a*) *The Son of God*. If God was indeed the Father,
then His ideal people would be a family of sons. God's
promises would be fulfilled when it could be said of His
people : " Ye are the sons of the living God " (Hosea i. 10).
To whatever origin we trace His self-consciousness Jesus
undoubtedly believed Himself to be in a unique sense *the
Son of God*. We may refer again to the remarkable saying in Matthew xi. 27 (derived from the source Q) regarding the relation of the Father and the Son. The revelation
which Jesus received at the Baptism implied that He was
the only Son the Father had. All other men were, like the
younger son in the parable, sons who had become lost to
the Father. And Jesus believed that His vocation was to
bring them again into their sonship.

(*b*) *The Son of Man*. The acute controversy which in
the last forty years has raged round this term has served
in various ways to clear the issue. In the Book of Enoch it
had come to be applied to the Messiah; but in the earlier
Book of Daniel (vii. 13) it was associated rather with the
ideal people of God—such a people, it is implied, was like
a man, while the other great peoples were but beasts. It
would seem to be of this people of God that Jesus is thinking when in the Gospels He speaks of the Son of Man,
though He uses the term with very special reference to
Himself as the central, and for the time the sole, representative of that people.

(*c*) *The Messiah*. As a corollary of these more intimate
beliefs Jesus further believed that He, with the people
whom He was to call into being, was God's chosen instrument for the judgment of the world and the establishment

of His Kingdom. In that sense He conceived of Himself as God's Messiah. But Jesus never lost touch with immediate realities; He based His authority on His present experience of "Sonship," not on His call to some future "office"; and so it is not till He stands in the presence of final condemnation and death that He openly avows His Messiahship (Mark xiv. 61 *f*.). A veiled indication of this claim may be seen in many of His predictions regarding the Son of Man.

(*d*) *Jesus' Teaching on His Death.* Jesus' consciousness of uniqueness comes out further in the significance which He attaches to His death. In the face of the evil of the world something more than teaching and example is needed to bring men into the family of God; and Jesus, who, as the Son, believed that He was called to be the Servant of God —that Servant of whom Isaiah (ch. liii.) had foretold that he would fulfil his mission by suffering—realized that a life of service must find its consummation in a sacrificial death. There was a purposefulness about His death that made it more than martyrdom. In a memorable sentence (Mark x. 45), which is not to be emptied of its meaning or dismissed as unauthentic, He Himself described it as " a ransom for many." Taken by itself that phrase does not answer for us all the questions that naturally arise regarding the meaning of His death, but it does enable us to see how He conceived of His death as a " deliverance " by which those who were called to be sons of God might enter on a life of freedom from which otherwise they were debarred.

(*e*) *Jesus and His Disciples.* We get a fresh light on the self-consciousness of Jesus if we study His relations to His disciples, more especially to that inner band called the Twelve. In them as they gather around their Master we see the nucleus of the new people of God. He chose them, says Mark (iii. 14), that they might be with Him; and so day by day they learned, not merely from His direct teaching, but from the unspoken lesson of His daily life of goodness and power. He trained them in the first great essential, a knowledge of God; and as a result they learned the other great lesson of love to man. He so influenced them that even in His lifetime they came to think of Him as the Messiah, the Son of the Living God (Matt. xvi. 16), and after His death they were convinced of His living Presence and looked forward to His Coming in power.

Shortly after the acknowledgment by the disciples of the Messiahship Jesus had an intensely real spiritual experience which in some way three chosen disciples were privileged to share with Him. In prayer on a mountainside they saw on His face a radiance which was not of earth, and they were made to feel that there stood by their Master Moses and Elijah, the two most representative prophets of God, who in some mysterious way had passed beyond death and who were expected to reappear as witnesses to the Messiah. Thereafter they turn their faces to Jerusalem, and on the way the supreme concern of Jesus seems to be to get the Twelve to reach a conception of Messiahship more in line with His own. Repeatedly they show that they associate Messiahship with pomp and victory; repeatedly, as in His blessing of the children and in His reply to the request of James and John, He leads them to associate it with humility and sacrifice. Repeatedly, too, He predicts to them His coming rejection, death, and resurrection (Mark viii. 31, ix. 31, x. 32 ff). It may be that in the form in which they have come down to us these predictions have acquired a definiteness of detail which at first did not belong to them. But their general substance we need not doubt. Jesus went to Jerusalem believing that it was the will of the Father that He should die there, and He went believing also that it was the purpose of the Father to raise Him from the dead. Our Gospels tell us that when He spoke to the disciples about these matters they failed to understand Him, and that when finally they saw their Master dead they were filled with confusion and fear. In the face of such an ordeal their obtuseness and confusion are not difficult to understand. But the faith of Jesus never wavered: He had sown the good seed in their hearts, and He knew that God would bring forth the fruit in good time.

On the night before He suffered He gathered the Twelve together for a meal. This has sometimes been represented as essentially a farewell supper, and because of the absence in Mark, Matthew, and the shorter text of Luke of the words " Do this in remembrance of me," we are asked to believe that it was never meant to be repeated. Arguments from silence are always precarious; and all that we know of the mind of Jesus and of His relations with the Twelve reminds us that at this time their thoughts were set on something far more than an earthly parting. This was but the last of many suppers at which the Master had sought to make real to the disciples all that He had otherwise taught them about the Fellowship of the Sons of God. On that evening as He passed to them the bread and the wine He reminded them again of the sacrificial significance of His death: it was for them that He was dying. But He and they formed a family, and He doubt-less meant them to realize that they too must share in His death as they had shared in all His other trials (Luke xxii. 28). It was, however, no occasion for sadness. Death had no power to break the fellowship; and the supper which they were celebrating now on earth was a foretaste of the feast of victory which He and they should celebrate together when all was fulfilled in the Kingdom of God.

The Resurrection. The Gospels testify that Jesus was crucified, dead, and buried; they testify equally, and without any suggestion that here they are passing from history into romance, that He rose from the dead. It is unfortunate that the final chapter in Mark has in some unknown way suffered mutilation—verses 9-20 are undoubtedly a later addition; but in the authentic part of his narrative we have clear evidence that Mark, like the other three evangelists, believed that Jesus after the Resurrection revealed Himself to His disciples and that the tomb was found empty. Of the actual rising from the tomb our Gospels, with characteristic reticence, tell us nothing. Additional evidence of first-rate importance comes to us from the fifteenth chapter of St. Paul's First Epistle to the Corinthians, written about the year 55; and what he asserts there bears the hall-mark of a much earlier date, for St. Paul, who became a Christian within a very few years of the crucifixion, tells that he is merely passing on what he himself had received. The facts to which St. Paul confidently appeals are the appearances of Christ to Peter, to James, to the Twelve, to an assembly of five hundred disciples, and finally to himself.

Neither St. Paul, nor the writers of the Gospels, seem to have any doubt about the reality of these appearances of the risen Christ; and their very assurance is a factor of which account must be taken and an explanation found. On the other hand we have no direct means today of testing their assertions, and we must also face the fact that there are serious discrepancies in the various accounts.

There is firstly the problem of the scene of the appearances. Matthew places them in Galilee, and for this there is corroboration in John's appendix-chapter (xxi.), and in certain anticipatory references in Mark; Luke and John (ch. xx.) place them in or near Jerusalem. These accounts cannot be fully harmonised—a fact which, though it may be disturbing to those whose sole test of truth is accuracy of detail, may usefully remind us that this is a case where harmonization ought not to be attempted. If we care to fall back on hypothesis where certainty is no longer attainable, we may conjecture that, whether at different times or to different individuals, there were appearances both in Galilee and at Jerusalem. There were two quite independent traditions in the early Church, and discrepancies arose only when, in good faith but on insufficient evidence, details were added of time, place, and participants. In themselves these discrepancies, however much we may regret them, are no argument against a basis of historical truth.

A more serious problem concerns the nature of the Resurrection appearances. The body in which Christ appeared was obviously not identical with the physical body which had been His during His earthly life—we may recall in this connection how after the Resurrection He was seen only by believers. But if on the other hand we introduce the conception of visions, we must be careful to safeguard the reality of the appearances. The disciples were not the victims of hallucinations—their subsequent confidence, which apparently never wavered, is sufficient evidence against that. Neither are we anywhere near the truth if we assert that all that happened was that the spirit of Christ came to new life in the souls of the disciples. St. Paul makes it plain that he regarded Christ as having risen with a " spiritual body," by which he apparently means a body adapted to the unhindered control and self-expression of the spirit.

This raises the question of the empty tomb. Here again we have an alleged historical fact which as such we have no means of verifying. It is easy on general grounds to deny it; but denial involves difficulties scarcely if any less serious than acceptance. The hypothesis of Dr. Kirsopp Lake that the tomb which the women found empty was not the tomb in which the body of Christ had been laid is too conjectural and improbable to carry conviction. On the other hand, if we imagine that the body had been removed, it is not easy to explain how either friends or enemies should have conceived the desire or could have successfully found the means to remove it. St. Paul's evidence here is interesting and important. He certainly does not mention the empty tomb, but on the other hand the whole structure of his thought in this and other passages is based on the conviction that there was in some sense a resurrection of the body. If we operate with the conception of a spiritual body, the question arises of the relation of such a body to the natural body. St. Paul faced that question (1 Cor. xv. 35 *ff.*): there are many different kinds of "body," he reminds us, and even in the realm of nature the sown seed dies to reappear as wheat. May it have been so with Christ? Did His dead body disappear to reappear transformed? If we have other sound reasons for believing that Christ rose from the dead, such a hypothesis is surely not impossible, and it seems the best explanation of the various scriptural *data*. But it is important that we put first things first. A resurrection faith that is built mainly on the disappearance of the natural body is no faith at all. What gave life and content to the faith of the early Christians was not that the Lord had somehow escaped from the grave, but that in a transformed state He had emerged triumphant from it.

No theory of the Resurrection can be regarded as satisfactory which does not adequately explain the faith of the early Christians and the rise and development of the Christian Church. A study of the content and the vitality of that faith would take us beyond the limits of this essay, but for our present enquiry it is essential to remember that the faith of the disciples did not spring, as it is too often represented to have done, *solely* from the Resurrection appearances and the discovery of the empty tomb. The soil had already been prepared for it by all their previous contacts with Jesus. The Resurrection had a meaning for them just because it was Jesus who had risen. And similarly we today in all our thought on the Resurrection must learn to view it, not as an isolated phenomenon, but in the context of the life and teaching of Jesus.

The Virgin Birth. The Christian assertion that Jesus is the Son of God does not in itself denote that He was born without a human father. Yet that He was so born is evidenced in the only two Gospels which relate His birth, Matthew and Luke. In these two Gospels the accounts of His birth and infancy are entirely different from one another, so that we must recognize two independent traditions: Luke's version may be said to represent Mary's point of view, and Matthew's that of Joseph. Nowhere else in the New Testament is appeal made to the Virgin Birth (though certain passages may be interpreted so as to appear to imply it); if it was generally known, it was apparently not regarded as an essential element in the Christian message. Passages may even be cited from the Gospels as telling against it, though in no case is the evidence conclusive. It has also been suggested that the sources employed by Luke for the first draft of his Gospel (which in some parts seems to have been left unchanged) did not know the tradition: Joseph and Mary, *e.g.*, are in Luke frequently referred to as the parents of Jesus, the genealogy is traced through Joseph (iii. 23), and even the birth-narrative in chapter i. ceases to be miraculous if we may regard verses 34, 35—or even the four words in verse 34 translated " seeing I know not a man "—as added (perhaps by Luke himself) at a later stage.

A sympathetic and detailed study of the traditions preserved both by Matthew and by Luke shows that they originated in circles of Jewish piety. That is important: the New Testament story is assuredly not a mere importation from heathen mythology. Much in these narratives, however, is obviously poetry rather than prose (*e.g.*, the visit of the angel Gabriel, and the song of the heavenly host). Other stories, like that of the shepherds at Bethlehem, the Wise Men from the East, and the Flight into Egypt, though they may have some basis in fact, are unmistakably akin to the exegetical stories of the Jewish Mishna. In such an atmosphere of poetry and devotion can one be certain that in the central narrative also there is not poetry as well as prose?

On purely critical grounds there is clearly room for doubt; but does the evidence justify emphatic denial? Here we may well hesitate. It is hard to see how (presumably in the fifties of the first century) in the Jewish Christian Church of Jerusalem, where there would be a national repugnance against anything that savoured of heathen mythology, and which was presided over by St. James, the brother of Jesus, the story of the Virgin Birth could have gained currency if there were not strong grounds for thinking it to be true. On the other hand early Christian thinking, just because it was so convinced of the genuineness of Jesus' Sonship, may have been driven to speculate on its origin, with the result that, while one tradition connected the Sonship with the Baptism, when the Spirit of God descended on Jesus, another carried it back to the conception, when the Spirit descended on Mary.

There are problems here which the historian cannot answer. Taken by themselves, the stories of the Virgin Birth can have no cogency save for those who on other grounds believe that Jesus is the Son of God. And even for them it may be held that the vital truth to which they witness is, not that He was *born miraculously*, but simply that He, the world's Redeemer and Judge, was *born*, entering into human history by the same portal as His

135

brethren. Thus the words "born of Mary the Virgin," like those other words "suffered under Pontius Pilate," are part of the Church's emphatic declaration that its faith is firmly rooted in history.

The Place of Jesus in History. It is not always realized that the view men take of Jesus, and of the historical value of the Gospels, depends ultimately on the view they take of human history. If history is a purely evolutionary process, then Jesus, however superlatively endowed in power and wisdom, must remain on essentially the same plane as His fellows, and if the Gospels present a different picture of Him their evidence must be set aside or interpreted according to our evolutionary preconceptions. We see this notably when a " pure historian " like Professor Guignebert of Paris, whose book on *Jesus* in the " History of Civilization " series has recently attracted a good deal of attention, sets out to reconstruct the Gospel story. Professing that his concern is not with beliefs but with events, he presents us with a picture of Jesus which is pathetically out of harmony with the evidence of the Gospels, and which is quite as fully the child of presupposition as any interpretation of Jesus current among Christian believers. But there is another view of history according to which it is not a mere record of the doings of men; it is also (if we can learn so to read it) a record of the self-disclosure of God—from first to last God is overruling history, working out His purposes of judgment and salvation. On this view it is reasonable to believe, as the Church has always believed, that Jesus occupies the pivotal place in the scheme of divine revelation and in the working out of the divine purposes. The Gospels are not concerned to tell how, in a particular setting of time and place, Jesus Christ emerged to make His contribution to the development of human thought and action. What they tell is how, by the appearance of Jesus, God Himself in a unique

and decisive way entered into human history, seeking not
merely to enlighten and encourage His human children,
but to deliver them from the evil of the world, to establish them in a perfect relationship with Himself, and so
to ally them with His advancing purposes. Such a Jesus
is the true " Jesus of History."

THE CHRISTIAN BELIEF IN CHRIST

By A. E. J. RAWLINSON, D.D.(Oxon), Hon. D.D.(Durham),
Bishop of Derby

THE CHRISTIAN BELIEF IN CHRIST

THE Christian belief in Christ is in the last resort the
affirmation of a spiritual conviction not primarily about
Christ, but about God. There is a sense, indeed, in which
faith in God—a specific and definite conviction with
regard to the ultimate Being who is behind all things—is
not so much the conclusion as it is rather the presupposition of Christianity. The Gospel of Jesus (whether or not
by that phrase we are to understand primarily the Good
News proclaimed by Him, or the Good News proclaimed
by Christians about Him) came into the world, in the
first instance, in the spiritual context, and against the historical background, of Judaism. There was presupposed
by it the distinctively Jewish belief in the living God. The
Christian belief in Christ is not simply a worship of Jesus.
In the ancient world it would have been all too fatally
easy for a worship of Jesus to have arisen upon a background, not of belief in the living God, but of polytheism.
The Church was preserved from this peril by the two facts
that its first preachers were Jews, and that it possessed the
Old Testament. Today, in a not wholly dissimilar fashion,
there exists the possibility of a quite genuinely religious
devotion to Jesus, considered as an adorable Person, which
can yet be combined with a characteristically modern
hesitancy or semi-agnosticism about God, which falls far
short of the true Christian theism. "Ye believe in God,"
says the Christ of the Fourth Gospel, "believe also in me."
The exhortation, for modern purposes, occasionally needs to
be reversed—" Ye believe in Christ; believe also in God!"

And by the term "God" must be meant not simply
the worshipful—not simply that (for example) which to

our human thinking appears to be good rather than bad, divine rather than diabolic, in *quality*. The term must at least denote the eternal Lord of our destiny, the inscrutable Source of all life, truth and being; who "dwells in light unapproachable, whom no man hath seen, nor can see"; who is the Maker and Indweller of this strange universe, in all its terror and in all its mystery—this universe with all its sin, tragedy, cruelty, suffering, and pain. It is in *this* sense that the Christian affirms his belief in God—in the living God, active and personal, "by whom all things were made"; and yet (by a strange paradox of faith) he affirms that God is supremely holy, supremely righteous, supremely adorable LOVE. He affirms that the living God, who "at sundry times and in divers manners spake in time past unto the fathers by the prophets, hath in these last days spoken" unto mankind "by his Son"; that "God so loved the world that he *gave*"—and that that which God gave was none other than the self-expression in manhood of His own proper Being, the eternal "Son of his love," Jesus Christ. The divinity of Christ is thus for the Christian not simply an honorary rank bestowed upon Jesus on the ground of the supreme excellence of His human and ethical character : it is the recognition of an ultimate mystery—the mystery of the paradoxical "coming" into this world of time and of history of an eternal Person who, in the roots of His being, is essentially God. The Christian believes that the Divine "Word," incarnate in Jesus, stands in the last resort on the other side of the boundary line between the Creator and all things created, where there can stand only God; and that to affirm, with a modern writer, that " the inner Reality of the universe has looked into human eyes through the eyes of Jesus Christ "[1] is to affirm simply the truth.

[1] Dr. Edwyn Bevan, *Hellenism and Christianity*, p. 242.

This Christian belief about Jesus did not, of course, in its developed and classical forms of expression, spring suddenly into life ready made; and, moreover, it cannot be demonstrated. It is an essential part of the affirmation of orthodoxy that Jesus Christ came " in the flesh." He is the Word *incarnate*; and the deity is in such wise " veiled " in the manhood as to be recognizable only by faith. Considered externally, and apart from the insight of faith, Jesus Christ is a Jew, and a first-century Jew; so much, at least, must be held to be common ground between Christians and non-Christians alike. It is admittedly common ground also that the Apostles and earliest disciples of Jesus proclaimed after His death and (so they themselves, at least, firmly believed) after His resurrection a religious message of Good News in His name. They believed that in Him God had in very truth " visited and redeemed his people," and that the salvation of God was through Him made available to all such as by faith should receive it. The traditions with regard to the historical life of our Lord which have been handed down and enshrined in the Gospels are all presented and told from the standpoint of " faith." They present Jesus Christ not simply as prophet and teacher (though they do so present Him), but as *the* Prophet, *the* Teacher, who is also the Christ, the Messiah, who, as such, speaks with authority. For the Evangelists themselves it is not primarily the originality of our Lord's teaching, it is rather the absoluteness of His claim, which is the main point. " The reader is confronted with the Messiah who demands the complete fulfilment of the Law of God, and who once stood in the midst of Palestine and called men to Himself."[1] Apart from mere questions of simplification, of arrangement, of editing, and of relative emphasis, there

[1] Hoskyns and Davey, *The Riddle of the New Testament*, p. 133.

are no real differences, of any fundamental importance, between the Synoptic writers in respect of their general conception of the story they have to tell. "All three evangelists record the intervention of the living God in the heart of Judaism at a particular period of history in the Words and Actions and Death of Jesus of Nazareth: all three describe this intervention in the context of Old Testament prophecy: and all three regard these happenings as one great Act of God by which His rule is inaugurated on earth, and as a result of which those who believe are enabled to do the will of God, are freed from the powers of evil, are forgiven their sins, and are given a confident hope that they will share in that life which belongs to the era which is to be."[1]

I have been quoting from a book published some five years ago by two Cambridge scholars. The writers, in the course of a careful argument, maintain (and, by my judgment, successfully) that the doctrinal or "Christological" interpretation of the story of Jesus was not simply imposed by the Evangelists upon their materials, but that it was implied already, at every turn and in every *stratum*, in the materials themselves at the pre-literary stage of the tradition. If this contention is sound, the conclusion ensues that at no recoverable stage in the transmission of the Gospel material is there presented to us the non-Christological Jesus of modern "Liberal" or Unitarian theology. The Gospels are not neutral documents: they are what has been called "testimony literature"; and that to which they bear witness and testify is primarily the faith of the Church, from the very beginning of Christianity (so far as our evidence goes), in Jesus of Nazareth as the Christ, the Anointed of the Spirit, the Fulfiller of Prophecy; the supernatural Son of God, who, despite His manifest manhood (for it is part of the very essence of the Christian

[1] *Op. cit.*, pp. 143 *sq.*

"Good News" about Christ to affirm that, as the Johannine writer expresses it, He "came in the flesh"), is yet, in His own Person and "coming," and not simply in respect of His *teaching*, of decisive and final significance for the religious salvation of man.

The Gospels—these ancient books, which come down to us out of the living heart of the worshipping Church of the first Christian century—are admittedly not modern documents; and their mental furniture (if the phrase may be allowed) is not modern. They have a message for modern times, as for all times : but their message requires to be understood. They speak home to the simple believer; but for the more sophisticated mind there is need of a real effort (which must be informed both by disciplined study, and by a genuine and sympathetic use of the historical imagination) if that which they have to convey to us is to be in any adequate fashion grasped. The reader will certainly not become adequately seized of their meaning by dint of pursuing simply the naïve methods of rationalism; or, in other words, by discarding, and without more ado, laying aside as of no special significance, everything which, at the first blush, does not appear to be immediately intelligible or congenial to the average cultivated mind of today.

The methods of rationalism have indeed often been tried : and the world is familiar enough with the results. The procedure is simple. From the Gospel according to St. Mark (chosen, in the period since Renan,[1] on the ground both that it is the earliest of the Gospels in date, and that it provides an alternative framework to that of St. John) there is stripped away, as being by the modern

[1] Renan's *Vie de Jésus*, first published in 1863, is a sentimentally coloured treatment of the Gospels which differs from most of the "Liberal" Lives in its relatively conservative view of the Fourth Gospel.

mind unassimilable, almost the whole of what to the Evangelist will have constituted the main point of the story—viz., the Messiahship of Jesus, together with the emphasis laid upon the Passion; the very numerous miracles; the supernatural voices from heaven; the testimony borne by the demons, as the denizens of a supernatural world, to the supernatural Christ; the eschatological setting in which the whole is presented, with the discourse of Jesus about the Last Things. The framework or outline of St. Mark's narrative is allowed (as I think, somewhat uncritically) to stand; and is commonly held, by the type of writer I have in mind, to supply a reliable *cadre* for the story, an itinerary of our Lord's movements, in chronological sequence. Beyond this, there may be taken over a few easily rationalized narratives of cures worked by suggestion, and the general picture of the enthusiasm of the Galilean crowds, set dramatically in contrast with the opposition of the Pharisees—those wicked ecclesiastics of the day—who in Jesus disliked a religious reformer, unorthodox in respect of the Law. There have been theological " Liberals " who have even somewhat optimistically described St. Mark's Gospel, by an overpressing of the tradition which connects Mark with St. Peter, as being virtually the work of an eye-witness— though, if so, it is clear that the " eye-witness " has succeeded in observing a great deal more than, on the assumptions of Liberalism, he ought to have done! Be that as it may, into the framework or *cadre*, with its few meagre contents, thus supplied by a rationalistically weakened Mark, there is inserted next (with the omission, as unauthentic, of a few of the more inconvenient or difficult sayings) the greater part of the teaching material from the supposed document " Q "[1] and the Lucan parables. The

[1] By the symbol " Q " is denoted a written document, other than Mark, and containing almost exclusively sayings of Jesus,

result—tricked out and seasoned to taste with descriptions of the scenery of Palestine, and with some account of the religious, social and political life of the time—is then finally presented to the world as a scientifically trustworthy account of the real Jesus as He actually lived, a Jesus uncoloured, because uninterpreted, by the presuppositions of Christian faith.

It has been done so often! And when it was first done, it appealed, certainly, to the modern world with a certain freshness and force. Vigorously presented, by a writer of sufficient skill, sympathy and imaginative power, the "Liberal" or humanitarian portrait of Jesus can still be made, to some modern minds, subtly attractive. There is literature still being produced in which the Jesus of Liberalism masquerades as the Jesus of history, and there are those still to whom the idea of a Christ stripped of dogmatic trappings, a Christ who is "simply human," and who is supposed to require no kind of interpretation in terms of theology—a plain teacher of righteousness, a human Master in the spheres of religious faith and of personal piety—very strongly appeals. But the sceptical doubt still persists: Is this really the Jesus of history? It is not the Christ of the documents, and it is not the Christ in whom Christians believe. Can we be *sure* that the faith of Christians in Christ is mistaken, and that the documents also are wrong? And is it really to be supposed that behind the phenomenon of Christianity, as an historical faith, there is nothing *more*, in the way of legitimate starting-point, than such a Jesus as in these modern humanitarian "Lives" is depicted? Alas! there are skeletons still in the theological cupboard. The ghosts of orthodoxy do not consent to be thus easily laid. The his-

which is believed by scholars to have once existed, and to have been used by the compilers of Matthew and Luke.

torical conscience of the modern theological Liberal is not
at rest. The question so penetratingly asked in the Gospels
themselves—"What think ye concerning the Christ?
Whose son is he?"—persists still with its challenge, and
confronts the minds of men still.

The considerations and arguments which have been set
forth in the last few paragraphs admittedly do not amount
to a demonstration : it has already been laid down that the
Christian faith cannot be demonstrated. There is a sense
in which, with regard to any historical subject-matter,
there remains always the alternative of scepticism : and
with regard to the Gospels, the most recent developments
of what has come to be known as " form-criticism " have,
in the hands of some writers, been given a perhaps need-
lessly sceptical turn. It has been argued above that the
Gospels are " testimony literature," and that in this respect
the tradition which has been handed down to us with regard to our Lord is, from first to last, all of one piece. But
behind the tradition, in its written forms, there was a
generation of unwritten preaching ; and the story is certainly told from the standpoint of " faith."

Apart from the inevitable possibilities of *detailed* scepticism at almost any given point in the narrative, it is the
writer's own personal conviction that the Gospel tradition
is, in general, rooted in history, and that the influences to
which it has been subjected in the course of its transmission have affected or altered its form far more than
they have affected or altered its substance. But this is because he believes that the actual historic facts with regard
to the person, work, teaching, life, death, and resurrection
of Jesus were really of such a kind as to require and to
justify the apostolic proclamation or " Gospel " of Jesus'
Messiahship, and of the redemptive action of God, in and
through Him. It is admittedly no part of the historian's
task, simply as such, to decide in respect of the issues of

faith. Admittedly "no man can say, Jesus is Lord, save in the Holy Ghost." It is the historian's part to interpret the evidence, to attempt simply to understand the New Testament, and to present an historical portrait. It is the conviction of the writer of this essay that the portrait of Jesus, fairly presented, upon the basis of a legitimately critical study of the evidence, turns out to be of such a kind as to involve and to imply a supremely staggering claim, and to challenge a decision in terms either of faith or of unfaith. He believes that we are confronted, in Jesus, with an historical Figure whose claims are of such a kind that, if they are admitted as valid, they must in the long run mean that the Person who makes them, however historical, must yet transcend history—must demand explanation in terms not of the historical merely, but of the super-historical. "An historical figure," writes the present Dean of King's College, London, "whose life and teaching are held to provide the ultimate values by which the meaning of history is to be determined and its course controlled, cannot be purely historical in the admitted scientific sense."[1] There is an issue here; and it is of a kind which is not finally to be evaded. It is precisely the newer and more radical criticism of the schools which have gone beyond Liberalism which is in process of bringing us back to the original sharpness and challenge of the Gospel.

To accept the Gospel (which is the alternative to scepticism) is, in effect, to share broadly the Evangelists' outlook. It is to take up the standpoint of "faith." And, just as the more modern forms of historical criticism have gone beyond Liberalism, so there is a sense also in which "faith" goes beyond criticism. Criticism, pursued honestly and for its own sake, may have exploded (I believe that it

[1] From a sermon on "The Historic Jesus," printed in *The Guardian* for September 4, 1931.

has exploded) the affirmations of Liberalism. It can never hope by itself either to reach, or in the strict sense to substantiate, the affirmations of "faith." For it is the historian's aim to be simply historical; and if the aim of the purely detached and external historian could in respect of the subject-matter of the Gospels be wholly achieved, the result (it is to be presumed) would be just such an insight, completely adequate as far as it went, into the actual and outward historical facts of our Saviour's life as would amount, in the phrase of St. Paul, to a "knowledge of Christ after the flesh." And in the knowledge of Christ "after the flesh" there is neither religious value nor saving power.

On the other hand, this does not mean that to know Christ "after the Spirit"—that is to say, to know Him by faith as the Son of God—is to depart from reality. Quite on the contrary; that which in Jesus Christ is discerned by faith is the truth—God's truth. Faith is no system of make-believe. It is the capacity to apprehend truth in the sphere of things spiritual; and the truth of Jesus is the truth of God in Him, as it is apprehended by those who in the power of the Spirit have been enabled to confess Him as Lord. It is not the case that the worldly world's secular, non-Christian interpretation of Jesus is the real truth, and that the Christian's insight is merely a more or less beautiful idealization. The "Word" really *was* "made flesh": and the crowds who, in the days of our Lord's life upon earth, perceived in Him merely a prophet were (in so far as regards the essential point) only a degree less mistaken than the High Priests who perceived in Him merely an impostor. But it belongs, as part of its very meaning, to that doctrine of the Incarnation in which the faith of Christians in Christ finds its fullest expression, that the Incarnate Lord, considered apart from the insight and from the presuppositions of faith, *must* present the appearance of being simply a man amongst men. Of all those who by faith are enabled to discern in the Man Christ Jesus the eternal Word of the Father, the scriptural words remain true—"Flesh and blood hath not revealed it unto thee, but my Father which is in heaven."

For in truth it is not a question here simply of a bare, intellectual assent. The revelation of God in Christ goes beyond the mere revelation or setting forth of a *truth*: it is the breaking forth also of *life*, whereby the believer is stirred and gripped, not in a part of his being only (for example, the intellect), but in the heart's core of his very self. There is no " light " here which is not at the same time " life "; no "belief " which does not also involve obedience, awe, and trust; no cognition or knowledge which does not involve also a personal act of decision. It is a question of a Word of God, or rather of *the* Word of God, absolute in its claim: it is God Himself, as the absolute Lord, speaking to us, and laying upon us His demands.[1]

Of the classical forms in which, in the general tradition of Christian theology, the doctrine of the Incarnation in Jesus Christ of the eternal Word of the Father " for us men and for our salvation " has found expression, it is perhaps in an essay of this kind hardly necessary in detail to speak. It is obvious, for example, that the succession of paradoxes comprised in the clauses referring to the Incarnation in the latter part of the document known as the *Quicunque Vult* in the Anglican Book of Common Prayer represents simply the attempt to affirm with the utmost clearness and definiteness at once the real and absolute Deity and the no less real and no less absolute Manhood

---

[1] The above paragraph is taken in substance from Emil Brunner's *Der Mittler,* p. 177 (*cf.* English Translation, *The Mediator,* by Olive Wyon, p. 203. I have preferred, however, to make my own translation from the German).

of the one Divine-human Person, Jesus Christ. Jesus Christ—such is the doctrine—is truly and genuinely God : and He is at the same time truly and genuinely Man. How, from the point of view of a thought-out theology, the two distinct and distinguishable " natures " (the Divine and the human) are in the one " person " of the Christ to be regarded as being related to one another, and what is the precise manner or mode of their union, the official formulæ of orthodoxy (and perhaps it is fortunate that it is so) do not explain. What appears to be important, from the point of view of the Christian faith, is that it should be possible to make the affirmations (1) that to have truly " seen " Jesus is to have " seen " God; (2) that in Jesus the " Word " was " made flesh "; and (3) that in Jesus we have to do, not with a human being who was deified, but with a Divine being who became man. As it has been expressed by some recent theologians, the coming of Jesus into the world is the coming of " the Word of God from beyond history "; and the coming of the Word from beyond history is the " breaking through " into history of that which is not in itself simply historical, and which, in respect of the ultimate secret of its being, cannot completely " go " into history, because it is eternal. There is, in effect, a mystery *behind* the historic " personality " of Jesus : and a distinction needs to be drawn between the historical and the human " personality," and the Divine and eternal " Person," whose secret is the ultimate mystery behind. It is the Divine " Person," incarnate in Jesus, who is to be adored, and who is a proper object of worship; to adore Jesus Himself, as to His simply historical and human " personality," would be creature-worship and heathenism.

The question may be raised, and in fact has been raised, whether a doctrine such as the one which has just been indicated, a doctrine which affirms the paradoxical

" coming " into the world of time and of history of an eternal Person, who in the full sense is God, is not in form mythological: and perhaps it may be so. It is in the form of a narrative, a *mythus* or story, that the Christian affirms his faith: he speaks of One who was " in the form of God," and who " was God," and who, for our sakes, " came down from heaven." It has been argued by Emil Brunner that the forms in which Christian faith finds expression not only are, but inevitably must be, in a certain sense mythological: that this so-called " mythological " form of expression is the only one possible. The human mind is continually and rightly making the attempt to translate into non-mythological forms (metaphysical or scientific) the Christian content of faith: but the attempt as continually breaks down, in the sense that what is expressed in the new forms always appears to be other, and less, than the full paradoxical challenge of the New Testament Gospel. But the Christian *mythus* or " story " is something quite other than what is ordinarily meant by mythology. Its whole point is that you could *not* say of it " These things never happened: they are eternally true ", and, in so saying, leave its religious and spiritual value or " truth " unimpaired. The Christian Gospel, in other words, is *not* simply the expression, in the pictorial form of a story not literally true, of a truth which is timeless. On the contrary, its whole point is that it is historical, it is something which happened; and it is also decisive, it is something which happened once and for all. The " childlike mythology " of the Bible story is the truth which God has Himself given us, and which He has wrought out in fact. It is something which *happened*, a " time-myth " which is also the act of God, God's own doing; a " mythology " of which God Himself is the author, and which came actually to pass; an act of God which, if it happened at all, is for all time decisive and final. " The Word was made flesh, and tabernacled amongst us, and we beheld his glory."

The Christian faith is in the last resort not a matter of proof but of testimony. The Church bears witness and testifies to the truth by which she lives. And the essential witness of faith can be stated quite simply. "A Light we can bear to look at" (so it is expressed by a recent writer), "and looking at must adore, comes to us from a Light we cannot bear to look at even whilst we worship it. The mystery of Reality enters history very gently by a human channel, and shows the character of Perfect Love within the life of man; gives us something to hold on to, a Truth which is also a Way and a Life. What we see is not very sensational: but if we look at it steadily, it pierces the heart. First we see a baby, and a long hidden growth; and then the unmeasured outpouring and self-spending of an other-worldly love and mercy, teaching, healing, rescuing and transforming, but never trying to get anything for itself. And when we look deeper, we see beyond this a mysterious self-imparting, and a more mysterious anguish and struggle; consummated at last by the most generous and lonely of deaths, issuing in a victory which has given life ever since to men's souls."[1]

The modern New Testament scholar is disposed for historical purpose to contrast the tradition of the first three of our canonical Gospels (the so-called "Synoptic" tradition, to which reference was made at an earlier stage in this essay) with the more admittedly interpretative presentation of the evangelical story in the Gospel according to St. John. The contrast should not be exaggerated. The Synoptic tradition is throughout penetrated actually, as we have seen, by an element of explicit or implicit "interpretation": and the Fourth Gospel, however interpretative, is in intention unquestionably based upon history.

Evelyn Underhill, *The School of Charity*, pp. 28 *sq.*

But the broad contrast exists: and the Fourth Gospel provides an interpretation which in certain important respects is on different lines from the one which the earlier Gospels set forth, and which may rightly be described as being not only an interpretation, but in large measure an interpretation in new terms. The new version of Christianity does not, indeed, cut the Gospel adrift from its roots either in history or (for that matter) in Judaism. It is an important part of the writer's avowed purpose to insist that the Lord Jesus Christ came "in the flesh": and he insists equally that "salvation is from the Jews." The author of the Fourth Gospel, as I think, is a Jew, and a Jew, moreover, who had been in intimate contact with Christianity, perhaps from its beginnings in Palestine. But he is a Jew who not only writes as a Christian, but who, as a Christian, is writing in Asia Minor towards the close of the first century: and he deliberately writes with the object of setting forth Jesus to the "Greeks"—that is, to the cosmopolitan world. He sets forth the Lord Jesus accordingly, not only in Jewish categories, hard to be understood (for example, such terms as Messiah, Son of God, Son of Man, Kingdom of God, End of the Age, Age that is coming), but in such terms as are universal and (without any need for translation) can make their appeal, and can speak home, to the general heart of mankind.

Man needs guidance; he needs, in the midst of the perplexities (intellectual and moral) of this dark world, the assurance of truth and of light. He needs to be able to know that he is moving in the right direction, and that his feet are upon the right road. He needs life—spiritual life—food for his soul, strength for the journey. He needs recovery and restoration—the assurance of the forgiveness of sins. He needs (to sum it all up in a sentence) spiritual light, life and love.

It is for this reason that the Gospel according to St. John

(despite many things, and a number of passages, contained in it which are difficult), because it sets forth our Lord as the Life and the Light, as the Way and the Truth, as the Bread that came down out of heaven, and as the Good Shepherd, the Saviour, the Lamb of God that taketh away the sin of the world, has been for millions of simple-hearted Christians what Luther (I think) called it—" the precious and only Gospel, far to be preferred above the others."

The Fourth Gospel presents Jesus in these terms: it presents Him also in terms of the doctrine which represents the maturest phase of the New Testament thought (and which underlies the theology of this essay), as the " Word " (or Self-expression) of God Himself in the " flesh " of our manhood. There is a sense in which " God can only be known by God "—a sense in which God, except He Himself, by His own will, take the initiative, and by the activity of His own Spirit make Himself known, is unknowable. " No man hath seen God at any time: the only-begotten Son, which is in the bosom of the Father, he hath declared him." Those who, by the grace and power of the Holy Spirit, have been enabled in Jesus Christ to see God: those who, beholding Jesus, have been enabled to cry, with St. Thomas, " My Lord, and my God "—to them (in the words of St. John's Gospel) there has been given " the right to become children of God, even to them that believe on his name."

THE PRIMITIVE CHURCH

By NATHANIEL MICKLEM, D.D., Principal
of Mansfield College, Oxford

VI

THE PRIMITIVE CHURCH

I

THE almost universal reverence paid to the Figure of Jesus Christ is not extended to the Christian Church. Men contrast the simple teaching of the Master with the complicated and remote theologizing of the institution; they contrast the freedom, the spontaneity, the divine compassion and tenderness of "the Jesus of History" with the rigidity, the formalism, the intolerance of organized Christianity.

The instinctive impression of a fundamental difference between Christ and the Church has received support in the arguments of certain Biblical scholars. Jesus Christ, they have said, neither founded nor contemplated the Christian Church. The simple and spiritual teaching of the Gospels, which is the real essence of Christianity, we owe to Jesus Christ; the Church, which has done so much to obscure that message, is the work of the apostle Paul, ecclesiastic and theologian.

Was St. Paul, then, the real founder of Christianity? Did Jesus Christ intend to found a Church? These are the two main questions to be discussed in this chapter. It will be well at the beginning to state as clearly and forcibly as possible the case we have to meet.

Jesus Christ, it is argued, was concerned with personal religion and with the proclamation of God's coming Kingdom. Only on two occasions is He said to have mentioned the Church, and both these passages are of very doubtful authenticity. Moreover, Jesus Christ could not have contemplated the Christian Church, for He expected the imminent end of the world and the rolling up of the book of history. The Christian Church, as we know it, is as remote from His thought as, only too often, it is out of harmony with His Spirit. No, when He died there was no Christian Church nor any thought of such a thing. After His death His followers kept together and may perhaps be regarded as a Jewish sect, but it was not till the Gentile mission of the apostle Paul that Christianity really breaks away from Judaism, and the Christian Church emerges as an institution. Further, this change in outward status corresponds with a fundamental change in thought. Hitherto the followers of Christ have accepted His teaching about God and the world and duty; they have, in fact, adopted the faith *of* Jesus Christ. Henceforward they appear with a Gospel *about* Him, a proclamation of His Death, Resurrection, and Second Coming as achieving man's salvation. Who cannot detect a fundamental difference between "the simple Gospel" of Galilee and St. Paul's doctrine of salvation "by the blood of Jesus"? Paul, therefore, was the true founder alike of the Church as an institution and of Christian theology. It behoves us to go back to the simple and uncontaminated faith and teaching of Jesus Christ and to regard the Church as a usurper and corrupter of the Gospel.

This may perhaps be regarded as the plain man's view, and, even if it has less support today than once it had from scholars, it needs and deserves frank consideration.

II

We may conveniently start from a consideration of the two texts whose authenticity is doubted. In Matt. xviii. 17, a passage dealing with the erring brother, we read " and if he refuse to hear them (the two or three witnesses), tell it unto the church (ecclesia): and if he refuse to hear the church also, let him be unto thee as the Gentile and the publican." It is often said that this text, which occurs in St. Matthew alone, presupposes the organized Christian Church and its problems of discipline and excommunication; therefore it cannot be an authentic saying of Jesus Christ. This may be so. On the other hand, our Lord may very well have used these words; but, if He did so, the Aramaic word corresponding to ecclesia or church would presumably have been understood by His hearers to refer, not to a Christian Church which did not exist, but to the Jewish synagogue. In either case, therefore, this text is indecisive.

But it should be noted that the passage continues thus: "Verily I say unto you, What things soever ye shall bind on earth shall be bound in heaven: and what things so-ever ye shall loose on earth shall be loosed in heaven." Binding and loosing according to Jewish legal terminology mean forbidding and allowing. This verse is like the promise to the Twelve that they shall sit on thrones judging the tribes of Israel (Matt. xix. 28). We cannot safely argue from this that our Lord anticipated the Christian Church as we know it, but it fits in with the many other passages which indicate that He looked forward to some community in which His apostles would play a ruling part.

The second passage to be considered is Matt. xvi. 18: "I say unto thee, thou art Peter, and upon this rock I will build my church." The question at issue here is the authenticity, not the truth, of this saying; for as a matter of history it seems clear that after the Resurrection the Church was founded upon Peter and Peter's faith. The difficulty, rather, is this: if we read in a natural way St. Mark's account of the scene at Cæsarea Philippi (Mark viii. 27 ff.), it would seem that our Lord received

St. Peter's confession, "Thou art the Christ," rather with anxiety and distress than with overwhelming joy. The word Messiah (or, in Greek, Christ) upon St. Peter's lips in those days might well have too political and militaristic a sound to be received with unqualified satisfaction. Hence our Lord begins at once to speak of the sufferings of the Son of Man, as if He could neither deny nor yet accept this title.

So understanding the narratives in St. Mark some scholars have supposed that St. Matthew for the purposes of his Gospel has brought together the two confessions of St. Peter, the first at Cæsarea Philippi when he said, "Thou art the Christ," and the second by the lakeside when the "gates of hell" had not prevailed against his Lord, and St. Peter said, "Lord, thou knowest that I love thee."

This is possible. On the other hand, these words as they stand may very well have been spoken by our Lord at this critical moment of His ministry. In that case we should have to understand by His "church" the Messianic community, the Remnant, the true Israel of obedience and faith. This is the kind of question where certainty is not attainable. On the one hand, we have no adequate reason, so far as New Testament scholarship is concerned, for denying the authenticity of either of these two passages in which our Lord is said to have referred to the "church." On the other hand, there is an element of uncertainty such that we cannot affirm with assurance that our Lord during His days on earth used the term "church" of the Christian community.

III

We must next consider the far-reaching contention that our Lord could not have contemplated the Christian

Church because He expected "the end of the world" within a few days or a few years at most. Certain texts seem to bear this out: "Ye shall not have gone through the cities of Israel, till the Son of man be come" (Matt. x. 23), or "There be some of them that stand here, which shall in no wise taste of death, till they see the Son of man coming in his kingdom" (Matt. xvi. 28).

Attempts to explain away these and other so-called "eschatological" passages by the suggestion that our Lord did not really mean anything but the slow processes which we call history and Evolution have definitely failed. On the other hand, there is ample evidence that this kind of "eschatological" language, familiar to the Jews as it is strange to us, is more akin to poetry than to the prosaic and exact language of science. There is no doubt that certain passages in the Gospels taken by themselves might seem to imply an imminent "end of the world" and therefore to be with difficulty reconciled with the idea of an enduring Church; but the teaching of our Lord must be taken as a whole, and it is obviously sensible to interpret these very difficult passages, if possible, in the light of the rest of His teaching.

It is quite impossible in a brief statement to give a summary of the vast literature that has discussed this matter in recent years. Upon many points there is still no kind of unanimity among scholars. But two things may in fairness be said of those scholars who have taken the expectation of the imminent end of the world to be the keynote of our Lord's teaching: first, that their theory has compelled them violently to explain away a very large part of the rest of His teaching, and, second, that their theory makes it impossible for them to give a rational account of the actual rise of the Christian Church.

It must suffice that we here lay down certain broad principles which will be universally intelligible, and which may claim the support of the great bulk of enlightened Christian scholarship.

First, then, we have no reason to think that our Lord, who even according to the strictest orthodoxy assumed a human mind, foresaw the Church of England or Nonconformity or the post-Tridentine Church of Rome. We cannot assert with confidence that He ever spoke of the "church" in the sense of the Christian community. We have no direct evidence in His recorded sayings that He laid down a constitution or rules for an organization that should arise after His death.

Second, He proclaimed the imminence of the Kingdom of God, which is almost the opposite of what we mean by Progress and Evolution. He declared, in fact, that God was about to intervene in some decisive way in human history. We must add that this prediction was indeed fulfilled. Not for nothing do we date a new era in world-history from the coming of Jesus Christ. Not only did He proclaim the Kingdom, but He also brought it. We may not with Roman Catholic scholars identify the Church with the Kingdom, but certainly those who are true members of His Church have received and are receiving the Kingdom under the conditions of our human life. Those who have had an experience in any way akin to that of St. Augustine or St. Francis of Assisi or Ignatius Loyola or John Bunyan or John Wesley know what it is to be reborn into a world made new. Their experience is essentially "eschatological"; it is an apprehension of a Coming of the Son of Man. St. Paul compares the act of God in Christ with His action at Creation's morning: "It is God that said Light shall shine out of darkness, who shined in our hearts, to give the light of the knowledge of the glory of God in the face of Jesus Christ" (2 Cor. iv. 6). That which in the first three Gospels is called "the Kingdom of God" is represented in the Fourth Gospel by "eternal life" and in the writings of St. Paul by life "in Christ" or "in the Spirit." It is, then, patently the teaching of the whole New Testament that a divine act of God has taken place, the Kingdom has come, or, to use Jewish phraseology, the powers of "the age to come" are already at work in this present age.

Certainly, however, the Kingdom is not yet consummated. It is possible, but quite undemonstrable, that our Lord expected the *consummation* of the Kingdom in a relatively short time; but the Kingdom of God is a spiritual reality, and the question of its sooner or later consummation is hardly a religious question. Its postponement for a million years or more would not affect the teaching of the Lord.

We accept, then, the view that our Lord did not contemplate the Christian Church as we know it, that we cannot assert with confidence that he ever spoke of His "Church," and that the Gospels give us no warrant for supposing that He laid down a constitution for the later Church. Further, we are bound to assert that He proclaimed the imminent advent of the Kingdom of God, but not that He necessarily expected the consummation of this Kingdom at any particular date or even in the near future, nor can we see that the question of date has any strict relevance to His teaching.

On the way we have come upon a principle of the utmost significance for our present enquiry. For we have seen that the Christian Church is intimately bound up with the "eschatological" teaching about the imminence of the Kingdom. We read that our Lord came into Galilee declaring, "The hour has struck; the kingdom of heaven is at hand." That He was not deluded is proved by the Church itself. The Church as the fellowship of believers, of the redeemed, of those who have been "translated out of darkness into the kingdom of his dear Son" is the direct result of the mighty act of God which Christ not only announced but in His own person realized. This is only hidden from us as we regard the Church from outside as a very imperfect and human institution; it is plain when we regard the Church from within as the fellowship of those who say in gratitude and awe, " He loved me and gave Himself for me."

Before we consider the great significance of all this for our second question concerning the alleged divergence between the teaching of Christ and that of St. Paul, we must consider one further general principle.

IV

Our Lord is reported to have said, "I came not but to the lost sheep of the house of Israel." His ministry was limited, or almost limited, to Jews. He does not appear at first sight to have contemplated the later " Gentile mission " of St. Paul. He spoke as one of Jewish race and Jewish religion to the Jewish people. How then can it be said that He planned a world mission or even a world religion? What place is here to be found for the idea of the Christian Church?

Yet we read that at the beginning of His ministry He was shown " all the kingdoms upon earth in a moment of time." He refused to win these kingdoms by doing obeisance to the devil—that is, by using the devil's weapons, but He did not renounce His claim to this world-wide dominion.

We must bear in mind the religion of the Old Testament, in which He was brought up. Israel, arising out of a group of Bedawin tribes, developed first a narrow but passionate nationalism. As there was no people like them, so was there no god like their God. The prophet Amos was possibly, but not certainly, the first to declare that the

God of Israel, holy and righteous, was God of the whole earth. From this conception arises in time the thought that it is the task of Israel to bring the knowledge of the true God to all the earth. The Old Testament reaches one of its highest points in the conception of the Servant of the Lord, which is Israel, or the faithful in Israel, or the ideal representative of Israel, as suffering martyrdom that the knowledge of the glory of God might be brought to the Gentile world. Thus the Servant of the Lord is depicted as in the extremity of wretchedness and dereliction—" his visage was so marred more than any man, and his form more than the sons of men . . . he hath no form nor comeliness; and when we see him, there is no beauty that we should desire him." Then the meaning of this suffering dawns upon the nations, and they declare in astonishment " Surely he hath borne our griefs and carried our sorrows; yet we did esteem him stricken, smitten of God and afflicted. But he was wounded for our transgressions, he was bruised for our iniquities; the chastisement of our peace was upon him; and with his stripes we are healed " (Isa. lii. 13-liii. 12).

In later years Israel fell far from that ideal. The wall which Nehemiah built round Jerusalem symbolized that terrible exclusiveness and utter separateness of Israel from all other peoples which is typified for us in the Pharisees. Yet even the Pharisees " compassed heaven and earth " to win a proselyte, and it was a commonplace even of the most bitter and nationalistic Jewish literature in the time of Christ that before " the End " there should be a gathering in of the Gentiles. We can say, therefore, on general grounds that, even if the ministry of Christ was limited to Israel, His outlook must have been world-wide (*cf.* Matt. viii. 11; Luke xiii. 29).

Indeed, from one point of view we may say that the purpose of His ministry was to recall Israel to its God-given task. He called men to repent and receive the good news. And what then? Surely to *be* Israel, to fulfil Israel's destiny, to be the medium through which the knowledge of God should spread through all the earth. In accordance with this, when He went up to Jerusalem to challenge His enemies in the seat of their power, and by one signal symbolic act to declare before all the world His purpose, He drove the traffickers out of the Temple, and, where it was written up in great letters, "Death to any Gentile who enters here," He declared that the Temple was to be "a house of prayer *for all nations*" (Mark xi. 17).

This does not prove or imply that He contemplated the Christian Church as we know it, but it plainly involves that the calling together of a Church was essential to His thought and mission. Had Israel hearkened to Him, Israel, the chosen people, would have been the Church that should gradually have gathered into itself all the fulness of the Gentiles. But when the invited guests refuse to come, the master of the feast must send out into the highways and hedges; the Church must be a Gentile Church.

We may thus summarize the foregoing argument. No attempt has been made so far to show that our Lord contemplated the Christian Church as it was in the fourth century or in the Middle Ages or as it is today. But it has been sufficiently indicated that the idea of a Church, a community to be the instrument in the hand of God for the salvation of men, was integral to His thought, and, further, that the Christian Church, regarded as the company of those who have been translated out of darkness into the light, corresponds with the promise contained in His "good news" and is most intimately connected with Himself.

V

We may now consider the contention that the apostle Paul radically altered the Christian faith by substituting "faith *in* Jesus" for the "faith *of* Jesus."

The case is presented in such terms as these : " Our Lord came calling men to repentance that they might enter into the Kingdom of God. Nothing was needed for their forgiveness beyond their repentance; let but the Prodigal start for home, and the Father will run to meet him. The essence of the Lord's teaching is the Fatherhood of God, and even this is set forth less as a dogma than as a matter of intimate and happy experience. Let men but treat God as their Father and all men as their brothers, and they will enter at once into the liberty and blessedness of the children of God. Love to God and love to man, the simple message of the Christmas angels, the acceptance of Christ as Teacher and Example and Friend—such is the Christian faith, the Christian Gospel.

" Contrast this simple, spiritual, intelligible, unsophisticated, all-satisfying message with the complicated theology, the dogmatism, the churchiness of the apostle Paul. In the place of simple trust in our Heavenly Father, St. Paul has put the acceptance of certain dogmas about Jesus Christ.

" What is there in the Gospels to suggest that a man can only be forgiven in virtue of the death of Christ? Did not Christ forgive men before His death and without reference to it? What in the Gospels corresponds to St. Paul's elaborate teaching about the Spirit, about justification, about the sacraments, and, not least, about the Church? To turn from the Gospels to St. Paul's epistles is like passing from the sunshine into a dim and ill-aired crypt.

"This seeming contrast might be further elaborated; it is felt by the plain man and is largely the ground upon which men seek to repudiate the Church and Christian theology in the supposed interests of loyalty to Jesus Christ Himself. St. Paul, it is said, shows no interest in the life of Christ; he hardly ever quotes or refers to the words of Christ; with his fierce, intolerant spirit, his dogmatic insistencies, his preoccupation with an institution called the Church, he offers us what is virtually a religion that is as new as it is inferior when compared with the religion of Jesus, with the Gospel of the Sermon on the Mount, and with the creed implied in the Lord's Prayer."

This point of view rests partly upon a misunderstanding of the apostle Paul, perhaps still more upon a misapprehension of his Master's teaching, and upon a serious underestimate of what had happened between the ministry in Galilee and the opening of the Gentile mission.

It is hard to exaggerate the importance of the labours of St. Paul, but we should remember that he was not the only missionary, and that he created neither the Christian creed nor the Christian Church. Not one of the three outstanding churches of the early centuries, Antioch, Alexandria, Rome, looked to St. Paul as its founder. During his life he was a doughty fighter and was for long regarded as a heretic in respect to justification apart from the law and, in general, to the place of the Gentiles in the Church; but in no other regard, so far as we know, was he ever accused of altering or misrepresenting the Christian faith. It is true that immediately after his conversion he "conferred not with flesh and blood," but the Christ to whom he surrendered on the road to Damascus was the Christ of whom he had learnt through the Church that he had persecuted. Later, as he tells us, he went up to Jerusalem "to learn Peter's story"; there also he conferred with St. James, the brother of the Lord (Gal. i. 16, 18 f.).

Most important of all, when in writing to the Corinthian Church he makes a synopsis of "the gospel which I preached unto you," he begins it in these words, " I delivered unto you first of all *that which also I received,* how that Christ died for our sins according to the scriptures; and that he was buried; and that he hath been raised on the third day according to the scriptures, and that he appeared to Cephas . . ." (1 Cor. xv. 1-5). Here we have the innermost core of the Christian creed in a form that must go back to the very first period of the Church's history before the conversion of St. Paul himself. It is quite certain that St. Paul neither founded the Church nor invented the creed.

VI

It may be objected, however, that, whether or not St. Paul was responsible for the change, an unmistakable and indeed a fundamental change in thought and teaching took place between the ministry of the Lord Himself and the theology of the Christian Church. This distortion took the form of putting the Figure of Jesus Christ Himself, and especially His death and Resurrection, in the forefront and centre of the picture, whereas in the Lord's own teaching the Fatherhood of God and the Kingdom of righteousness are central.

The plausibility of this view rests largely upon an exclusive concentration of attention upon the Galilean ministry and public teaching of our Lord.

It is usually thought that the scene at Cæsarea Philippi where St. Peter first confesses, "Thou art the Christ," marks a crisis and turning-point in the Lord's ministry. From that time on, it appears, He began to speak about His sufferings, and, in general, He began to speak about Himself. The Baptism narratives at the beginning of His ministry indicate that from the start He realized clearly His own central place in the drama of God's redemption, and it is not here suggested that prior to Cæsarea Philippi He never spoke of His own personal task directly or by implication, but from that time onwards He had necessarily to speak about Himself, for now He had "set his face to go to Jerusalem."

This was openly to challenge His enemies in their own stronghold. It is as if the time for preaching is over, and the time for action, dramatic, decisive action, is at hand. He warns His disciples that, if they go up with Him, they take their lives in their hands; He must require of them not merely assent to His message, but personal loyalty to Himself.

If our Lord be regarded simply as a Teacher of sublime and spiritual truths, that journey to Jerusalem must appear as inexplicable or inexcusable. If they will not hear Him in Galilee or Judæa, why should He not, as did St. Paul, shake out His tunic and say, " Your blood be on your own heads; I go to the Gentiles "? He might have travelled to Athens where any new thing was welcome, or He might have journeyed about Asia Minor like a wandering Stoic preacher. At the very least He might have gone to Alexandria, where the Jews were liberal and might be expected to give Him a more favourable hearing. But He was not mere Teacher; He was the Son of Man, whose function it was to receive the Kingdom from God and to bring it to mankind (Dan. vii. 13 *f.*).

The latter part of the ministry, the story of the Passion (as we call it), which really starts with Cæsarea Philippi, is the complement of the earlier preaching ministry. The Kingdom of God is at hand, or, in modern speech, a decisive act of God for man's redemption is to be immediately expected. But how? By a rending of the heavens or a driving of the Romans into the sea? Such was the

Jewish expectation; and we who mock the blindness of the Jews are ourselves so blind that we cannot even see that the promise of God *has* been fulfilled: "He *hath* visited and *hath* redeemed his people."

The redemption of God could only come through the Passion of His Son; only from the Cross could He win dominion from sea to sea and from the river to the ends of the earth. His mind is revealed at the Last Supper on the night on which He was betrayed.

Six hundred years before, the prophet Jeremiah, realizing that preaching is not enough, and that there is an impotence and deep-seated perversion at the heart of mankind, had cast all his faith upon God and uttered the memorable prophecy: " Behold the days come, saith the Lord, that I will make a new covenant with the house of Israel, and with the house of Judah, not according to the covenant which I made with their fathers in the day that I took them by the hand to bring them out of the land of Egypt; which my covenant they brake, though I was an husband unto them, saith the Lord. But this shall be the covenant that I will make with the house of Israel; After those days, saith the Lord, I will put my law in their inward parts, and write it in their hearts, and will be their God, and they shall be my people . . . for I will forgive their iniquity, and I will remember their sin no more " (Jer. xxxi. 31 *ff.*).

We are so accustomed to think of the death of Christ as His Passion that we miss the recognition that even more it is His action. This new covenant, this redeeming intervention of God, could only come through the death of the Messiah; " it is *necessary* that the Son of man should suffer many things "; the covenant must be sealed with blood. In moments of our deepest intuition, when, for instance, we are most deeply aware of the guilt and degradation of sin, or when the tragedy and pathos of man's sufferings and impotence come most nearly home to us, we glimpse the *necessity* of the Cross of Christ. We must not here develop this theme; it is enough to insist that the sense of this necessity was laid upon our Lord. We must not think that His teaching was confined to general spiritual principles and ethical requirements. " This cup is the new testament in my blood " is also part of His teaching; but, since with these words He hands to them the cup, it is His action not less than His teaching.

This supposed contrast or contradiction between the teaching of Christ and the teaching of St. Paul is connected with the failure to recognize that the teaching of Christ is secondary to His action. It was suggested above that the Galilean ministry was a time of preaching, whereas the later part of the ministry after Cæsarea Philippi was the time of action. The contrast here is only relative. The true significance of the whole ministry of Christ is recognized in the collect wherein we pray to Him " whose blessed Son was manifested that he might destroy the works of the devil and make us sons of God and heirs of eternal life." Christ was manifested not primarily to teach but to destroy the works of the devil. The teaching was incidental to the great campaign against the enemy.

We are apt to exalt the teaching and to relegate the miracles to a very secondary place. Modern New Testament scholarship has shown that the miracles are primary. At what must seem a crucial point in the ministry His enemies accuse Him of casting out devils by Beelzebub the prince of the devils. He answers, " If I by the finger of God cast out devils, without doubt the kingdom of heaven has come upon you " (Luke xi. 20). Our Lord proclaimed the imminence of the Kingdom; His miracles attested it; Satan's house already was being despoiled, the strong man was bound. It is, therefore, quite inaccurate to say that at first He exercised a preaching ministry, and afterwards, when that failed, He went up to Jerusalem. His death was but His *final* grapple with the enemy, the Resurrection was His victory.

Once it be grasped that the Lord's ministry was rather action than teaching, that we are studying not a doctrine but a campaign, it is not difficult to meet both contentions, that St. Paul fundamentally altered the message of Christ, and that the Church had no place in the thought of Christ. We may consider these two points separately.

The charge against St. Paul is that he altered the whole thought of the disciples of Christ—so much so that he is really the founder of the Christianity we know—by converting the teaching of Jesus, which is, in other words, the religion of Jesus, into a Gospel of the Cross and Resurrection which is a Gospel about Jesus; our Lord instead of being the supreme believer, the subject of faith, takes the place which belongs only to God and becomes Himself the object of the believer's faith.

At first sight St. Paul appears to have little interest in the teaching of our Lord or in His life. It is true that he rarely quotes a saying of Christ and refers to scarcely an incident in His life except His birth and death and Resurrection. On the other hand, in his teaching about the Spirit, which is the Spirit of Christ, he indicates again and again what manner of men Christians will be if they " walk by the Spirit " (*cf.*, in particular, 1 Corinthians xiii. and Romans xii.). Herein he offers us incidentally but unmistakably a portrait of what the Lord Himself was like, and shows how deeply he had entered into the Master's mind and teaching. Indeed, it is not

175

strictly proper to say that the Gospels here corroborate St. Paul. Rather, it is St. Paul who corroborates the Gospels, for not only were the epistles written before the Gospels, but St. Paul alone offers us what is indubitably contemporary evidence about our Lord.

The complicated or, rather, the allusive and unsystematic, theology of St. Paul is best understood as his attempt to explain the significance of the *action* of Christ, that ultimately victorious struggle with the enemy, which, as we have seen, is the primary element in His life, and of which His teaching is the reflection.

Two outstanding elements in the theology of St. Paul have struck the modern reader as remote from the thought or teaching of " the Jesus of History ": first, his doctrine of Christ as the eternal, pre-existing Son of God, " in whom dwelleth all the fulness of the Godhead under bodily limitations " (Col. ii. 9); and second, his doctrine of justification by " the blood of Christ "; or, in other words, his doctrines of the " divinity " of Jesus Christ and of the Atonement.

This, as has been explained, is because in a quite unscientific way, which modern scholarship is making more and more impossible, we are apt to take the Sermon on the Mount and perhaps the fifteenth chapter of St. Luke as a summary of the message of Christ, to regard His miracles and His mission to seek and to save the lost as secondary, and to regard the Crucifixion as the tragic conclusion of His ministry due to the social, political, and religious conditions of His day.

The Sermon on the Mount, as we may say with confidence, is a summary of the Lord's teaching put together in order to answer the question of an enquirer or candidate for baptism, How must I live if I would follow Christ? The fifteenth chapter of St. Luke represents God as the father who runs to meet his returning prodigal, as the shepherd who goes out over the mountains to seek for his lost sheep "till he find." But is God really like that? Has He done it? The answer is Jesus Christ Himself. Apart from Jesus Christ, who came to seek and to save, who gave His life having loved His own " unto the end," this doctrine of God is but an idea, a hope, at most an ultimate probability; it is no Gospel.

All the elaborate theology of St. Paul is but a commentary upon such sayings as these: "The Son of Man came to seek and to save that which was lost" (Luke xix. 10); "The Son of man came not to be ministered unto, but to minister, and to give his life a ransom for many" (Mark x. 45); "No man knoweth the Father save the Son" (Matt. xi. 27); "Come unto me all ye that labour and are heavy laden, and I will give you rest" (Matt. xi. 28); "This cup is the new covenant in my blood" (Luke xxii. 20).

For our present purpose it is not necessary to expound nor to attempt to justify all the Pauline theology, but enough has been said to show that the representation of St. Paul as the virtual framer of the Christian creed, the perverter of the whole basis of Christian thought, the real founder of the Christian religion as we know it, is simply not true to the evidence.

VIII

Again, the recognition that the life and work of Christ is to be regarded rather as action than primarily as teaching goes far to answer the question, Did Jesus Christ contemplate the Christian Church? Historical science cannot prove that He spoke of "the Church" as such, that He legislated for the Church or visualized the historical forms which it was destined to assume. Indeed, when we regard the actual historical Churches which are known to us and consider the Church as a human institution or corporation, we may, perhaps, say with some confidence that Jesus Christ never contemplated the Christian Church. Yet we have clearly seen that the Church—not in any particular form, but the Church in some form—is not merely integral to the thought of Him who is depicted in the Gospels, but is most intimately associated with and necessary to His work; indeed, it *is* His work. We may quite truthfully say that the creation of the Church is the very purpose of the Incarnation.

Our Lord not merely proclaimed the coming Kingdom, He also brought it. He declared the imminence of a decisive act of God for the redemption of mankind; His coming, His life seeking the lost, forgiving the sinner, casting out demons by the finger of God, His death, His Resurrection—all this *was* the decisive act of God, a redemption not yet consummated, but in principle accomplished and actually, though but partially, realized in the new Israel, the company of those who have been translated out of darkness into light, who, once strangers to the promises of God and without hope in the world, now know themselves forgiven and His children. The decisive act of God was nothing else than the coming of the Redeemer and the gathering of the redeemed, or, in other words, the Person of Christ Himself and the Christian Church. If we eliminate the Church from the thought of our Lord, we throw away the one clue which interprets all He was and said and did.

IX

To some readers the argument put forward above may appear too facile and too triumphant; they will suspect a catch somewhere. In conclusion, then, it may be admitted that there is a catch, or, at least, that it has not really been proved to logical demonstration that our Lord intended to found the Christian Church, and that St. Paul was not the Church's founder.

The whole argument turns upon the contention that our Lord came in the first instance, not to teach, but to " destroy the works of the devil and to make us sons of God and heirs of eternal life." If it is correct to suppose that His life and death were part of a divine campaign, a struggle with the enemy on man's behalf culminating in victory through death, we can recognize that the theology of St. Paul is simply an attempt to explain that which was implied in the Christian faith which he received from the first disciples and which they had learnt from the Lord Himself; we can see, further, that the raising up of a Church is integral to the work and purpose of the Lord.

Now, this contention that the work of Christ is action rather than doctrine, and that the doctrine is but the commentary on the action, is increasingly recognized by modern scholarship, but it can never be demonstrated beyond cavil that such is the only possible interpretation of the facts. The argument, therefore, may be rebutted in either of two ways. On the one hand, it may be said that the Gospels and epistles of the New Testament misrepresent " the Jesus of History," who was a great spiritual and ethical teacher, the Prophet of Galilee, who lost His life through the implacable enmity of the religious authorities of His day and (we should add) through His own ill-advised and unnecessary journey to Jerusalem; the later Christian doctrine about His divine Person and the imminence of the Kingdom and His Coming Again are an addition to, and a contortion of, His original message; He was concerned purely with personal religion, and His outlook was limited to Palestine.

This answer may take innumerable forms, but in the end it may always be reduced to the contention that the Gospels and epistles (for the two cannot be separated in this connection) misrepresent " the Jesus of History." The view should be regarded sympathetically, for no one should suggest that it is *easy* to credit the apostolic testimony. But it must be firmly insisted that if Jesus Christ was not such as the Gospels and epistles represent, we have no means whatever for guessing what He may have been. Beyond question this so-called " Jesus of History," the " real " Jesus in distinction from the Jesus of the Church's faith, is a creation of phantasy, the arbitrary invention of the unbeliever. Still, it always remains possible and quite intelligible that men should declare the Figure revealed by scholarship to be impossible.

The second way of meeting the argument of this chapter is really a variant of the first. It may be maintained that the thought of Christ has not here been misrepresented, but that it was based on a pathetic and demonstrable illusion; Christ really expected some divine intervention, some winding up of the world order, some act of redemption wrought by God; but nothing happened, and the Church is the society which under the stimulus of the apostle Paul has adopted a substitute for the discredited expectation of its nominal Founder. The fundamental basis of this as of the former objection is that the Kingdom has not come, nothing supernatural has happened, our world is the same old world with only some deep ethical teaching and some attractive religious hopes added to its stock of ideas.

This final issue can never be settled upon the basis of historical research alone. It is ultimately a matter of faith or unbelief. It has been shown that, if the Gospels be taken seriously, our Lord contemplated that which we may call a " Church," and that St. Paul is the expositor of the Christian faith, not the real founder of the Church. Further than that we cannot go.

*　　　*　　　*　　　*　　　*

But Christians constantly fail to recognize that they must decide between alternatives, the acceptance of either of which is almost more than human nature can endure. To reject Jesus Christ as deceived and a deceiver—that, says the Christian, would be to take all colour, all meaning, all hope out of life; it would be death itself far more truly than is the mere dissolution of the body. We cannot declare Jesus Christ a liar. In denying Him, we should deny ourselves and life and everything. On the other hand, to accept Him and His teaching means in the frankest way to accept the supernatural; it implies the faith that "God from on high *hath* heard," that He "*hath* visited and *hath* redeemed his people," that the powers of the age to come are already at work in this world, that the divine Son of God has come to earth, that He has died and risen again, that the Church is so intimately connected with His Person and His work that it may not inappropriately be called His Body. To accept this doctrine, however, with its implications, implies a miracle of faith or, as the Schoolmen put it, the supernatural gift of faith, for such teaching is to the formalist a stumbling-block and to the superior person foolishness.

It may seem a far cry from this spiritual conception of the Church to the various Christian "denominations" with their wide differences of thought and practice and, not infrequently, their exclusive claims to be *the* Church. From the pages of the Gospels we can vindicate the Church, but we cannot vindicate ourselves—that is, we cannot vindicate and justify the Church in so far as it displays not the divine life of its Head but the all too human infirmities of its members. At this point, however, the subject must be referred to later chapters and other pens. But whatever changes, deformities, and perversions there may have been in history, the Church remains self-identical with the community of disciples gathered in the Upper Room in virtue of the unchanging apostolic Gospel and the breaking of the bread in fellowship.

SIN AND THE NEED OF REDEMPTION

By J. S. WHALE, President, Cheshunt College

VII

SIN AND THE NEED OF REDEMPTION

CHRISTIANITY has always refused to be reduced to an intellectual system for philosophers or to an ethical programme for moralists, though it obviously implies and includes both. As a religion it is primarily and distinctively concerned with redemption; it presupposes not only the fact and universality of moral evil in the world, but also man's inalienable responsibility for it. The very *raison d'être* of a gospel of forgiveness is sin.

Much modern hostility or indifference to Christianity is understandable, therefore, if one of the striking differences between preceding ages and our own lies in our changed attitude to sin, as is constantly alleged. The modern world is reputed to take sin lightly. According to rather facile generalizations now current, there is a widespread decay in the sense of sin and a diminished severity of judgment towards it, few things giving more vivid testimony to a new temper of easy tolerance than the dislike of the very word sin by great numbers of people, not all of them young. Presumably, then, the title of this chapter would irritate many and rouse their antagonism.

I leave others to judge whether this is just the healthy anti-clericalism of the natural man, or whether it is more accurately diagnosed by Jane Austen's remark in *Sense and Sensibility* that when people are determined on a mode of conduct which they know to be wrong they feel injured by the expectation of anything better from them. Again, I can only glance at Mr. Lippmann's argument in his somewhat splenetic yet deservedly famous book *A*

Preface to Morals, that for many people the very name of moralist has become a term of disparagement because it is too nearly synonymous with antipathy to the genius and vitality of the modern age. Probably the alleged relaxation of moral earnestness in ages of disintegration and rapid change like our own requires some such interpretation. To Leonardo da Vinci the mediæval world must have been what classical Protestantism was to Rousseau with his philosophy of self-expression, or what nineteenth-century piety is to Mr. Lippmann himself. It is no moralist who looks out at us in Leonardo's picture of John the Baptist in the Louvre, but the magnificent yet wistful paganism of all such ages of Renaissance, crying out against a world grown grey with the breath of a stuffy moralism.

However we are to account for it, then, a louder and more articulate expression is being given in our day to the unanalyzed notion (it is no more!) that a lot of unnecessary fuss can be made about the mystery of iniquity; that to bother much about one's sins is morbid, while to bother at all about the sins of others is impertinent.

A religion of redemption is plainly superfluous on such premisses; the antidote is unnecessary if we have been mistaken all along about the bane. Thus a modern defence of Christianity has to face and answer once again four successive questions about sin which the gospel of salvation necessarily presupposes, and which our age is making its own. (i.) Is there such a thing as sin? (the problem of evil in general). (ii.) Even if sin be real, does it matter very much? (the problem of moral judgment). (iii.) Even though sin matters, is it our fault? (the problem of guilt). (iv.) If sin is our fault, what is at stake? (the problem of redemption in a moral universe).

I

Is there such a thing as sin? or, to put this fundamental question in another way, how can evil of any kind exist in a universe created and sustained by God? This is no mere academic question which may be dismissed as a puzzle for philosophers or as a subject for mystic meditation. After all, the possibility that evil is an illusion, a subjective interpretation by the human mind, is the basis of at least one great religious system in the East, the non-moral monism of Hindu thought, according to which Good and Evil are alike only appearances, albeit necessary, of an Absolute which transcends both. Again, the same hypothesis provides the philosophical basis (in so far as there is one) of those theosophical movements whose most notable modern representative is Christian Science. Yet again, the naturalistic ethic of secularism, which has had some vogue in the West, arrives at the same result, based as it is on a crude form of determinism. Thorough-going mechanistic materialism is not only incompatible with the absoluteness of moral distinctions; our question is one of its plainest implications.

Thus our question raises one branch of that problem of evil which we can neither fully solve nor disregard, and which has vexed thought and tried faith through the centuries; how can evil co-exist with God if He be the source and ground of all that is? If everything that exists follows of necessity from the Final Reality in all its perfection, can anything be evil?

There are two classic and contrasted types of solution to this problem, neither of which is satisfactory to a truly Christian philosophy yet each of which expresses truth it may not ignore—the monistic and the dualistic. Philosophers are said to incline to the former, moralists to the latter. The philosopher seeks some unifying principle which will embrace reality as a whole and leave no loose ends or awkward facts unexplained; he tends to sacrifice the reality of individual experience to philosophical unity. The moralist, on the other hand, seeks to safeguard the indubitable reality of evil and its clear distinction from good, this being the root fact in ethics; he tends to sacrifice the absoluteness and sole causality of God. The one repudiates deism which virtually denies the reality of the divine omnipotence since it postulates a world of existents somehow independent of the supreme source of existence. The other repudiates pantheism which virtually denies the reality of sin. To quote Dean Inge's epigram on the dilemma, " the notion of a finite God is one that the moralist can never afford to forget nor the metaphysician to remember."

Our sole concern here is with the so-called pantheistic view. It is ironical that its classic statement comes from a descendant of the race that produced the Old Testament, the great Jew Spinoza. For him evil is an illusion due to our necessarily limited point of view, our inability to see things as they really are, *sub specie æternitatis*. Since there can be no intrinsic disorder in the universe it is our finite imagination, viewing the world *sub specie temporis*, which gives to evil a fictitious substantiality. Evil is the unreal assuming the semblance of the real, false appearance caused by darkness in ourselves. Moreover, since God is all and all is God, the finite ego is also an illusion; the creature is not an independent self but, as merged in God, is only a mode in His mind. The reality of the finite subject being done away, to speak of its sinfulness or goodness is meaningless.

Two objections are obvious. First, the theory that sin is illusion would leave unexplained and inexplicable vital elements in our moral consciousness—our indefeasible

sense of selfhood, personal freedom and ethical self-determination, and all those feelings of obligation and responsibility which are bound up with it. Secondly, we do not
dispose of a positive and terrible fact common to all
human experience by explaining it away as illusion or
defective cognition. As Tennant remarks, such a defect
of cognition is itself an evil; darkness in ourselves is itself
a problem requiring a solution.

This pantheist or absolutist solution of our problem
takes various forms; evil is sometimes regarded as mere
appearance, in the sense that so far from being absolutely
evil it is relatively good, a necessary element in or step
towards perfection. Hegel, for example, regarded " sin "
as the necessary way whereby we move from the non-
moral stage of innocence to the final synthesis of positive
virtue. But here again, cogent objections spring from
common experience; the reality of the finite subject and
of its experiences is dissolved by such a philosophy; if sin
is only a stage, though a necessary one, it ceases to be
what the religious consciousness knows as sin—namely,
that which has its seat and ultimate source in the will, and
for which the free subject's moral responsibility is therefore inalienable. If moral evil be an absolute necessity in
the evolution of spirit, guilt clearly ceases to be its correlative. Necessary moral evil is a contradiction in terms,
since evil which is necessary thereby ceases to be moral.
Indeed, moral evil like moral good is an abstraction, without an agent; it originates in the will of man. When we
speak of sin we mean sinners, free agents who are individually responsible to God. A fact which the familiar
distinction between, say, manslaughter and wilful murder
sufficiently illustrates is that a sinful act is what it is only
as it expresses a personal choice, a will in action; strictly
speaking, guilt can be predicated only of persons. Sin is
real, but only as moral evil for which man is responsible

in the sight of God. Moreover, in that it concerns God it is of supreme moment.

This, however, raises a new and important question to which we must now pass.

II

Even if sin be real, does it matter very much? This question, which follows naturally on what has gone before, virtually asks how sin is to be defined. Granted its reality, wherein lies its gravity? Is it any more than the vice which is solely the affair of the individual concerned (short of the point at which it becomes a nuisance to others), or the crime which admittedly offends against the law, but only because it violates the social convenience which the law exists to preserve? Or does it matter in the sense that the pervert has perverted the eternal spiritual order and offended against holy laws; that the criminal has not only sinned against his neighbour and society, but also against Heaven? Moral evil is no illusion, clearly enough. But is it more than dust in the balance of eternity and can it conceivably matter to Him who is from everlasting to everlasting; may not our plaguing sense of responsibility before God be an illusion, and the age-long idea of redemption a moral puzzle of man's own making? There are those who claim (with some apparent justification!) to have no particular sense of sin at all, those for whom what is called sin is no more than stupid miscalculation or mistake; they contend that though our moral distinctions are necessary, inasmuch as they obviously fulfil a necessary social function, they are not in any sense absolute. It is this sincere, widespread, though often inarticulate contention for which we have to account and with which we have to deal here.

First of all it may be remarked that our modern emphasis on relativity goes a long way towards accounting for it.

Notoriously enough our age cannot sound out the positive note; having lost the absolute standards of earlier generations, very many in the modern world are certain only of their uncertainties, in almost every department of thought and action. It is our misfortune, even if it is not our fault, that we cannot answer our questions; we can only ask them and leave them open. "Everything being now relative, there is no longer absolute dependence to be placed on God, free trade, marriage, consols, coal or caste." That is our modern situation, seen from the satiric angle of Galsworthy's vision. A boundless relativism everywhere throws the old landmarks down, and the more men feel their deep need of a palpable, self-authenticating authority —that unwritten law, eternal in the heavens, to whose objective truth Antigone could appeal with the serene confidence of the martyr—the more wistfully do they confess in deed and word their obvious lack of it. When incertitude is the mark of the hour, men are less inclined to listen for the everlasting Yea, and one point of view seems as likely to be true as another. In that very phrase "point of view" the fetters of the dungeon of subjectivism clank ominously.

In the second place this anthropocentric temper may be accounted for by a heightening of man's immemorial sense of insignificance and loneliness as he looks out upon the inconceivable vastness of the universe and feels what has been described in our day as its astronomical intimidation. With scientific knowledge greater than that of the Psalmist or of Pascal, the modern man stands like them under the stars, alone in all his magnificent frailty; he is so small amid this terrible immensity; his life is but a vapour that appeareth for a little time and then vanisheth away. A speck of wayside dust is to the globe what the globe itself is to a universe whose measurement in light-years man can only guess at, whose centre is everywhere and whose circumference is nowhere. Is this wayside planet, measured in terms of electron and geological epoch, any more in comparison with the whole universe than a raindrop of a few seconds' duration? The modern man finds it increasingly hard to believe that it is. He does not easily rid himself of the depressing conviction that things human are too trivial to matter; that human iniquity has no cosmic significance, nor its condemnation at the bar of man's moral consciousness any eternal validity. His sense of the gravity of sin as offence against God is subtly undermined as he asks the defeatist question, Does it matter what I do? In explanation of this modern pessimism Freud argues in a well-known passage that man's self-esteem has suffered three successive shocks from blows delivered against it during the modern epoch. The first was the cosmological blow struck by Copernicus, the proof that the earth is not the centre of the universe. The second was Darwin's biological blow, the argument that man is no special creation but linked by evolution with the animal world. The third was the psychological blow, a knock-out given presumably by Freud himself, the contention that since man's life is determined by complexes and psychical heritage, his sense of freedom and responsibility is an illusion; "the ego is not master in its own house." Thus, with man's uniqueness trebly discredited, his pessimistic refusal to bother about his sins is natural enough.

In the third place, what is generally known as Humanism is associated with the foregoing both as cause and effect. Humanism rejects the Christian doctrine of man as *imago dei*—a supernatural being having his very origin and existence in the Word of God—and boldly makes man the measure of all things. It starts with anthropocentric premises, but is so far from pessimistic conclusions that it is almost truculent in its optimism. Indeed, if what I do does not ultimately matter, Humanism has logic on its side in recommending me to do as I like. If nothing matters, why be " good "? Or rather, since it is impossible to desire evil as such and strictly for its own sake, if I think a thing is good it *is* good for me whatever others may think. This is the doctrine which sophists from Protagoras to Aldous Huxley have bravely proclaimed and which a few have even tried to translate into practice.

So much for the threefold contention underlying our question, Does sin matter much? In dealing with it the religious man need do no more than appeal to the tremendous testimony of human experience. Any candid person can verify the significance and power of sin by invoking the threefold testimony of man's moral judgment, as revealed in his literature, his history, and his conscience.

Look first at the conscious and deliberate testimony of literature. Literature *is* testimony by its very nature. It holds the mirror up to life and reveals all that is distinctive and abiding therein. In the great literature of the world the spirit of man witnesses to moral realities, the eternal rock upon which his being is built. A sense of sin is not only expressed in all great literature worthy the name; it is a creative element therein. The sublimest utterances of man in all their poignancy and tragic grandeur would have been impossible if the sense of guilt had not been a terrible and enduring reality. To omit from Æschylus or Dante, Shakespeare or Goethe, the sense of sin and the fact of man's responsibility for it would be to read them with one eye shut; indeed, one could not begin to read them at all. Speaking of the certainty that nothing in earth or heaven can overthrow the sanctions of the moral law, Professor H. R. Mackintosh observes truly that if the teacher of religion will not keep a man right on this point, the novelist and dramatist will. He goes on to say that

" if the evil things he has done and the evil person he has made himself do not justly pierce and wound a man's conscience, the tragic dramatist cannot make a beginning."[1]

Look in the second place at the same testimony in human history. It is impossible, while looking steadily at history, to say that there are no eternal sanctities to which it bears witness. If morality is an illusion, everything is an illusion including existence itself. There have ever been men and women who have done the painful right and so vindicated the eternal moral order in the midst of time, finding blessedness and peace, not in the reward of virtue, but in virtue itself. They have been sure that the good is an end in itself, and therefore that the question, Why be good? is essentially immoral. History is also eloquent of the opposite fact that " even on the view of the universe as physical process, there are some rampant lies and degradations and brutalities which, not without a measure of plausibility, are called sin."[2] The historian cannot turn a blind eye to these things and remain a historian. He may not deliberately cultivate the " smiling, intelligent detachment " of an artist like Jane Austen, whose theme is high comedy and whose pages are therefore never darkened by the shadow of the Industrial Revolution or the Napoleonic War through both of which she lived. Though she exclaims with sprightly candour, " Let other pens dwell on guilt and misery; I quit such odious subjects as soon as I can," the facts remain, and they remain odious. Further, if language means anything and if history be objectively real, they are odious to God.

Moreover, history, which is biography writ large and the study of man in his social relations, also testifies to law, whose very existence is a monument to wrong-doing

[1] *The Christian Experience of Forgiveness*, pp. 8, 16.
[2] J. Oman, *The Natural and the Supernatural*, p. 292.

both empirical and potential, and to the fact that rights can be universal only if they imply duties. A do-what-you-will individualism, which means business and wishes to be taken seriously, will very soon be taken seriously by the law, if only because it depends on the principle that all our desires and impulses are equal in value and ought to be satisfied[1]—a principle which is plainly anti-social, breaking down at the merest whisper of universal application. It is this obvious fact which leads the thorough-going individualist to say that sin is no more than miscalculation or mistake, an offence against the man-made rules of the prevailing social code. Even for him all things, though lawful, are not always convenient or expedient; he finds out by experience what is desirable or undesirable, taking the consequences when he is mistaken. It is all a question of social expediency, not divine sanction; duty is only a high-sounding name for herd instinct, while conscience for all its undoubted authority is purely of social origin.

Now no one with an eye on history will deny that there has been variety in the demands made by conscience at different periods and in different places, or that even the trained conscience derives something from its social environment. But it is the *fact* of conscience rather than its content the significance of which is writ large in history; and variety in the content cannot discredit that uncompromising sense of obligation which is distinctive of and vital to the fact. This consciousness of obligation is essentially the possession of the individual, and it is not the testimony of history that it is no more than " dread of society," to use Freud's phrase, or group disapproval in action. If conscience can be analyzed without remainder into a spontaneous tendency to obey "that monster Custom," it is difficult to explain why it has so often com-

[1] *The New Morality,* p. 317, appendix on Aldous Huxley's *Do What You Will.*

pelled the individual to defy custom, and to meet herd disapproval with the words, Here stand I; I can do no other; God help me. History is too eloquent of the lonely witness of an Antigone, a Jeremiah, a Luther, or an Edmund Campion, for so easy a hypothesis to be convincing.

Thus we have already arrived, in the third place, at that testimony of conscience which is the presupposition and basis of all the foregoing testimony; volumes have been written about it, and here a brief treatment must suffice. First of all, conscience is a fact, as universal as it is indubitable. In all human experience there is an inexpugnable consciousness of moral obligation, an "I ought" and an "I ought not." Secondly, the masterful intensity of this fact is an ultimate of experience, an irreducible datum refusing to be explained in terms of any other principle; its compelling character completely resists analysis. The wisdom of the ages knows justice, truth, magnanimity, faithfulness and love as cardinal virtues because they have a self-evidencing claim on man's allegiance; there is therefore an obvious and objective wrongness about their opposites—meanness, cruelty, greed, and lust. Thirdly, the consciousness of moral obligation has transcendent implications; our religious certainties are built upon it. Our inevitable moral judgment that sin is always more than mere miscalculation is a religious judgment based on our sense of an eternal spiritual order, whose divine sanctions are never manufactured by man, but found by him. The sense of the sacred is no mirage; it is rather a potential ever demanding actualization, an ideal always ahead of man and waiting to be realized, a seeming mirage that becomes a pool as soon as he advances towards it. To put this in another way: man is aware of himself as a personality carrying its own witness to its unique value and end; to realize this end in himself and to respect

196

it in others is a sacred obligation, far transcending the obligation to obey tribal custom. Indeed, it points man beyond himself, and finds its sanction in God.

Here, moreover, lies the answer to astronomical intimidation. To use Pascal's famous words, man is only a reed, the weakest in nature, but he is a thinking reed. It needs no universe but only a drop of water to kill him, yet man is more noble than the universe which crushes him because he knows that he dies, while of the advantage which the universe has over him it knows nothing. Man is therefore greater than the process, if only because he is able to comprehend it as it can never comprehend him; he alone looks before and after and has immortal longings in him; he alone has been given the capacity for prayer. And it is his profound conviction that the categories of quantity and quality may not be confused; that size has nothing to do with greatness.

Sin matters, if only because the moral law within him is more significant for man than the starry heavens above him. His moral and religious judgment is the rock on which all relativist sophistries founder.

III

Even though sin matters, is it our fault? This third question is prompted by a vague but increasingly popular notion which may be summarized as follows: " Are sin and guilt correlative terms? Granted the reality of wrongdoing, can we really be held responsible and blameworthy, in view of all that we now know about the power of heredity and environment in human life, and of all that modern psychology has to say about the subconscious and its complexes? Sin obviously presupposes responsibility, and responsibility freedom, but are we really free? Has the son of a dipsomaniac, born and brought up in a slum, "any chance"; is his drunkenness any more blameworthy than the normal thirst of one who has had the advantages of a good home and a good education? Is he ultimately any more responsible for his sin than a thermometer for frost? Surely the stern moralist is further from the truth here than the old proverb, "Tout savoir est tout pardonner."

Here we are at the heart of our problem. No one in England has discussed it more thoroughly or acutely than Dr. Tennant, and it is worth while setting down his four well-known conditions for sin to happen at all.[1] His first condition is the existence in the social enviroment of an objective standard whereof sin is a transgression. Without law there can be no sin. There may be imperfection; but sin and imperfection, so frequently confused, must be sharply distinguished. His second condition is awareness on the part of the individual agent—at the time of his moral activity which is to be designated as sinful—both of the content of the moral law or standard and of its bindingness on himself. Sin due to ignorance cannot, strickly speaking, be called sin.[2] If sin is to be an ethical concept it must be correlated with self-determination; it cannot be made to include inevitable imperfection (like that of the human infant or of the adult savage) without forfeiting all that makes it *sui generis*. Unless morality postulates awareness and freedom, one logical consequence will be the pagan notion that sin is attributable to physical objects, and we shall be right in punishing the stool against which we have barked our shins, as earlier phases of law have actually done. Dr. Tennant's third condition is the existence in men of certain inborn dispositions—natural

[1] *The Origin of Sin*, 1906; *The Concept of Sin*, 1912.
[2] Theoretically considered, the legal argument that ignorance is no excuse (ignorantia juris neminem excusat) is not an ethical argument.

instincts, appetites and passions—which are not only non-moral and neutral in themselves, but necessary to human life. Biologically considered, they are essential to the continuance and health of the human race. They are not abnormal but natural, belonging to man as God has made him; they are non-moral because non-volitional. They are not only the raw material of sin and the conditions of its emergence, but also the basis of man's highest virtues; the " vital spark " of evil is also, of necessity, that of good. Tennant adds that it has been nothing short of disastrous that these conative tendencies have so often been identified with the activity of the will in regard to them. Propensities which are non-volitional cannot be called sin; it is the will which shapes and not the raw material which is shaped which alone calls for moral approval or disapproval. Thus the fourth condition is volition, which must include intention. Sin has its source and seat in the will; otherwise we might speak of matter as evil or of animals as sinners. To quote Kant's famous words, there is nothing in the world or even out of it that can be called good without qualification except a good will. Thus Tennant rightly insists on the voluntary aspect of sin, and on the sinner's freedom and responsibility as the presupposition of guilt.

But just here we have to meet the awkward question, why is sin universal? Granted that this is how sin happens, why does it happen always and everywhere? How are we to explain that seeming bias or perversion of the human will which makes sin an empirically universal fact? As the very condition of moral action men must be free to choose the evil, but why do all without exception do so, unless a sinful tendency is part of their very nature? All serious thought about the mystery of sin has had to grapple with this, its constitutional, as well as its voluntary, aspect. St. Paul, for example, argues that where there is no law there is no sin; guilty sin is found only when a man is aware of the demands of the divine law and consciously disobeys it, sin and guilt being correlative terms. But, on the other hand, St. Paul uses the same term " sin " to describe guiltless sin " where no law is "—that deadly spiritual wrongness which pervades all humanity and which, being objectively contrary to God's purpose and glory, alienates men from God even though they are not strictly blameworthy. Sin is there, even when there is no law to challenge and convict men, but it is " not imputed " (Rom. v. 13). We may deplore St. Paul's ambiguous terminology, but we cannot fail to know from our own experience what he is driving at. To take an extreme example, the cannibal, *who cannot possibly know any better*, is admittedly not guilty of sin, but his cannibalism certainly grieves the Holy Spirit; inasmuch as he is not a python nor a gorilla, but a man, his " sin " is an objective reality, even though it is " not imputed."

The same unfortunate ambiguity of language appears in the term Original Sin used by theologians to describe this universal human tendency to evil. The ecclesiastical doctrine of the fall, based largely on St. Augustine, explained the racial tendency to evil as original sin, by referring it back to Adam's fall in the Garden as its centre and sufficient cause, and so imputing guilt to it. Because of its unity in Adam the race shared in the results of Adam's fall by the doctrine of " corporate personality." Moreover (and this is a second and distinct point in the Augustinian doctrine), original sin made actual sin inevitable, every man being a sinner in spite of himself because of the corruption of his very nature by his first parents through the act of " concupiscence." The Augustinian doctrine of original sin on this twofold basis thus implied the doctrine of original guilt, which is not only contrary to reason and morality, but is incompatible with our modern conception of individual personality, and our conviction that " sin " lacks the essential element of guilt if the four conditions already set down are lacking.

The awkward question remains, however, and though we abandon the classical doctrine of original sin we are still left with the historical fact of universal moral imperfection in the race, whose reality that doctrine attested.[1]

It is not surprising therefore to find three present-day explanations of the all-pervading fact of sin, which are virtually the modern equivalents of the doctrine of original sin, save that they are poles asunder from it in one vital respect. Popular inferences from modern psychology, biology and sociology, so far from explaining guilty sin, very often only succeed in explaining it away. Before we glance at them we ought to notice that the root fallacy in them all lies in the attempt to explain what must be *ex hypothesi* inexplicable. We have seen that moral action is bound up with freedom, in the sense of real alternatives; the very essence of personality lies here. But if man is free no scientific explanation of sin is possible; you cannot explain the universality of sin without altering sin's very character by taking away that freedom which makes it *sui generis*. To formulate an absolute and universal cause of sin in terms of a " collective unconscious " or heredity or social environment would be to abandon the spiritual fact

---

[1] In passing we ought to notice carefully that the word " universality " can be used in a dangerously doctrinaire and misleading sense here; there is good in man as well as evil, and anything like a formula of universal depravity breaks down before the immense variety in the moral life of man. To quote Dr. Wheeler Robinson, "The practical universality of sin must not be taken as a single fact, capable of explanation by some single dogmatic hypothesis; it is a collection of facts, covering the widest range. . . . There are many grades of sinners which the mouth-filling word Universality tends to obscure." *The Christian Doctrine of Man* (3rd ed., pp. 303, 365), a great and authoritative work to which I am closely indebted here.

of personality which is rooted in freedom and which makes man what he is. You may account in this way for the mechanism of the actual sins which men commit, but not for their mainspring. Even so, the words "mechanism" and "mainspring" are misleading metaphors. Any alleged explanation of the fact that all men sin is only a new determinism, making moral evil a necessary element in human personality as we know it, and thereby affirming that it has no more moral quality than breathing or perspiration or the growth of the beard. "The Christian consciousness of sin . . . is the very repudiation of necessity in every form. How then can we be true to that consciousness and expect to find any cause for the universality of sin more ultimate than personal freedom?"[1] This brings us to the threefold argument which would lower our sense of responsibility and guilt by suggesting that we are not really free.

First of all, can man fairly be made morally accountable for what he is and does in view of the modern psychological discovery of the existence and power of the unconscious in each human life, and of the complexes generated therein as the result of repressions from the conscious? "Surely," it is said, "the power of this uncontrolled unconscious in our mental life to dominate thought and action means that what we do is not to be explained on a conscious rational basis at all; is the ego 'master in its own house'?" This is largely the classic problem of free will in a modern form, and a brief answer to it must therefore begin where the famous academic discussion ends—namely, with an appeal to experience. In asserting that whatever it may be in speculation, freedom is a fact, Bishop Butler said the last word here. For the fact of freedom, so difficult to analyze and define, is unmistakable. Remorse is a monument to it. If "I ought"

[1] H. W. Robinson, *op. cit.*, p. 304.

is an ultimate of experience, so is " I ought not to have done as I did." But freedom is not the sheer indeterminism of doing anything whatever at any moment, as though our successive actions were absolutely unrelated and disconnected. No true psychology of volition can be built on the palpably false hypothesis that the setting of our physical and psychical life is a chaos of indeterminacy. Chaos is not freedom. We live in a cosmos, which means that a relatively settled order is the very condition of purposive activity. This is as true of psychical as of physical activity. The self which wills and chooses does so, inevitably, in terms of previous willing and choosing; volition is always caused or conditioned by circumstances and character, which provide a precedent setting or sphere within which the self initiates and creates.

Of course, the will does not function at all without motives, but it is never completely determined by motives, " as a cannon ball is completely determined by the impulse of explosion within the gun." Motives and impulses are the material determining the stage whereon choice is to be exercised and moral defeat or victory wrought out. It is true that psychological analysis of an act of will seems to imply a closed circle of determinism, for behind my active choice lies my motive which owes its efficiency to and presupposes "attention"; but attention depends on my interests and these spring from my general character; yet my character is, after all, the deposit of all my previous acts of choice, and thus I have come round full circle to the point from which I started. But if this were the whole story, a man would be a machine, and facts of experience such as conversion and reformation become inexplicable. The truth is that there are reserves of psychic energy in "personality" making spontaneity and fresh starts possible; the closed circle is really a spiral staircase. By mistaken or wrong choice a man may descend, thus hindering the true progress of his whole, enduring personality; by right choice he may ascend, and so fulfil his life purpose. For by personality we mean "that which cannot be reduced to the purely natural sequence of cause and effect; that in which new beginnings are made. . . . The self is always more than its previously formed character . . . it is not exhausted by the sum of its motives."[1]

Moreover, modern psychology with its valuable analysis of the rôle of the unconscious confirms this. If it were deterministic as is popularly supposed, its own therapy of psycho-analysis would be logically impossible. Dr. Barbour points out that Freud, in spite of his formal determinism, disproves his own position by stating that the method of treatment in psycho-analysis is to make the unconscious conscious. "Our therapy," he says, "does its work by transforming something unconscious into something conscious, and only succeeds in its work in so far as it is able to effect this transformation." Thus Freud repudiates his own theory every time he cures a patient, because he thereby provides definite evidence of the power of the consciousness to redirect unconscious impulses and their accompanying power towards higher ends.[2] For the Christian, of course, whose doctrine of personality implies a doctrine of divine grace, the last word cannot rest with psychology or any other scientific description of sin's operation. But the vital point here is that all redirection is done of necessity by the individual, who is ultimately responsible not only for every fully sinful disposition and for much of the content of the unconscious, but also for his cure.

The second argument, a popular inference from biology, is at bottom a variant of the first. "Sin is not our fault if it be attributable to the fact of heredity; it is merely the

[1] H. W. Robinson, *op. cit.*, especially pp. 292-293.
[2] C. E. Barbour, *Sin and the New Psychology*, pp. 36.

survival of necessary appetites inherited from the sub-human world to which man is akin by evolution." But here again, the facts which are summed up in heredity do not exhaust the being of one who, though rooted in Nature, is also its sovereign. Heredity does not destroy the moral consciousness. In asserting that no man ever with a clear conscience put down his sin to his father's account, James Denney said the last word. To it we need only add that an appeal to man's animal origin in explanation of universal sin is to make that sin as inevitable as the ecclesiastical doctrine of the Fall made it; inevitable sin is a contradiction in terms. Moreover, we have no right to assume that the science of biology teaches the inheritance of acquired characteristics, or to base upon it the possibility of the transmission of sin by physical heredity. Evolution will explain the actual content of my heredity, since the present is continuous with the past; but the whole meaning of evolution is that with continuity of process goes the emergence of real differences all along the way. Facts arise which, though continuous with the past, are new. Here the new fact is morally responsible personality; to attempt to go behind it is to destroy it altogether.

Similarly with the third argument, which is drawn from sociology. No one will deny that there is a social inheritance and environment of moral evil which handicaps every child born into the world, and vitiates the world-wide context of social life. Sin is never a man's private affair; your failure matches mine, and our lives, interlocking, form an organized system or kingdom of evil. "We mortal millions" do not "live alone," but in society together. The social solidarity of the race is a fact, and, in view of the reality of sin, a terrible fact. As Dostoievsky puts it somewhere, we are each responsible to all for all. Therefore, we cannot ignore social heredity and environment, for the will as the source of sin cannot be abstracted altogether from it. The individual has an organic connexion with the race, past and present, a fact which is fully recognized by a great historian like Carlyle, who has been described as belonging to the Homeric Age of historical science because he conceives of history more in terms of personalities than of conditions. But Carlyle sees history as the complex resultant of character and conditions, as every historian must do. Describing the decadent years preceding the French Revolution, and seeking causes, he makes the characteristic outburst: " Woe to all men that live in such a time of world-abomination and world-destruction. ' Nay,' answer the courtiers, ' it was Turgot, it was Necker, with their mad innovating. It was the Queen's want of etiquette: it was he, it was she, it was that.' Friends—it was every scoundrel that had lived, and quack-like pretended to be doing, and been only eating and misdoing, as shoeblack or as sovereign lord, each in his degree, from the time of Charlemagne and earlier."

Nevertheless, the handicap due to environment is never the last word in the moral race which all men have to run from infancy to old age. Social environment shapes personality but does not control it; nor may it replace heredity as an " explanation " of the universality of sin, without emptying sin of its moral meaning. Temptation is not sin nor its cause, but its occasion. Sin implies freedom, and it is the testimony of the awakened and remorseful conscience that sin is our fault.

IV

If sin is our fault what is at stake? The decay in the sense of sin with which we started is ultimately due to a weakened sense of God in the modern world. For sin is a concept involving the language not of philosophy nor of law nor of ethics, but of religion. Sin is more than moral evil as soon as it is seen in relation to God the Father of our spirits. A man who realizes the ultimate implications of his wrong-doing makes confession not only to his wronged neighbour or before the law of the community, but to God in His holiness; he cries: "I have sinned against Heaven . . . against Thee and Thee only have I sinned." From the high viewpoint of religious experience sin—as the conscious disturbance of a man's filial relation to God, as the deliberate distrust and frustration of His proffered love — always means estrangement from God. The religious vocabulary in all ages has been eloquent of the sinner's sense of ritual uncleanness; he feels polluted by his guilt; he experiences the reaction of the divine perfection and holiness against it and must needs cry, "Depart from me for I am a sinful man."

Further, as a man yields again and again to temptation and becomes morally weaker, he can use only the language of the prison house about his condition. He is progressively tied and bound with the chain of his sin until he finds himself enslaved, his sense of guilt and his impotence under the tyranny of sin intensifying one another. Yielding to sin, as someone has acutely observed, is like drinking sea-water to quench thirst.

Again, the sting of *death* is sin. If our life in time in any way conditions our eternal salvation, that life is seen for what it is—final and unalterable—in death, which has been called the supreme external manifestation of temporality. The life-long drama of the soul comes to its climax here; a man is never so aware of the meaning of sin as at the moment when his sin confronts him in all its irrevocability. Death is " the sacrament of sin " (James Denney's phrase) if only because it is the outward sign of opportunities gone for ever. Through its approach, man is often brought face to face with God, and made conscious of a need that is far more than physical. He needs forgiveness and he needs redemption. "Against Thee and Thee only have I sinned " . . . "Thou must save and Thou alone." Unless the Creator is also the Redeemer, we are lost men and women; this is what Luther meant when he said, "The Word that has created the heavens and the earth must do this, or it will be left undone."

THE CHRISTIAN GOSPEL OF REDEMPTION

By H. WHEELER ROBINSON, D.D., Principal of
Regent's Park College, Oxford

THE CHRISTIAN GOSPEL OF REDEMPTION

THERE are three dark shadows that fall across every human pathway—death, suffering and moral evil. Each of them is what it is because man is not only a physical organism but also a conscious self. If man could be regarded, and could regard himself, simply as a biological unit, death would be as natural as birth, the suffering of disease or accident would be the misfortune of an organism capable of pain because capable of pleasure, whilst there would be no such thing as moral evil. But every man is a conscious self indissolubly linked within his present experience with a body. He is a self so capable of cherishing lofty dreams and purposes, so conscious of belonging to a world that protests against slavery to death and suffering, that instinctively he cries for deliverance from these tyrant masters. Most men also, in most generations, become conscious of a tyrant more to be feared, because he rules from within through purposes of the self which are traitorous to its best hopes and truest aims. This is the moral evil which religion calls " sin ". It is more than the physical passions and desires with which it is largely interwoven, and it is regarded by the man himself as something for which he is responsible, something that *ought* not to have been and *need* not have been, had the true self chosen the better part. This consciousness can never be wholly eliminated by our evasions and excuses to others and to ourselves.

Every religion worthy the name must offer some sort of deliverance or " redemption " (in the widest sense of the word) from these three tyrants, and the quality of the religion is seen in the kind of deliverance it offers. The religion may seek to persuade the man that either his self or the world about him is an illusion; or it may nerve him to a "stoical" endurance of the common lot; or it may promise him (on certain conditions) a happiness beyond death more than compensatory. It is characteristic of Christianity, because it was cradled in a religion unique in its moral demands, that all its emphasis is thrown on emancipation from moral evil. Apart from that emancipation it has nothing to offer; with it there goes the power to transform suffering from loss to gain, and the promise of a deathless life already begun here. (We may contrast the Indian emphasis on redemption from suffering and the Egyptian emphasis on redemption from death.)

Let us try to frame, in broadest outline, the Christian Gospel of Redemption as we may find it in the New Testament. The New Testament itself has more than one way of putting it, but Paul's way is the richest and most suggestive in detail, though it is by no means a fully wrought-out system of theology. In his most important epistle, that to the Romans, the true starting-point is to be found in the seventh chapter, when he portrays that perennial fact of our human consciousness, the divided self. There is a struggle between the higher and the lower, as in the overture to Tannhäuser or Nathaniel Hawthorne's *The Scarlet Letter*, and we hear the cry "O, wretched man that I am! Who shall deliver me from the body of this death?" The answer is "Jesus Christ", by which Paul means not the teaching or the example of Jesus whilst He lived on earth, but a new spiritual dynamic which reinforces the spirit of man and makes possible the impossible. That dynamic works in man so far as he identifies himself by "faith" with the risen Christ. It gives him a present moral victory. It enables him to face the greatest suffering in a joyous and triumphant spirit. It declares that death itself cannot separate us from the love of God, which is in Christ Jesus our Lord. All this for Paul is based on a great redemptive work wrought in the historical Cross of Jesus Christ. There can be no doubt that this has been the experience of a great multitude of men and women through nineteen centuries, as it was for Paul himself. But here rises the first and most general objection of the modern man. As we may hear him say in so many words, " This is a beautiful dream. It works, so long as you can persuade yourself to believe it. But who can, when he remembers the mind's trick of objectifying its own dreams? After all, Paul is not offering us even the historical Jesus, but a phantom Christ, whose death he has interpreted by a whole host of outworn forms of Jewish and Hellenistic thought sublimated into a Christian mythology." We cannot possibly meet so radical an objection as this by an appeal to authority, even authority in the very respectable form of experience through nineteen centuries. All that we are entitled to say is that a faith which wears so well and has been so widely tested is at least deserving of more respect and attention than it gets from so many in the present generation. After all, faith must always be directed towards the unseen, as the Epistle to the Hebrews reminds us. That is no disqualification of faith, which deals with intangibles because it is precisely those intangibles which most press upon us. If we knew for certainty that death was a negligible incident in our career, if we could successfully ignore suffering, if we could eliminate the self-rebuking conscience as a socially begotten illusion, then we could reasonably dismiss religious faith as equally unreal and certainly unnecessary. Faith always takes us beyond sight; that is its *raison d'être*. In doing so, it must of necessity use the forms of contemporary experience and thought, or it would not be even intelligible. It is no objection that the

Pauline Gospel is expressed in ancient forms of thought derived from the Apostle's personal life and his social and religious environment. The real point at issue is whether the Christian faith (1) meets a real and permanent need in offering the forgiveness of sins; (2) provides a real and necessary redemption from moral evil and its consequences; (3) derives a genuine moral dynamic from this religious redemption; (4) obtains redemption from suffering and death.

(1) Does the Christian Gospel of Redemption, then, meet a real and permanent human need, when it promises the forgiveness of sins, and puts this first and foremost in its programme as the primary necessity? That question can be answered briefly, since it has been faced at length in the previous chapter of this book, where it was seen that "sin" is not a subjective illusion, encouraged by religion that it may thus heal the (imaginary) disease it has fostered, in the manner of the advertisements of some patent medicines. "Sin" is the religious name for the great and universal fact of moral evil, which is at the root of most of our distresses. That fact has witness borne to it by history and literature, by law and conscience. We hold ourselves, and we hold others, to be responsible for evil choices, and by public and private means every society seeks to restrain or prevent those evil choices. Moreover, both from within the conscience and in social judgments from without we regard that responsibility as extending into the past, even though the present attitude is changed and the evil act would no longer be done. The whole structure of personal life and social intercourse depends on this continuity of the self of today with the self of many yesterdays. Every one of us who is frank and honest with himself knows that he carries the burden of a whole series of evil acts, for which, in greater or less degree, he and he alone is responsible. As events of the past, they

are irrevocable and unalterable. His present self may dis-
own them, but they remain *his*, in a sense in which they
are no one else's. The proper name for this responsibility
is guilt. Moreover, no one can think about the course of
his own life without seeing how closely it has been bound
up in " the bundle of life " with other lives, both for good
and for evil. He sees that a particular sin, that has become
a habit sapping and destroying his happiness and usefulness, goes back to the evil example or direct incentive of
another, and he realizes that his own unconsidered
example or influence may equally have helped to spoil
other lives. The chain seems unending; the fatal inheritance of evil through social life makes it practically, if not
logically, certain that every individual will be exposed to,
and will sometimes yield to, the temptation of this evil
environment. For the consequences to others as well as
for those confined to his own life, the honest man will
accept his own measure of responsibility. The plausible
suggestions drawn from psychology or biology or sociology may lower this sense of personal responsibility (as
they certainly do today), but the fashion will pass, and
with it no little of the unrest and anxiety and inefficiency
which the suppression of truth always entails. The
Christian Gospel of a redemption from the pitiful misery,
the ugly selfishness, the admitted disillusionment of our
modern life, stands or falls with its initial condemnation
of that life, in the individual and the society, as " sinful "
—that is, as something that ought not to be, and need not
be, and would not be but for our evil choices. The first
demand of the Gospel is for " repentance ", which means
our own judgment of ourselves as " sinners ", our own
change of purpose, and our own acceptance of responsibility
for the evil we have done. It is the very nature of the
" grace " which underlies that Gospel that it often initiates
and always deepens the repentance which it demands.

The raw material of repentance is in every heart that cares to be honest with itself, and only when there is repentance can the individual have any concern with, or any interest in, that forgiveness of sins which is central in the Gospel of Redemption.

(2) But is there not an unwarranted assumption in the claim that moral evil does concern God so intimately, and that anything to be called a " redemption " is necessary? We cannot, it might be said, deny that there is such a thing as moral evil, and we must deal with it as best we can, individually and socially. But, after all, it is a purely human affair, a transient and negligible feature when we think of the God of the starry sky. Can we, as Kant did in another connection, couple together the starry sky and the moral law? Are we really to believe that our petty sins concern the God of the universe? Well, the sinner cannot look into God's eyes as he can look into those of a man he has wronged, and read there the condemnation of his sin and the suffering it has brought to his friend. We cannot hope to prove anything about God, even His very existence, by the evidence of the senses (which ought to hinder us also from trying to measure His character and interests simply by the evidence of the telescope). But if we believe in God at all, we must credit Him with the best and highest we know, and if we have rejected that best and highest in ourselves, we have rejected it in Him, or we make God less than ourselves. If my sin wrongs myself and my neighbour, much more must it wrong God.

How, then, does sin affect God and what is His reaction to it? This is the crucial question of our theme, and all we say about " redemption " or " atonement " or " reconciliation " will obviously be conditioned by the answer we give to it. It is of the essence of the New Testament answer that it is not framed on *a priori* lines, simply from a philosophical argument concerning the nature of God.

The answer is given in a historical event, the way in which Jesus Christ was affected by man's sin, and the reaction of Jesus to it. This is not the place to consider in general the historical element in Christianity (see Cc. IV., V.). But the fundamental principle must be grasped, viz. that the effective speech of God to man must always, directly and indirectly, be in terms of history. God can say nothing intelligible to us in a vacuum. Every mysticism that has any meaning at all must be linked to human history, racial and individual, even if, relatively, we may speak of an " immediate " communion with God. The prophets of Israel, those supreme agents of revelation, owed the occasion and the content of their message to historical events. Every " word " of God is a fragment of human history, and His speech to us must always accept the limitations of our historical experience. For the Christian, the Incarnation is the limiting case of this universal principle of revelation. The Christian faith is essentially and in origin an interpretation of God in terms of Jesus Christ. With innumerable differences of emphasis, it always says, " God is like this, and the best and truest I can know of Him will be based on what I know of Jesus." But it says more, for it declares, " The words and deeds of this Man are the unique act of God in human history."

The Cross is central in this divine act of redemption and revelation, not only because it marks the culminating and most intense moment of the life of Jesus in His fullest surrender to the will of God (as known to Him through God's providential control of events), but also because Jesus on His Cross comes to closest grips with man's sin, the primary fact for the Christian Gospel and Redemption. There is nothing artificial or even theological in this historical juxtaposition of sin and grace. It has a natural and human history to explain it. Whatever we think of God, it is a historical fact beyond question that the moral

evil of man crucified Jesus. But equally the " grace " of
Jesus, seen in His forgiving love and loving forgiveness
of those who killed Him, is a fact of history beyond
denial by any reasonable criticism. Here in this world of
ours, we find the actuality of " sin " and " grace ". If
there is a God and Father of Jesus Christ, this is where
we may best know what sin does to God, and how God
reacts to sin. If Christ's forgiveness is a costly one, then
so is God's. We have no right to draw an arbitrary line,
in the interests of Greek metaphysics, and say that Christ's
forgiveness on the Cross was costly to *Him* in the agony
of suffering, physical and mental, but cost nothing to
God, who is *ipso facto* incapable of suffering. Of course,
all our interpretation of God in terms of Jesus is so far
" anthropomorphic "; we are consciously using finite
symbols of the infinite, just as when we call God
" Father ". But the love of God, on which any Gospel of
forgiveness is based, must be a sacrificial and costly love
to be worthy of its human parallel and its revelation in
human history. We cannot evade this issue by appeal to
the " two-nature " theory of Christ's Person, in such a
way as to make His revelation of God an artificial one,
so that he is said to suffer as man, but not as God. We
must at all costs hold fast to the " actuality " of redemption. It is historical fact, not theological fiction, that Jesus
Christ in the unmistakable unity of His personality bore
the worst that man could do to Him, and transformed it
into the best that we dare to believe of God. The actual
need for redemption was met at Calvary by an actual forgiveness of sin; this is our datum for any Christian interpretation of God's concern with sin. But, obviously, we
need to go deeper, if we can, into the question of the
" cost " of forgiveness, because this is just where the
variety in the types of doctrine becomes noticeable. Christian theologians in general would agree that the forgiving

love of God is revealed in Christ and especially in His
Cross. This is common ground; whatever else is believed
to be necessary, it is held that the love of God displayed
in Christ both moves man to repentance and establishes
his confidence that his sin is forgiven by God. But here
comes a great division of thought. From the time of
Abelard some theologians have held that the forgiveness
of sins means no more than this. God says, in Jesus
Christ, "I forgive you," and there's an end of it. Appeal
is often made to the parable of the Prodigal Son as war-
ranting this view of forgiveness. The simplicity and intel-
ligibility of this view seem to commend it; moreover, we
escape by it from all the repulsiveness of "commercial"
transactions between Christ and the Father, all the arti-
ficiality of the formal recognition by Christ of a broken
law, all the injustice of one being punished for another's
guilt, all the anachronism of supposing God requires a
"sacrifice" before He can be approached. But it is
very doubtful whether such simplicity is a virtue in any
interpretation of God's ways. There is a mystery of god-
liness as well as of iniquity; is human goodness itself so
simple as it looks? In fact, as Professor H. R. Mackintosh
has rightly urged in his book *The Christian Experience
of Forgiveness*, the real forgiveness of one man by another
is not anything like so simple as saying "I forgive you."
There is no forgiveness worthy the name without suffering. The saint's forgiveness of the sinner is always a
costly thing; from the first contact of the holy with the
unholy, and through the struggle of one soul to save
another, right up to the triumphant restoration of the
sinner to the fellowship of God, there is for the saint the
agony of a spiritual suffering, which we lesser men, for
whom "to forgive is to forget," hardly know. If it be
said that all this voluntary suffering with and for the
sinner is more than forgiveness ought to mean, that is

just the point at issue. It is more than what most of us Christians mean by forgiveness. But is it more than forgiveness in the saints of God, such as St. Teresa, of whom it was said that the way to make her your friend was to do her an injury? And is it more than the forgiveness of Christ, who came to seek and to save the sinner with whom He was ready to identify Himself? If, then, we are to interpret God through Christ, it does not seem possible to make Him an "unmoved Mover" of men to repentance. The holy God must in some sense we cannot fully imagine suffer through the sin of man, to whom He has given the awful power to defy Him for a season. The creature is always within the comprehensive circle of the Creator, or he could not continue to exist. But the impact of his sin on Holy Being must bring to Holiness that which corresponds to suffering in our experience. One reaction of the holiness which we can conceive, and a true one, so far as it goes, is Holy Wrath. Even man can feel indignation and anger against wrong-doing; shall God be less than man in this respect? But there is a deeper reaction of Holy *Love* to sin, and that is the voluntary acceptance of the suffering in order to save the sinner. That is grace, not deduced by any *a priori* argument about the nature of God, but ascribed to God because of what man has actually seen in Jesus Christ. Once seen, it becomes convincing by its own intrinsic quality. We feel that this is how God, being God, must react against sin. In the ways of eternity, which our speech can but imperfectly symbolize, the divine suffering transforms the sin of man into the grace of God. God does in the unseen world what Christ did in the seen, by a sort of spiritual alchemy. Just as the first key-word for the Christian Gospel of Redemption is "actuality", the reality of history, so the second is "transformation", by the miracle of grace.

There is nothing new in this conception of God, the great burden-bearer by His own will and not a weary Titan on whom an unwilling burden has been thrust. The conception goes back to Hebrew prophecy, the true cradle of the Christian faith. The nameless prophet of the exile contrasts the God of Israel with the gods of Babylon (Isa. xlvi. 1-4). They themselves, as seen in their idols, are a burden to be carried; but the God of Israel can say, " Even to old age I am He, and even to hoar hairs will I carry you : I have made, and I will bear; yea, I will carry and will deliver." God's chief burden is the sin of man. The penitent sinner *knows* that his sin does not concern himself alone; indeed, when face to face with God he is moved to cry, "Against thee, thee only have I sinned " (Ps. li. 4). However deep and sincere his penitence, he knows that he cannot loose the burden of his sin from his own shoulders or carry it alone. God, the very God he has wronged by his sin, must help him not by *saying* but by *doing* something. The discovery through Christ that God *is* doing something all the time, that God is carrying this burden with him and for him even as the earth carries his body—this discovery is the beginning of the revelation of the love of God, the knowledge of the Gospel. On the other view, indicated above—the Abelardian—revelation *is* redemption; on this view, which goes so much deeper in meeting the ultimate needs of penitence, redemption is revelation and God is known, as indeed He is known throughout the Bible, by what He does. It is a matter of secondary importance what metaphor we use to describe this, for indeed all our doctrines of redemption are expanded metaphors. When they are worked out logically they break up the indivisible unity of reconciliation with God—the consciousness of something done for us both *by* God and *to* God. In fact, we cannot hope to include the consciousness of God in our own or hold at the same moment the objectivity of Christ's work towards God and its subjectivity in God, until our philosophy can solve the problem of the relation of time and eternity. But even the crudest of the metaphors, such as the ransom paid to the devil that he might release his captives, bears witness to the conviction that God must do something with sin, and that He must not simply agree to ignore it. Anselm, who so fully recognized the objectivity of this burden, conceived sin as a violation of God's honour, for which "satisfaction" is rendered by the death of Christ. The Reformers, working with the conception of a public law of righteousness, regarded Christ as taking the place of guilty sinners and bearing the punishment instead. Nearer our own times, escape from the law court metaphor has been sought in the theory of a vicarious confession of sin, or of a vicarious penitence, rendered by Christ on behalf of the sinner. All these and scores of other theories or varieties of theories can easily be criticized, and they are all vulnerable to criticism, if only because they all conceive the work of Christ as in some sense apart from God and rendered to God. But, as is said by Paul himself, who could conceive the redeeming work of Christ in such sharply forensic terms, " God commendeth his own love toward us, in that while we were yet sinners, Christ died for us " (Rom. v. 8). That is not an " Abelardian " text, as has sometimes been claimed, for Paul has just said that " Christ died for the ungodly," and is just about to say that we are "justified by His blood," the sacrificial blood which guilty man needed, according to ancient conceptions, in order to approach God. But the text does suggest that an adequate doctrine of redemption must bring together all that Christ did at a particular moment of history, and all that God does throughout all our history, and see them as one—not simply because the historical reveals the eternal, true as that is, but also because the historical *is* the eternal at that moment of time and under the limiting conditions of human history; it is God's act in time. That is the ultimate ground, however difficult be its explication, which assures the sinner that God has dealt with his sin by transforming it into His grace. Through that great act in time, we are enabled to penetrate the secret of eternity, and the visible redemption reveals the invisible.

(3) Moreover, the deeper and higher the idea of redemption as a work of God, the more powerful is the moral dynamic which it yields for man. Redemption means more than revelation, but the more it means the richer is its meaning as revelation. If in Christ and His Cross we see God actually doing something with our sin that costs Him suffering we have a greater revelation of His love than any prophetic utterance or deed could bring. The historic faith is that " God so loved the world that He gave ": the more costly the giving the greater the measure of the love. This is where the " romance " of the Gospel is seen; the poetry of religion excels the prose of theology. We see that poetry breaking out again and again in the New Testament, as when Paul describes the voluntary descent of the Eternal Son of God to empty Himself in the death of the Cross, that He may win a new and glorious " name " (Phil. ii.); the whole passage is modelled on the poetry of Isaiah liii., and " He emptied himself . . . unto death " reproduces the Hebrew of Isaiah liii. 12. Again in the story of the feet-washing (John xiii.) Jesus is represented as moving in a great arc of descent and ascent which touches its lowest point just here: " Knowing . . . that he came forth from God and goeth unto God, he riseth from supper, and layeth aside his garments and took a towel and girded himself " (verses 3, 4). In such poetry the beauty of truth is made manifest. If, as Francis Thompson said, " every great poem is a sacrifice,"

223

it is not less true that every great sacrifice is a poem, and most of all the sacrifice of Jesus. We cannot dismiss the Pauline and Johannine way of stating the Gospel as simply Christian mythology. All we can ever say of the eternal must be in the symbolic and imperfect forms of time; the greater their beauty, the greater will be their truth; criticism of particular features does not touch the truth they seek to express, the truth of which the beauty gleams through the muddy vesture of our earthly language. The Gospel is poetry, for it is the romance of God's love story, but none the less it is rooted and grounded in historic fact; it is actual with the sweat and blood of Gethsemane and Calvary. As the forgiving love of Christ becomes actual in and through the drama of the Cross, so the costly forgiveness of God continues to make its appeal through the historic incidents and circumstances of the life and death of Jesus. It is so high and beautiful a thing that when men have once seen it they cannot escape from it. It moves them as nothing else could do. To remain indifferent to such costly love, offering itself to us and for us, seems the one unpardonable sin, the act of a churl, for whom there can be no redemption. So the love of the highest becomes a deliverance from the lowest—which is a profound psychological truth, for it is what we attend to that at last shapes our thought and our motive; moral evil remains possible only when we will not attend to that which condemns it. We may be impelled to believe, as has been said, from the direct perception that "a particular kind of life is the life most worth living" (Dr. Edwyn Bevan, *Christianity*, p. 254). But we are enabled to share that life in whatever degree by the conviction that it is the life of God whose redemptive work has become the effective revelation of His being and of His purpose.

Our deepest moral consciousness is met by the essential

and intrinsic rightness of God's way in Christ. Our emotional nature can be stirred by the beauty of the human story of Jesus and of the grace of the living God seen through it. Our intellect, when its necessary criticism of historic detail or metaphysical speculation has been wrought out to the full, can rest in the belief that this is the truest of all theisms. Such an appeal as this is necessarily individual. But its essential nature is social. It is no accident of expression that the supreme work attributed to the Holy Spirit in the New Testament is the creation of " fellowship" or " communion " (as is the meaning in the triple Benediction). The " fruit " of the Spirit (Gal. v. 22, 23) largely consists in the right moral relation of man to man; the " gifts " of the Spirit (1 Cor. xii. 4 ff.) are not meant for individual glory, but for the service of the community. Christian ethics are social ethics in origin as well as in application. They spring from the Gospel. They depend for their moral dynamic on the altruism of Christ, which is the altruism of God. Their accomplishment is represented as dependent on the reproduction of Christ's Spirit in us. That is why Christian " casuistry" always runs a certain peril. Even to try to systematize the teaching of the Sermon on the Mount has its danger—the danger of forgetting that Christianity is not a new law so much as a new life. We may compare the ethics of Stoicism with the ethics of Christianity and be left wondering why the one failed to move the mass of men and the other succeeded—till we take into account the new dynamic of the Gospel. The Christian Gospel brings a man into a new relation to his fellows, and then largely leaves him to work out the redeemed life for himself, *because* it is God who works in him. The " social solidarity " of that new life will have countless forms and experiences, but it will necessarily go back for its principle as well as for its inspiration to the vicarious suffering that created it, the principle expressed in the Cross as Christ endured it. The member of the "Body of Christ"—to use the Pauline phrase to describe the community of the redeemed—will therefore "fill up that which is lacking of the afflictions of Christ for his body's sake" (Col. i. 24); that is, the union with Christ brings with it the joy of suffering as He suffered, of sharing His purpose, and of continuing (in this sense) His work.

The "Spirit of the Cross" can claim more than anything else to be the principle of unity in the Body of Christ so far as its conduct and character are concerned. Underneath the countless differences of speech and dress, of climate and country, of organization and worship, that mark successive generations of Christians, the altruism of the Cross stands out as the most abiding feature. The redeemed man is the man who in some degree lives or tries to live according to this principle, and for most men "Christian" conduct means the forgiving and gentle spirit. The admitted inadequacy of achievement in the individual life or in its corporate expression is perhaps the greatest of all objections to the Christian Gospel of Redemption—at any rate, it is that which weighs most with the outsider, and especially in such times as these, when there are many rival theories of life which do not present striking differences of result. Several things ought to be remembered, however, before a hasty judgment dismisses Christianity as no better than the rest of the theories. One is the degree to which Christian ideals have penetrated modern society, so helping to produce "humanism" as a theory as well as "humanity" in practice; the truth in humanism is largely borrowed from Christianity. Another is that the finest Christian qualities are those which advertise themselves least; the best Christians are usually those least in the limelight, and ecclesiastical statesmen are not always "saints". Further, it is the very altitude of the aim that explains the considerable and widespread failure to reach it. The Spirit of the Cross seems the very antithesis of the dominant principle of nature and has supervened far later in time upon it, though the sympathetic eye may discern much in nature that prophesies from afar of the realm of grace. When we consider the momentum of that natural order from which we have come and in which we live, the wonder may well be not that the Christian Gospel has done so little with us, but that it has done so much, in the relatively short space of time for which it has worked on the product of countless ages of physical evolution.

(4) It is in the relation of man to the order of physical nature of which he is part through his body that we meet our fourth and final question — how can the Christian emphasis on redemption from moral evil be enlarged to a redemption from the other two tyrannies of suffering and death? This is a particular aspect of the perennial problem of the relation of the natural and the spiritual, which has engaged the attention of philosophers throughout the centuries. We cannot here, of course, even pass in review the varied solutions that have been offered, the attempts to reduce the spiritual to the material, or to sublimate the material into a form of the spiritual, or to remain content with an unresolved dualism. In the New Testament Paul was so far conscious of the problem that he spoke of the whole creation groaning and travailing in pain together and earnestly expecting that very redemption from the bondage of corruption into which Christians had partially entered (Rom. viii. 19 *ff*.). Just as along the lines of Jewish thought he conceived the " fall " of man to have brought a curse on nature (Gen. iii. 17), so Paul conceived a future restoration of nature of the kind described by Jewish apocalyptic when, for example, " the wolf and the lamb shall feed together " (lxv. 25). The modern man

cannot easily accept so direct an inter-relation of morality
with the natural order, even though he may speculate on
some degree of "freedom" and of resultant evil within
sub-human forms of life. As Ward has said (*The Realm
of Ends*, p. 358), "How far down within this seemingly
fixed mechanism the fluent processes of life extend we do
not know; if there are such processes their *tempo*, so to
say, is so different from ours that their significance escapes
us." He goes on to point out that it is in their comparative fixity, not in their possible secular transformation,
that they concern us for good or evil. It is from the comparative fixity, the ruthless neutrality or indifference of
nature as seen in the incidence of suffering and of death,
that man seeks redemption.

Now there are certain postulates of the Christian faith
without which its content is unintelligible or quite unconvincing. We cannot form an adequate judgment of
the whole process as detached spectators of it, since we
are never that; we must study it from *within* the process
where we actually are. Readers of Dostoievsky's *The
Brothers Karamazov* will recall the comment made on
an instance of cruelty: "Imagine that you are creating a
fabric of human destiny with the object of making men
happy in the end, giving them peace and rest at last, but
that it was essential and inevitable to torture to death only
one tiny creature—that babe beating its breast with its
fist—and to found that edifice on its unavenged tears,
would you consent to be the architect on those conditions?" (E. T., by C. Garnett, p. 258). The detached spectator can give no adequate reply to that indictment of the
universe, but the Christian *within the process* is not without an answer, though it is necessarily incomplete.

Further, the Christian "values", the kind of life presented as the "redeemed" life, can be achieved only
through the actuality of living. In the words of Pringle-

Pattison (who shows so keen an insight into what those values are), "Nature is more than a training-school of the moral virtues in the specific sense; it is an element, savage and dangerous, into which the human being is thrown to show what stuff he is made of—an element testing with merciless severity his powers of courage and endurance, but drawing from him thereby the utmost of which he is capable" (*The Idea of God*, p. 416).

Yet again, Christian faith does not profess to supply a complete philosophy of nature and of its relation to grace; it flings itself upon God in prayer and looks for the miracle of His providential dealing with the individual life to which He has given this consciousness of itself and of Him. It is faith in "an overruling power, who if great enough to manage the universe must be great enough to answer prayer without upsetting the balance of the machinery" (G. Atherton, *Rulers of Kings*, p. 309). These three postulates, the inner point of view, the actuality of living, and the power of prayer, are of the essence of the Christian Gospel of Redemption as applied to suffering and death. The life that is built on these postulates does find a triple redemption. In the first place, the natural or social consequences of sin are accepted as more than penalty by the repentant and believing. They become part of the discipline of life; they are transformed in meaning and therefore in value. Further, the suffering which is in no way the result of the sufferer's wrong-doing can be welcomed as privilege. To bear it in the right way becomes an opportunity of witness-bearing that is Christian service at its highest and noblest (*cf.* the prologue to the Book of Job). The suffering has changed its nature and lost its bitterness because of the transformation wrought in it by a new attitude towards it. This view of suffering extends to all costly and sacrificial service "for Christ's sake" voluntarily endured. The creation of such new values as these *is* a redemption, beyond all comparison with any evasion of penalty, any fortunate escape from suffering and most of all any skilful avoidance of the troubles of others.

At the same time (as we may learn supremely from Gethsemane) the creation of these new values by the Christian attitude does not deny the truth of the instinct that makes us pray to be delivered from this or that misfortune or burden or even this or that penalty of our sin. It is only when such prayer seems unanswered in that way that we can look for its answer in another and deeper way, as Jesus did. The inevitability we face is accepted as God's inevitability for us, and God can redeem us from the pain of its mystery and bring us into the discipline of its sequence or the privilege of its service.

The Christian values of this redemption from suffering are to be estimated, of course, not quantitatively but qualitatively. There can be no question of striking a balance between the evils of suffering regarded as a set-off from human happiness and the spiritual qualities of redeemed lives. As well might we try to compare the physical suffering of the Cross and its spiritual achievement. But for those who hold these spiritual values to be incomparably great, there can be no question that the result has justified the means, and that the goal is worth the journey. They constitute a prophecy of that final and complete " atonement " when God shall look on the new creation as on the old and see that it is good—in the light of its final *meaning*.

The redemption from death is obvious enough in the light of what has been written. The incident of physical death is transient and has no power over the values that have been achieved, which belong already to the eternal world. Christian personality, by its very nature, projects itself into that unseen world beyond physical death.

Whatever may await it, whatever be the new discipline and service, fellowship and growth, it has passed beyond the powers of nature. The stern schoolmaster has done his necessary work, and the youthful spirit enters eagerly upon the greater freedom of the university and all that new world of promise for which he has been equipped.

Such is Christian redemption from the three tyrannies of life, such at least in that ideal form which belongs to the saints. Lesser men may never wholly enter in this life into the peace of complete and perfect deliverance. But they know at least that this is their true life and that by these things they live. Whatever unanswered questions remain, which necessarily spring from a life of partial freedom set in what seems to be an unyielding order, the mystery of whence we come and whither we go, the mystery of other lives that offer no promise of any real life beyond death, the burden of wrong done to others that seems irrevocable, the sorrow over lost opportunities of growth and of service—this at least Christians know, that nothing can separate them from the love of God in Jesus Christ, and that God has taken on Himself the greatest burden of all, the sin and guilt which in act and in memory alienate man from God and demand a divine redemption.

THE CHURCH

By EDWYN BEVAN, LL.D., D.Litt.

IX

THE CHURCH

GOD might have created a single finite spiritual being to hold communion with Himself. In that case, the whole spiritual life of this unique person would have consisted in the relations between itself and God. It would have been indeed, in the full sense of the phrase sometimes used to describe the mystical elevation, a case of *solus cum solo*. The wonderful thing is that God has created a plurality—an innumerable plurality—of different centres of finite consciousness capable of communion with Himself. The fact hardly seems wonderful to us now, because we have been so familiar with it as a fact of the universe from the beginning of our own conscious life. And yet when we reflect on this co-existence of innumerable conscious persons, each in a way a universe in himself or herself, in so far as each reflects the whole universe in a peculiar mode—as Leibnitz says that each of his monads does—we may feel it a truth staggering for thought. Some forms of religion have felt the plurality something so uncomfortable that they have tried to get rid of it by declaring it to be an illusion. When the individual soul, it is said, apprehends the ultimate Reality, all plurality fades away: there is only One Being, which to the soul on the lower level appears falsely as many; even the duality between God and the soul is done away; there is only God. It is in certain forms of Hinduism that this Monism is taught most emphatically. But the religions which stand on the Hebraic foundation reject this simplification as not doing justice to the complexities which are really there.

Difficult as the fact may be to construe philosophically, I am a universe beside which innumerable other universes exist, no one of them setting frontiers to my potential infinitude, each one in its own peculiar personal relation to God. It is sometimes affirmed by Hindus that, instead of saying a man should love his neighbour as he loves himself, one may equally well say that a man should recognize his neighbour as being in truth himself. This is to blur the essential difference between Christianity and Hinduism. I could not, in the Christian view, love my neighbour as myself unless my neighbour were *not* myself, unless the duality continued to be always there for love to transcend. If you took the Hindu view seriously as a basis for ethics, it would indeed make it absurd for me to desire to appropriate some good to myself rather than resign it to my neighbour, to be selfish in that way, but it would make it equally absurd for me to labour that my neighbour might have some good rather than myself, to be unselfish in that way; the logical consequence of the Hindu view would be that it is a matter of complete indifference whether I appropriate the good or let my neighbour have it; it would in reality come to the same thing. You cannot, on the Hindu supposition, be really unselfish. Mr. Chesterton indicated, I think, something fundamental when he described the difference between the Christian and the Hindu idea of heaven by saying that the Christian conceived of heaven as a state in which we should all *love* one another, and the Hindu as a state in which we should all *be* one another. But if Christianity, and the other Hebraic religions, take seriously this strange and difficult fact, the existence of a multitude of different persons, religion cannot be simply a matter of the relation between each individual person and God, a matter of *solus cum solo*; it must include a right adjustment of the relations between each finite person and the others.

Charles Bigg contrasts somewhere the Christian view of
life with that of the ancient Stoics, the old Western
thinkers who showed in many points an affinity to the
Hindu monists, as against those who stand on the Hebraic
foundation; for the Stoic, Bigg said, religion was a matter
of "My soul and God"; for the Christian it was a matter
of "My soul, my brother's soul, and God."

When the Hindu monist found the plurality of
different persons something uncomfortable, when he tried
to escape from the Many to the One, his feeling was not,
according to the Christian view, altogether unjustified.
The plurality of persons *is*, according to the Christian
view, something uncomfortable, in so far as plurality
means disharmony; it is right to desire unity, only the
unity should not be of the kind that blurs the differences
of individual persons in one uniform Being, but of the
kind which unites the many persons, with all their individual differences unimpaired, in one harmony. A bar of
music is a unity, the total impression it makes is one impression, but the perfection of the unity depends on the
notes which compose it being distinct and clear in their
several characters. The plurality of persons, each a unique
centre of consciousness, can offer the contemplating spirit
something satisfactory only when all these persons together
form one perfectly harmonious system. That is very far
from being the case today on the earth: what we see
when we look round us is rather an unhappy scene of
clashing wills and mutual hatreds. But even where enmity
is not there, there is for the most part a dull indifference
of one person to another. This is by no means entirely
due to defects in the spirit of men, which they could
remedy if they would. It is largely due to the laws of
space and time which govern the earthly phase of our
existence. If we suppose a man absolutely perfect in his
spiritual temper, it would nevertheless be impossible for

him to know more than a relatively small number of other persons, and without acquaintance love cannot become actual. A saint might show exceptional courtesy and consideration to the other persons occupying together with himself a crowded railway compartment, but he could hardly be said to love these unknown persons in corporal proximity to him—the elderly lady in the opposite corner, the bank clerk beside him, and the publican on beyond. The number of persons anyone really knows and loves in this life is likely to be well under a hundred. But where love and mutual understanding between two persons is greatest it still falls short of perfection. All means of communication we know here, words, looks, gestures—even, if it exists, the transference of thought without bodily means—cannot communicate thought without some distortions, some omissions. In the intercourse of the people who know each other best there occur misunderstandings, failures of sympathy. A perfect harmony of a plurality of persons could not possibly be realized under earthly conditions.

Christian doctrine asserts that the perfect Society, which is an impossibility under our present laws of space and time, will be realized in another mode of existence. The "divine event," in fact, "to which the whole creation moves," is the realization of this Society "in heaven." If there are personal spirits in the unseen world other than human ones, the perfect Society in its fullest sense would include all these; angels and archangels together with redeemed men would form, in the pleasant phrase of our Prayer Book, "the *company* of heaven." But, within that larger unity, human persons who had passed through life on earth, who, if their life on earth extended beyond infancy, had sinned and been saved, would form a special body, the Body of Christ, the Church. What we ordinarily call the Church, the community of Christians alive in the world around us, is just a small fraction of the perfect Society in its making, and, like anything else in the making, its significance can be understood only in reference to what it is intended to be when made. There is no entity of which it is more true that, in order to consider of it properly, we must begin at the end than the Christian Church. This may be expressed in the jargon of theology by saying that the significance of the Church is essentially eschatological.

If the union of persons by love is the supreme good, the perfect Society would imply that each individual comprised in it would know all the others and would enter by love into their experiences and interests in a harmony with no discords and no deficiencies. A knowledge so intimate extending to numberless millions of other persons is, of course, utterly unimaginable to us in our present condition. It may be that it does not come all at once to any person even in the heavenly mode of existence. But we can see that so long as the range of a person's knowledge and love has limits beyond which there are members of the Society unknown and unloved, the Society so far still falls short of ideal perfection. If a person makes progress in the other life, one part of such progress may be indeed a continuous enlargement of his capacity to know and love other persons, and if the multitude of other persons to be known exceeds all numerical expression, there is eternity for the enterprise.

In such an ideal state of the Divine Society we should have indeed something to which Leibnitz's description of his monads could be applied in full reality, at any rate in so far as each member of the Society would reflect the whole Society from a unique individual standpoint. Because the whole of the Society would be included in each individual's apprehension, there would be no member of it whom he did not know and love, but because his standpoint was a unique one, it would not be necessary to suppose that he knew and loved all other members equally. The harmony would present to each a different aspect, in so far as some of the other souls composing it were, from each particular standpoint, nearer, others more remote. We need not therefore accept as true the pronouncement that there will be no private friendships in heaven. Baron von Hügel used to assert his conviction that the relation of a person in heaven to that other person who in this life had been his mother would for all eternity have a peculiar quality which belonged to no other relation. And in regard to the saying of Christ that in heaven the marriage relation which had existed between persons here would exist no longer, it is to be noted that He was speaking about the legal bond which attached a woman successively to seven husbands, and that His words do not forbid our believing that where the conjugal association of two persons in this life is not only a legal bond but a close spiritual fellowship each continues in the eternal world to be specially near the other.

But we have not yet asked what it is that joins together all these different persons into one great Society—for we can see, even in the fragmentary associations of all kinds which make up human life on earth, that it is never simply and solely a relation between the persons who constitute that particular group, but a common relation in which they all stand for someone or something beyond the group. A common interest in some task to be achieved by the group as a whole creates the fellowship between its members. The love between husband and wife is corroborated when there is a common interest in their children. We can hardly imagine any vivid friendship between two persons in which there is not a common interest in something outside themselves—art or literature or sport or religion, or whatever it may be. Each contributes for the common enjoyment the impressions he or she has gathered individually from the world around. Without this material supplied by the outside world the bare relation between two persons, however much they might love each other, would be a vacancy, like two mirrors set simply face to face and each reflecting nothing but the other.

The ultimate Society, as Christianity conceives it, will be bound together into one by a common interest in God—an interest described by such words as love, wonder, gratitude, worship, joy. The interest may contain the element of ever fresh discovery, for since God is infinite and no created being, to whatever height it may be raised, can cease to be finite, there must always be something more in God to discover. But this common interest, implying a direction of all the members of the Society *to* God, will be produced by that which comes *from* God. The divine life of the God-Man, Jesus Christ, communicated to all the human beings who constitute His mystical Body, will be the ground of that Body's organic unity. And this diffusion of the life of Christ carries with it the diffusion of the Holy Spirit. It is, first and foremost, as the Spirit of the community that the early Christians came to know the " Holy Spirit " (*ruaḥ qodshā, τὸ πνεῦμα τὸ ἅγιον*). It was the One animating Spirit which made the community consisting of " believers " one.

When the Christian Church speaks of men and women as having the " life " of Christ it is not using a mere metaphor for a particular attitude to the world or direction of interest. It does not mean simply that such people's behaviour is governed by an acceptance of the " values " enunciated by Jesus of Nazareth or illustrated by His earthly life, though, of course, a man's having the life of Christ would imply, among other things, that his behaviour was governed by an acceptance of those values. A man who has been " born again " is regarded as having a new principle in him which makes just as real a distinction between those who have it and those who do not have it as the distinction between creatures who possess animal life and creatures who do not. Of course, it is impossible to explain by any analysis what that principle is; but then it is impossible to say what animal life is; the principle is called " life " because animal life is the thing most nearly analogous to it in the realm of things from which human language draws its ordinary meanings. The New Testament does not seem to regard the life possessed by Jesus of Nazareth before His death as being communicated to members of His " Church " (the word used by early Christians for " Church " was the old word denoting Israel in the Old Testament); it was the new life of the risen and exalted Jesus which baptized believers had in them.

This belief that something as real and distinctive as animal life, something " supernatural " in the sense that it comes into the life of men on this planet from quite another sphere, is communicated to those who are " born again " is still held by all Catholic Christians, Roman, Anglican, or Orthodox, and by all those Protestants who still believe that the religion of the New Testament is true. Of course, people who are not Christians think it a delusion, and try to account for it by the analogy of various kinds of belief in the transmission of divine substances, realistically conceived, in the world surrounding the primitive Church. Some kinds of " Modern Churchmen " would agree with them. It would be quite beyond the scope of this paper to enter upon the question what grounds there are for accepting Christian belief as true, or to go into the various shades and degrees of denial marking different brands of " Modern Churchmen." No doubt practically all well-informed Anglicans and Protestants are today Modernist in some respects. All I am

trying to do here is to state the belief about regeneration
which has been handed down from primitive times in the
Christian Church, and to which the majority of Christians
who take their religion seriously (even many who admit a
good degree of " Modernism ") still adhere, and to indicate the consequences which follow, if that belief is true.

It will not be necessary for our present purpose to take
sides on the controversies which divide those who share
this belief in regard to some questions connected with it.
While Catholics and Protestants alike believe in the communication to men of the supernatural life of Christ, there
is, of course, considerable disagreement as to the mode
and conditions of its communication. In the first days of
the Christian Church any man whose heart was won by
the Christian message—who, that is to say, " believed "—
was formally attached by baptism to the Divine Society in
which the new Life was embodied. Since his baptism was
also the declaration of his belief and his incorporation in
the Body of Christ, the two things which initiated his life
as a member of the Society—the faith in his heart and the
external rite of admission—ran together in the conception
of his fellow-Christians; he was born again " of water and
of the Spirit," and either his faith or his baptism might
be pointed to as the beginning of his life as a member of
Christ; it was felt that in either case what was meant was
the same thing. When later on the rite of baptism was
often conferred apart from any individual apprehension
of Christ in faith—on infants, for instance, or on persons
whose profession of Christianity was merely external—it
might become a question whether it was the inner act of
faith or the rite of baptism by which a human person
acquired the supernatural life. Protestants take the former
of these two views and Catholics the second. But the
difference between the two views seems mitigated, when
one remembers that Protestants, although they maintain

that the new life can begin only with an act of personal faith, nevertheless insist (with few exceptions, such as that of the Quakers) that, unless the rite of baptism has been conferred on a person before his inner act of faith, it is obligatory for the person, once he is regenerate by faith, to present himself, with no unnecessary delay, for baptism. If baptism has been conferred before the inner act of faith, it does not indeed, Protestants think, produce regeneration, but it may be justified by other considerations; for most Protestants hold that there are good reasons for baptizing the babies of Christian parents. On the other hand, while Catholics maintain that baptized children possess already the supernatural life, before any act of personal faith on their part, this life remains, they think, in a latent and ineffective condition, till the personal faith calls it into activity, and if the personal faith never supervenes, the supernatural life acquired by baptism will cease at bodily death. Thus both Catholics and Evangelical Protestants agree that the only persons in whom the supernatural life of Christ is active are persons who have apprehended Christ by faith, and that all such persons are, normally, baptized persons—whether the baptism preceded or succeeded the act of faith.

We might make such a view of the Church clearer to ourselves, if we imagined the spiritual connexion between Christ and the members of His Body represented to a spectator looking on from the unseen world by a visible connexion. Such a spectator would see filaments going out from the Person of Christ in heaven to millions of human individuals. Some of these individuals would be, as Christ Himself is, in the unseen world; some would be here living the life of men on this planet. Each of those filaments would represent a community of life by which the individuals participating in it would be actuated in their feelings and volitions, though those on earth only imperfectly, inasmuch as the action of the new life would still to a greater or less extent be interfered with by impulses or tendencies belonging to unregenerate human nature. The spectator would not see all men and women connected by such filaments with Christ, but only those into whom the new life had come. To men on earth the filaments would be invisible: those attached by them and those not attached would present an exactly similar appearance as ordinary men and women; but the spectator would see some of them actuated through the filaments by the new life, and some not. Christ and all those "members" attached to Him would thus form one single organism extending at its extremities both through the world of men now living on this planet and through the unseen world. And the common connexion with Christ would constitute an extraordinary fellowship between one member of the Body and another. The bond, unseen by men here, connecting one regenerate person with another would be without parallel in any earthly relationship, an eternal bond to which bodily death made no difference. And while on this earth the operation of the new life was restricted by the conditions of space and time, the organism in its perfected state would be such a community as was described just now, a community in which the mutual knowledge and love between members was universal and unconfined. The organism as a whole, animated by the life of Christ, may be called "Christ." When St. Paul wants to say that the ultimate end for which the world-process exists is the perfection of Spirit in the community of the one Body, he describes it as "the summing up of all things in Christ" (Eph. i.).

This is the view of things to which Catholic Christianity and Evangelical Protestantism is committed. One must recognize frankly that it makes a staggering claim, that in many people it excites vehement repugnance. So realistic a conception of a supernatural life is naturally abhorrent to those commonly described as " Rationalists," for whom the universe must be regarded as confined to the material world and the phenomena of life on this planet. Many Modernists and humanitarians hate the idea of such a distinction between the regenerate and the unregenerate. All men alike are children of God. It has been a favourite doctrine in the " Broad Church " that the Church in England is the whole English people in its religious aspect, an idea which, if the view of the Church just propounded is the really Christian one, denies the very basis of Christianity. Further, it must be admitted that, if you are going to confine genuine Christian doctrine to what can be extracted from the words attributed to Jesus in the first three Gospels, it will hardly be possible to substantiate such a view as the Catholic and Evangelical one. Of course, if you allow the Fourth Gospel to represent the mind of Jesus, there is very substantial ground for the Catholic and Evangelical view; it is recognized by New Testament scholars generally that the sharp distinction made between the regenerate and the unregenerate is a salient characteristic of the Johannine Jesus; Modernist theologians often regard it as a regrettable and disagreeable characteristic. How different the view of the Synoptic Jesus, for whom God remains the loving Father of the prodigal all the time he is in the foreign land!

In the chapter which Dr. Micklem contributes to this volume there are some valuable observations on the view just alluded to, that genuine Christianity consists solely in the Sermon on the Mount or the sayings attributed to Jesus in the first three Gospels—the Gospel preached *by* Jesus— and that the beliefs *about* Jesus embodied in the writings of St. Paul and St. John (including the sayings which St. John attributes to Jesus Himself) are an unfortunate mystification. To people who lightly adopt such a view

Dr. Micklem's remarks may give ground for doubting its validity, and I may refer them to him. But one must, I think, admit that if the Catholic-Evangelical view in its massive supernaturalism is to be accepted as true, it must be safeguarded by the recognition of a number of qualifying considerations. Granted that the regenerate amongst men on earth are really different in nature from the unregenerate, it is surely an unwarrantable presumption for any of us to attempt to say where the line between them comes. One of the things which made the older Evangelicalism seem so unamiable was its readiness to pronounce who was " saved " or who was " unsaved." It could do this because it held that the faith which brought about the new birth must include a definite apprehension by the intelligence of the doctrines of the Trinity embodied in the Catholic creeds and of a particular doctrine about the Atonement: if this was so, everyone who could not declare their distinct acceptance of these doctrines was, by his or her own confession, to be set among the unregenerate. If, on the other hand, saving faith is the right response of mind and heart to whatever is recognized as the Voice of God, then it is impossible for any man to pronounce in what cases it is there, since we can never say how much of the truth has been recognized as divinely authoritative by any particular person. It might be that an atheist whose recognition extended only to the categorical imperative enjoining a certain direction of the will, but who made the right response to what he recognized, had a faith by which he acquired, though he did not know it, the new life of Christ. Of course, if the Christian belief about God is true, the spiritual life, where that truth is not recognized, must lack many important elements which it should normally have, and be to that extent impoverished. The new life can be fully actual only when the whole of revealed truth is recognized and the right

247

response made to every bit of it, but that is the ideal perhaps never reached by any individual Christian, and below it there are innumerable degrees of imperfect recognition and imperfect response. Just as animal life may exist in cases where it manifests itself so poorly that the creature possessing it is hardly to be distinguished by external observation from the inanimate, so the supernatural life may be there, but in so rudimentary a form that it may be perceptible only to the eye of God. When we look on the world of men and women round about us we may see a number of persons in whose lives there is a special quality which we recognize as the Spirit of Christ. Here, we may say, there is definitely a new life in operation, but in other lives there seems so strange a mixture of good will and selfish impulse that the new life, if it is there, can have prevailed in but a low degree over the raw stuff of human nature. God perhaps sees it in many people where we cannot. So far as we ourselves recognize the truth, we know that the Christian life, where it is normal and true to type, must include recognition of what we see and a right response to it. It is enough for us to know what is normal, what the Christian life ought to be; it is for God alone to judge the various imperfect modes in which life, under earthly conditions, comes into some sort of existence.

It has to be remembered that, though animal life in low forms of manifestation seems to make but small distinction to external observation between the animate and inanimate, there is really an incalculable difference between a conscious being and an inanimate thing, because it is the difference between two orders or planes of being. Similarly, it may be held that though it may be impossible for the eye of man to distinguish cases where the supernatural life is present in a very low form from cases where it is not present at all, mankind are really divided into the two classes of those who possess the new life and those who do not. The spectator whom we supposed able to see the new life in the form of filaments connecting persons on earth with Christ in heaven, would see some persons connected by such filaments and some not. Would such a division of mankind into the regenerate and unregenerate contradict the parable of the Prodigal Son, which declares God to be the Father of men even when they are in a state of alienation? A contradiction could be proved only if a figurative expression, such as that which speaks of God as a Father, must always be used in precisely the same sense. God is the Father of all men in the sense that He is the author of their natural being and has for all men, however sinful, a fatherly love and care, a readiness, as is shown in the parable, to welcome them home. But if the new life comes from God, those who acquire it become the children of God in a sense in which those who are without that life are not children of God. That is recognized generally by Catholic and Evangelical Christianity; the Prayer Book, for instance, going on the Catholic supposition that the new life is imparted to babies by baptism, speaks of baptism as a sacrament " by which I *was made* a child of God." In the Pauline and Johannine conception it is the Holy Spirit, binding those who possess the new life together into one Body, which authorizes them to address God, the author of the *new* life, as Abba, Father. Those outside the Body are not, *in this sense*, " children of God."

"Outside the Church no salvation," an ancient maxim of Catholic Christianity, does, it is true, seem a maxim of terrible harshness, if it is taken to mean, as Catholics and Protestants in the past have indeed taken it, that every person who passes out of earthly life without acquiring the new life, is doomed to an eternity of misery. Some modern tendencies in theological opinion are perhaps short-sighted, but the change in the last two or three generations which has made the view just mentioned incredible goes, I believe, with a truer apprehension of the character and power of God. We may cherish the hope that ultimately all human beings will be brought into the organism of Christ's Body and become members of the perfect Society which was spoken of at the beginning of this chapter. I do not think that we can affirm this, with any certainty, on the ground of God's love. For God's love evidently does not exclude inequalities of level and value in the universe of His creatures: it is no failure of God's love that one creature is a pig and another a man, or that one man is a St. Paul or a Dante and another man ordained to humbler functions. It would not therefore necessarily mean a failure of God's love if some part of mankind were destined ultimately to a level of being inferior to that of the perfect Society which is Christ's Body. We may remember how Baron Friedrich von Hügel held that a large number of human beings never received the supernatural call, and therefore never rejected it; such persons, he thought, could not attain the Beatific Vision which is man's fullest felicity, but would enjoy in eternity well-being of a lower order. God has set before us the riches of glory and knowledge to which those who become members of the supernatural organism before they quit earthly life are destined, but how, in His love and wisdom, He will deal with those who pass from earthly life unregenerate, that the Father has hidden from us in His own secret councils. All we can say with confidence is that *if* any human being ultimately attains man's full felicity— "salvation" in that sense—that can only be as a member of the heavenly Society which shares the life of Christ, and that, in this sense, it is strictly true " outside the Church no salvation."

Similarly, the " damnation clauses " of the Athanasian

Creed, which have been so grave a stumbling-block in time past, may be given a meaning in which they become almost truisms. If we grant that the view of the Trinity stated in the creed is true, it follows necessarily that man's full felicity must involve a recognition of it. The life of the perfect Society must involve a knowledge of the truth about God (" Then shall I know, even as I am known "). If anyone were destined never to apprehend the truth about God, he would thereby be destined to eternal exclusion from the perfect Society. And if we call such failure to attain man's full felicity " perishing," then he who never apprehended the truth about God would " without doubt perish everlastingly." Of course, the people who drew up the creed meant that unless a man believed the doctrine of the Trinity before he passed out of earthly life, he would perish everlastingly, but they do not actually say this, and we may regard the meaning attached to a theological statement by those who first framed it as having often been the partially erroneous apprehension of something true, and we may use the old formula to express that something true, as we have now come to understand it.

But we have not yet come face to face with the practical problems involved in the existence of the Church as a fact in this world. We have been speaking hitherto of the Church on earth as consisting of all the men and women who share the new life by a spiritual connexion with Christ, but the term " Church " is also used for one among the visibly organized institutions in the complex of earthly society—an institution with its formally appointed office-bearers and established practices and legal possessions and times and places of meeting. In this sense there is not one Church, but many, the Roman Church, the Anglican Church, the Scottish Presbyterian Church, and so on. These many churches are visible societies, but the one

Church of the really regenerate is an invisible Society. This does not mean that the people in whom the new life operates are invisible, or that the actions in which the new life issues are invisible, but it means that you cannot see the outlines or contours of the Society, you cannot say precisely who belong to it and who do not, as you can say who belong to the Church of England and who do not. The spiritual filaments connecting its individual members with Christ and making them one living Body are invisible. Ideally, the visible Society of Christians on earth would include all those who are really regenerate and would include no one else : even if the filaments connecting individual Christians with Christ were invisible you could hardly speak of an invisible Church, because the contours of the visible Society would then be exactly the contours marking off the really regenerate from the rest of mankind. Unless by the " invisible Church " were meant that part of the Body which has already passed beyond earthly life, there *ought not* to be any invisible Church at all. The trouble is that in the anomalous state of things brought about by human sins and imperfections the contours of the really regenerate community and the contours of the visible Churches do not coincide. A large number of those included in the visible Churches are not really regenerate, and there are many who possess the new life and yet are not members of a visible Church. This is a wrong state of things, but it exists, and, so long as men on earth are sinful and imperfect, it seems inevitable. Even the Roman Church, which more than any other insists upon the divine authority and worth of the visible community, admits the existence of the invisible Church, for it admits that there are people who, in consequence of some unhappy impediment, have failed to join the visible organization, and who yet, as the phrase is, " belong to the soul of the Church."

Because persons connected with Christ in heaven by the invisible bond of the new life are also persons who have to live the life of men on earth, the fellowship of the new life has to form a visible organization whose functions are arranged by rational contrivance just as the functions of any other earthly society must be. There is a tendency in some quarters to despise the visible churches just because the contours of none of them coincide with the fellowship of the really regenerate, and it is perfectly true that the arrangements by which the business of a visible church is carried on may become mechanical, unspiritual, dead, and so hinder the new life and conceal it from men, instead of furthering and revealing it. But it is a mistake to suppose that the activities of the new life or its transmission from generation to generation of men on earth could go on without any framework of rational contrivance. Such a framework is a necessity, even if it is liable to become a hindrance. I have been told, I think, that the music produced on a piano is to some extent, though this is not ordinarily perceived, impaired by the tapping sounds of the wooden mechanism. If this is so, it would be a mistake to suppose that you could have the music purer if you did away with the wooden framework altogether. In some societies of Christians an attempt has been made to dispense with rational contrivance by trusting to direct promptings of the Holy Spirit on each several occasion, and it may well be that rational organization might profitably in some cases give place to such dependence on the Spirit. But you could never get rid of rational contrivance altogether without making the life of fellowship impossible. The Society of Friends has gone as far as any Christian community in abandoning fixed forms and trusting to direct inner guidance. But even the Quakers in any locality are not supernaturally moved at a particular hour each Sunday morning to start up from their seats at home and proceed to a meeting at a place never previously arranged.

If the fellowship of the new life had the maximum of spirituality, its life on earth would still be carried on in the framework of some visible organization. But there would be only one visible Church. Sometimes the existence of a number of different Christian communions side by side is justified by the consideration that these communions express different sides or aspects of the truth or of the Christian life. There is some confusion of thought here. The Church, in an ideal condition on earth, would, it is true, include a great richness of varieties—differences, according to vocation and temperament, of forms of worship and social fellowship, of emphasis and expression in teaching. But these differences would involve no contradiction or disagreement. The differences in teaching and practice between churches today do involve contradiction and disagreement. This is a definite evil. Two different statements may both be true, but two contradictory statements cannot possibly both be true. The existence of different churches with contradictory doctrines arises from the imperfections of the human mind. It could not be done away by a greater exercise of charity, because good men often honestly believe contradictory things. It must be recognized as an evil, inevitable so long as men's minds are imperfect, but an evil nevertheless. All any of us can do for the time being is to exercise a charity which preserves mutual love in spite of disagreement and to try by friendly communications to remove the error, whether in our own mind or in that of the other side, by which the disagreement came about. We can also co-operate, as Christians, in tasks within the field of our agreement. Even scholars of the Roman Church, for instance, co-operate with Anglican and Protestant scholars today in interpreting the language of Scripture.

One sometimes hears the *naïve* view expressed that when Christianity is presented to non-Christian peoples, the old controversies which have divided Christians in Europe might well be left aside. This, unhappily, is quite untrue. The differences which divide European Christendom are different paths chosen in regard to practical problems presented in the past, problems which must be presented in the same manner to Indian or Chinese Christians and in regard to which they must choose one or other of the alternative paths. The question, for instance, which divides the Church of Rome from other Christian communions, whether the Lord Jesus did or did not give His Church a constitution which makes submission to the authority of the Bishop of Rome a matter of obedience to Him, is a question to which an Indian or a Chinese Christian must answer " Yes " or " No," just as an English or French Christian must, and follow a different line of conduct accordingly. Or take a much smaller point—the baptism of babies. There are three possible views about this: (1) that it is obligatory, the view of Catholics and most other Christians; (2) that it is wrong, the view of Baptists and Quakers, though these two again disagree in so far as Baptists hold that it is right to baptize grown-up persons and Quakers hold that it is superstitious to baptize anybody; (3) that it is a matter of no religious importance whether babies are baptized or not, and might be left in each place to local custom. Indian and Chinese Christians have to decide, just as European Christians have to do, which of these three contradictory views they are going to follow in practice. That the disagreements between European Christians are a grievous hindrance to the spread of Christianity is no doubt true, but you cannot dispense Indian and Chinese Christians from having to make a decision in regard to them.

Great problems have come up in our own time about

the right line for the Church to take—whether by this is meant individual Christians belonging to the fellowship of the really regenerate or the visible Churches as earthly organizations—in regard to the earthly interests of men, to the material well-being or intellectual culture of contemporary society, to the State, to international politics, to class-war and international war. It is impossible to deal with these problems here. This only may be affirmed, that the main task of the Church must be to bring men into the community of the new life, whose future perfection lies beyond the earthly sphere of things, but that the Church can do this only by loving men as persons, and that if it loves them as persons, it will care for their temporal well-being.

Only in the perfect Society, free from the limitations of earthly space and time, can man's exigence for fellowship be fully satisfied. But all the various kinds of association by which life on earth brings men into partial fellowship and co-operation may be regarded as adumbrations of that transcendent community. They may have value both as images which help men to realize, in some degree, what the perfect Society will be, and as temporary frameworks within which man's social nature may find provisional exercise and expansion. It is noteworthy how Dante uses, to denote the company of heaven, words drawn from almost every kind of human association on earth. He calls it a *family* (*Paradiso* x. 49), a *kingdom* (very often), a *city* (*Paradiso* xxx. 130), royal *court* (*Paradiso* xxxii. 98, etc.), a *council* (*Purgatorio* xxi. 16), a *religious community* (*Purgatorio* xxvi. 129), an *army* (*Paradiso* xviii. 124), a *feast* (*Paradiso* xii. 22), a *marriage-festival* (*Paradiso* xxx. 135), a *dance* (*Paradiso* vii. 7; xii. 22), a *triumph* (*Paradiso* xxx. 98), even a company *at play* (*a questo gioco!* *Paradiso* xx. 117). All these different kinds of interest and activity may seem on earth to be incompatible: a man cannot simultaneously be taking part in the political activities of a citizen and the military exercises of a soldier and playing a game. But each of the modes of association named by the poet has its own order and beauty and calls out in some particular way man's capacity of fellowship. And Dante would seem to have felt that in the fellowship of Paradise the peculiar value belonging to each mode in which that capacity is called out on earth finds its supreme and perfect realization, in a society which all our various associations and friendships on earth can only shadow in some broken and partial way, but can never make fully apprehensible to our imagination.

CHRISTIAN WORSHIP

By FRANCIS UNDERHILL, D.D., DEAN OF ROCHESTER

X

CHRISTIAN WORSHIP

THE aim and end of religion is worship. A vigorous faith no doubt has many other valuable products : morality, the love and service of humanity, intellectual satisfaction, peace of mind. But these, important as they are, are secondary to the access of the human spirit to God. Faith without worship is dead. These two aspects of vital religion are indeed inseparable; in the individual and the community alike neglect of worship leads directly to weakness of belief. On the other hand, if it is desired to reinvigorate belief it is a mistake to deal primarily with the intellect. The first necessity is the restoration of disciplined habits of worship. Moreover, living faith finds itself first in worship; the believer in God adores Him, not because it is the correct thing to do, nor because he hopes to gain advantage from it, but because he cannot help it. He must.

The subject of this essay is Christian worship. The word will be used to cover all kinds of approach to God; but we shall fail to see it in any completeness unless we first consider briefly the origin of worship in human history. Christianity did not make an entirely new start in man's knowledge of God. The coming of our Lord Jesus Christ in the flesh did indeed profoundly affect worship; but Christian prayer has its roots deep in the past. The Church claimed, sanctified, developed, in the Name of Christ what was already there in the world and in men's hearts. We believe that everywhere God has been teaching man as he was able to bear it.

THE OBJECT OF WORSHIP

Always, from the most primitive times onward, man's worship has had an object; it is offered to some power or powers outside himself. Man does not first desire to worship or make up his mind to do so and then invent somebody or something to whom to address himself. In all the records we find man conscious of objects, spirits or gods mightier than himself and able to assist him if duly propitiated. These powers, spirits, persons, are of many varieties. We find an elementary personification of natural objects; the snowy mountain peak, with its avalanches and torrents, its rain and snow; a strange shaped stone; the spring, hot or cold, so beneficent to the primitive community; the strong river with its falls and rapids; the sacred tree in which dwells the benevolent or evil spirit; the tree of life or death; the tree of knowledge. There are, too, the ever present forces of nature: thunder, lightning, wind; fire, warming, protecting and cooking; the soil out of which all good things come; the corn, the wine, and the oil; the seasons, spring, midsummer, winter; sun, moon, and stars with their profound influence on human fate; the "wild", full of spirits, kindly and generous, menacing and dangerous; the totem animal of the clan or tribe, even the cult of the dreaded serpent. All these and many other phenomena are thought of as animated by spirits mysteriously other than man, to be placated and used as best may be.

Again, a strange power attaches to man's own works, particularly the useful ones; the axe, the saw, the knife and other tools, especially sacrificial objects. Here is the first appearance of images; the odd stone, shaped by nature or improved by man into the semblance of some animated object; this, too, is somehow indwelt by a higher power.

Nobler than these is the genius, the soul, or the material of which the soul is made. Of this class are the ancestral spirits which played so large a part in ancient Roman religion. These are thought of as still alive, interested in the family, to be propitiated and even fed. Spirits of this kind, especially in Greece, merged into the heroes, half-divine, half-human persons, of whom marvellous stories are related. More advanced still are the " gods " as they came to be called. Thus very early we find man's own activities personified; we get the god of War, of Love, of Song and Dance, of the Crops, of Hunting and the Arts, of Wine; together with those powerful beings who watch over man's most critical moments, the gods of Marriage and Birth, of Death and the Hereafter.

From these, who are often local and tribal, we pass to the "high gods." These are on a more exalted plane than the primitive spirits, though they may be more re-mote than their predecessors. Two points must be noticed about them : First, they are somehow the sources of exist-ence; they have life in themselves, they give it and pre-serve it. And secondly, more important still, they are the sources of values; they stand, insecurely enough at first, for good and evil, wisdom and folly, love and hatred, peace and strife, beauty and ugliness, truth and falsehood. The high gods tend to coalesce; an Egyptian god is recog-nized as being the counterpart of a Greek or Roman god. Thus they become universalized and come to have a common mind about those values, the emergence of which is so vital a point in the development of the religious sense in man.

So at last there comes the splendid conception, realized by man, of one supreme God, superseding all the im-perfect spirits in whom humanity had so far placed its trust. He is the Father of all; remote perhaps at first and less approachable than the smaller deities who still survived for a time. But more and more He is adored and loved as the Creator of man and the world, a very present help in trouble.

The attitude of man towards the primitive objects of his cults can hardly be called worship in any developed sense. Yet he has a dim idea attaching to them of strength, holiness, of that which has been called the " numinous." He may fear these strange powers, but he is fascinated by them, drawn to them. From them go out blessing and life, harm and destruction. The spirits may be change-able, pleased and angry, jealous and beneficent; they can be persuaded or worked by magic arts. But above all they are mightier than man and may be made useful to him if properly dealt with. They are therefore of the highest importance for man, both in this life and beyond it.

THE IDEA OF GOD

Here a fact of the first importance comes into sight. The attitude of man towards the higher powers is condi-tioned by his thoughts about them. To use at once the language of developed religion, man's worship depends on his conception of God. In order to illustrate this pro-found truth we may leave the cults of primitive times and turn to the immediate precursor of Christian worship, the religion of Israel. No period of the world's history before the coming of Christ is of such significance in the evolu-tion of worship as the time of the great Hebrew prophets, since to them God granted a revelation of Himself which had not previously been given. We need not concern our-selves with details of the worship of Israel. Animal sacri-fice in the Temple, which had formed a part of it for centuries, though we do not know when it began, evidently made the prophets uneasy, and ceased very soon after the foundation of the Christian Church. The essential thing about the later pre-Christian forms of Jewish worship is the noble view of God held by the best men, and the exalted spiritual worship enshrined in the Old Testament. We see in that collection of books the change from naïve pictures of a tribal god, righteous indeed in some aspects, but also testy, irascible, vengeful, unaccountable, into that of the judge of all the earth, the maker and lover of mankind whom we meet in the writings of the later prophets and in the books influenced by them. There are many problems concerning God still to be solved. But we must look far down the ages to match the thoughts about Him which we find in the books of Isaiah, Micah and Jeremiah.

These lofty conceptions, this tender love and trust, find their expressions in the prophetic and other writings. But the classic example of pre-Christian worship is reached in the Psalms. These magnificent songs of praise, strangely mingled as they are with darker and more primitive elements, go far beyond the present worshipping capacity of most of us. The words of such Psalms as the 23rd, the 63rd, or the 104th shame the poverty of spirit and weakness in prayer of most Christians. In his deepest moments of insight the seer of today still finds in them a more than sufficient vehicle for his adoration of God. Behind them lies a conception of God's love, power, and goodness, which calls out the most heartfelt prayer his mind and lips can offer.

JESUS CHRIST AS WORSHIPPER

This preparation leads us directly to the New Testament and to the main principles of specific Christian worship. These we shall study first in the example of our Lord Himself. At the time of His birth and life on earth there were three modes of worship known to His country-

265

men. First, the Services of the Temple at Jerusalem. After a long historical process these had come to be unique, in the sense that they could only be performed in one place. There was to be seen the whole ritual of animal sacrifice; the offerings of the fruits of the earth, of incense, psalm and prayer. In these rites our Lord took part on the occasions when He, in common with other devout Jews, went up to Jerusalem for the Feasts. Secondly, there were the much less formal Services of the Synagogue, the local meeting place of town or village. Here were no sacrifices, but regular, probably rather formless, acts of praise, reading of the Scriptures and instruction in the Word of God. Jesus quite regularly took part in these Services on the Sabbath Days, sometimes led them, and constantly preached in the Synagogues. But there was a third form of worship of which we hear much in the Gospels. It was the custom of Christ often to spend long periods, whole nights, for instance, in the mountain in private prayer to His Father. Most often He seems to have been alone. But sometimes He would say to His closest followers, " Come ye yourselves apart into a quiet place and rest awhile." It seems clear that such times as these were used for informal corporate meditation and prayer.

It is important that we should carefully distinguish these forms of our Lord's worship, since that of the Church has with varying emphasis been derived from them. We must notice also that the prayer of Christ, as recorded in the Gospel, covers the whole range of man's approach to God. The clause " give us this day our daily bread " in the Lord's Prayer was meant to be used in the first place as the simplest kind of petition for the supply of food needed day by day for the nourishment of the body. We find also exhortation to vigour in prayer of this kind, and to detailed expression of ordinary needs. Importunity, even some kind of violence, are recommended.

We are told of a widow who *will* have justice; of a man who hammered on his unwilling friend's door at midnight; the command to cut off a hand or a foot in order to enter into life. "Ask, and ye shall receive; seek, and ye shall find; knock, and it shall be opened unto you," cries Jesus.

Higher, as we believe, than these, are pure praise, adoration and thanksgiving, constantly on the lips of Jesus, His worship culminates in the complete conformity with His will with that of His Father. In this He sets His followers a perfect example; for it is the final desire of the human spirit to be at one with the Divine. It has been well said (Heiler, *Prayer*, p. 123) that " the intercourse of Jesus with God is through and through a heartfelt relationship with the Father. Though He has passed through the school of the psalmists and prophets, He rises head and shoulders above them. He is . . . the most powerful man of prayer in history."

The ending of this might seem to some of us not wholly orthodox. But the same writer quotes the following words from another source. The words of Jesus in the garden— " My God, not my will but thine be done "—are " the highest moment in the history of prayer, the most perfect word in religion that has ever been uttered." The heart of Christianity is found in following Jesus Christ in His worship of the Father.

WORSHIP IN THE EARLY CHURCH

The early Christian Church took over much from the worship of Israel; but it was profoundly modified by the teaching of Christ. At first His followers joined as before in the worship of the Temple at Jerusalem and in the synagogues in their home towns. But within forty years of the Crucifixion the Temple was finally destroyed, never again to rise from its ashes. We may believe that some of the disciples of Christ breathed a quiet sigh of relief at the passing of that which had long been a cause of uneasiness to the noblest Israelites. There came gradually a second development. As time passed, divergences of belief and practice appeared between Jew and Christian. The cry of heresy was raised; some were cast out of the synagogues and others quietly withdrew. The first Christian churches were private houses rather larger than the rest, and meetings for worship were sometimes held out of doors. But nothing was fixed as to *places* of worship until a somewhat later period.

The *occasions* were also at first doubtful. The habit of meeting daily which obtained in the first days of enthusiasm soon dropped out of use. No special day is mentioned in the New Testament, nor indeed before the second century. But quite early the first day of the week became a fixed occasion of worship in commemoration of the Resurrection. This was a revolutionary change from the Jewish observance of Saturday as the Sabbath, and resulted in the shaking off of many strict rules for the keeping of that day.

As to *forms* of early Christian worship; it is probable that during the time of the Apostles, as since, the worship of the Church centred on the Lord's Supper and the " love feast " which preceded or followed it. This was supplemented with canticles and hymns, particularly the psalter, and those other ancient songs which are still used in the public prayer of the Church. There were also readings from the Old Testament Scriptures, from the letters of prominent teachers such as St. Paul, and from the sayings of the Lord Jesus, treasured up long before our Gospels were committed to writing. There was also " prophesying," preaching and instruction, as is so often seen in that interesting book the Acts of the Apostles, and in the writings of the early Christians. Together with worship went collections or contributions for the poor, the sick, and the propagation of the Gospel.

The *object* of early Christian worship was God the Father of our Lord Jesus Christ and of all Christians; but the point of difference from the past was that praise and prayer were offered in the name of Jesus Christ the Lord. Worship was also very early offered to Christ as God, though there has always been reasoned objection to "Jesus-worship." This is one of those points at which popular feeling will always transcend strict theology.

Liturgical *forms* appear early, fixing the words and acts of public worship. We shall have more to write on this point later, but it must be mentioned here in its historical place. An exquisite picture of Christian worship at a celebration of the Holy Communion is to be found in the twenty-third chapter of Walter Pater's book *Marius the Epicurean*. The description may be in part idealized, but it is the work of a fine scholar and literary artist who has used his documents accurately. The dignity, beauty, and spirituality of the rite, the rapt attention of the worshippers, the vigour of the singing, form together an inspiring glimpse of a Service in the Christian Church in the second century, Marcus Aurelius being then Emperor. The leaders of the Service are personages recognized as having the right to conduct it; they wore some kind of special vestments. The air of the whole company was a grave one, an air of recollection. The worshippers were of all ranks and ages, from old people to children. The table or altar was the tomb of a youthful martyr of the family of the Cecilii, who had shed his blood not many years before, and whose relics were still in this place.

There would seem to have been a fairly orderly progression in the historical evolution of Christian worship. We have indeed evidence of experiments on somewhat

different lines; but before the time when the Emperor
Constantine caused persecution to cease, and recognized
Christianity as a permitted cult in the Roman Empire, the
principal Service had taken on essentially that Eucharistic
form which it has retained ever since, and which is still
the most usual mode among the vast majority of Christians today.

Evidence of this fact is to be seen in the arrangements
and traditions of the great early Churches, such as those
at Rome, Ravenna, and other places, as well as in the
slight remains we still have in our own country. In these
buildings the Lord's Supper was central from the first.
The church is a rough parallelogram, with or without
aisles or chapels; at one or both ends is a rounded apse,
and in the chord of the apse, or thereabouts, the altar at
which the Bishop or priest celebrated, facing the congregation assembled in the nave. This arrangement persists
in the plan of some of the most ancient remaining
churches. The splendid mosaics which cover the wall
above the arch and fill the semi-dome behind it in so
many of the basilicas symbolically carry on the same
thought.

Of what then did, and does, this central act of worship
of the Christian Church consist? There are variations in
the liturgies, but the main constituents of all of them
descend from a common source and from a very early
date. At the beginning a penitential note is struck, proclaiming the humility of the worshippers and their need
of God's pity. The words "Lord have mercy" occur at
this point, often in their Greek form, surviving when the
rest of the Service has been translated into some other
language. At this point, in most liturgies comes the Gloria
in Excelsis. Prayer, generally in the form of petition,
follows; it is noteworthy that many of the collects still
used in the English Prayer-Book, and in those liturgies

which are derived from it, come down from the fourth, fifth, and sixth centuries of the Christian era. Readings from the Old and New Testaments, generally from the letters of the Apostles, and always a passage from the Gospels follow the prayers. Somewhere about this point comes provision for instruction in the faith, and the recitation of the Creed, though neither of these is a necessary part of the Service. Hereabouts too occurs a great act of intercession for the Church, for kings and rulers, and for all sorts and condtions of men.

All, however, leads up to the hymn of Heaven, "Holy, Holy, Holy," and the recital by the priest of the words used by Christ at the institution of the Lord's Supper. This again is followed by the communion of ministers and people, with a commemoration of the Sacrifice of the death of Christ. Other prayers and thanksgivings are then used, and the liturgy concludes, as a rule, with some kind of blessing in the name of the Trinity.

It is important to realize how ancient and persistent is the central form of Christian worship. Whatever controversies may range about this or that part of it, this or that theological explanation of the Presence of Christ, no intelligent worshipper at the Eucharist of the Roman Catholic Church, the Russian or Greek Church, the English, Scottish, American, or South African Churches, can fail to see that the main characteristics of all are the same, whatever difference there may be in detail. Dogmas may be restated, faith may grow warmer or colder, but the normal mode of worship, sanctioned by many centuries of use, remains constant.

Again, the heart of it all is the adoration of God the Father through the Sacrifice of Jesus Christ in the power of the Holy Spirit. Here, to use St. Paul's words, "we have boldness and access with confidence to God through our faith in Jesus Christ."

THE RELATION OF PUBLIC AND PRIVATE WORSHIP

The discussion of liturgical worship will raise in many minds the fundamental question of the relation between fixed forms of praise and prayer and that which is sometimes called "free worship"; the immediate access to God of the individual soul in private, unhelped or little helped by outward things such as consecrated buildings, music and ceremonial, or the presence of other persons. Two tendencies are to be noted here; that which holds strongly to the fixed form, and that which rebels against any strict adherence to outward signs, or even to corporate worship. There has been always and everywhere, in a much wider sphere than that of Christianity, a tendency to fix the words spoken and the actions employed in divine worship. It is not merely that "the clergy," using the expression in its most extended sense, almost instinctively fall into habits of worship; the laity are at least as conservative as their ministers. Both have been ready to maintain that the ancient form, and that alone, is valid; variations from it must be resisted strongly by those who hold to the old and good paths. The power of outward expression is mighty; it matters not very much what preachers may say, provided that the words and ceremonies of the Service remain unchanged. Worship is more powerful than theology.

All this goes very deep into human nature; liturgical forms are almost immortal. An illustration may be seen in the Book of Common Prayer of the Church of England, and in those other Churches which first derived their life from her. Much in that book, especially in the Communion Service, is very ancient, some of it pre-Christian; and much dates back to the days of the early Church. It is just those earliest parts which are shared with the sister liturgies of other branches of the Church; the variations, which have usually been bitterly contested, are comparatively modern.

That danger may attend any fixed forms of worship is obvious, particularly in times when faith is weak. The most superb words and ideas easily slip over men's minds almost unnoticed just because they are so ancient and familiar. Expressions used for instance in some of those psalms or in those ancient collects, to which reference has already been made, fine as they are, and compelling as their influence should be to lift up men's minds to God, may act as a soporific just because they have been heard so often. Words much less magnificent, because they are homely and less familiar, may for the moment hold the mind more firmly, may arrest the attention and arouse the will to fresh efforts to seek God.

Attempts therefore have from time to time been made in the Church to abandon fixed forms, and to retain only modes of worship which are variable and more personal. The comparative failure of such attempts is significant. No doubt even the finest and most ancient forms of worship need supplementing by freer kinds of Service, more modern and topical. But no large part of the Christian Church has ever finally abandoned ancient and fixed forms. Today, in our country as well as in America and other English-speaking communities, there is a marked tendency to return to liturgies, particularly for the central Service of the Lord's Supper. Good preachers are not rare : the really inspiring leader in extempore worship is much less commonly found.

The age-long instinct proves itself to be right. There is great power in fixed modes of prayer provided that they are worthy ones. Their survival through so long a period of history proves that they have been found good. They have stood the test of time because they were fit to stand it. The central act of Christian worship, enshrined as it has been for so many centuries in splendid poetry and prose, has the finest quality; it is in the grand manner. It invigorates the individual worship of each Christian; we cannot do without it.

We have now, however, arrived at the central point of this essay. If venerable and beautiful Services are the heritage of the Christian Church, it is in the end because they express the deepest mind of each Christian man and woman. The outward cannot long subsist unless it is the true expression of an inner hidden devotion. Any part of the Church which attempted to express its approach to God solely in public worship and neglected to train its children in the art of private prayer would be on the road to collapse. A great part of the reason why church-going is rare and lifeless in some parts of Christendom today is not that the Services are dull, the music inferior, or the preaching uninspiring. It is because the practice of daily prayer and meditation has declined. As soon as we see a revival of interior prayer in the heart of each believer, so soon will renewed vigour appear in the public Services of the Church. We must therefore now turn our attention to the private worship of the individual Christian.

This falls very roughly into three main divisions. Every child is taught, or should be taught, at the earliest possible moment in his life to say daily some simple prayers in the morning and in the evening. Men and women will not be able to carry the thought of God in their minds unless they are accustomed to seek Him at fixed and definite moments. Moreover, the times of prayer themselves must be definitely articulated. In the morning it is natural to thank God for safety during the night; to dedicate the day to His service, and to ask help for any definite work or difficulty which may be in sight. In the evening there will again be thanksgiving for safety and peace during the day; penitence for anything which may have been wrong; intercession, if it is not made at some other time; and a prayer for safety through the night. These simplest modes of prayer have been emphasized in some detail, since they are the earliest of all prayers which most Christians learn to say, and form the basis of all other kinds of personal worship. Our Lord's own prayer would naturally be said morning and evening.

To what was said about intercession it must be added that no one can get very far in the art of worship who is not constant in his prayers for other people and for those causes in which each of us is interested.

Besides spoken prayer, it has been the custom of men and women in every age and class to spend times in thinking about God. The word meditation is that generally used; but no definite expression is needed. It is to be feared that those who so spend any perceptible part of their time are today comparatively the few. On the other hand, most persons are accustomed to give careful thought to other matters of importance—to study, scientific research, pleasure, business, the home. It may be asked whether it is less important or less possible to spend time in thinking about God and Eternity. Only thus can fulness of life be reached by intelligent human beings.

But if any success is to be reached in this high attempt, definite times must be fenced off for it, either daily or on some other occasions which are regarded as of obligation. Such discipline may be unwelcome at first, but it soon becomes natural and has been found by many people to be an exceedingly fruitful source of knowledge of God. The aim, however, of such mental prayer, as of all other forms of worship, is not that it should be an end in itself. The outcome of it should be a constant realizing of God's Presence, and the habit of turning thought into prayer many times a day. Such prayer may be of infinite variety

—petition, penitence, intercession, aspiration, thanksgiving, praise. There is no limit to the power which may be gained and used in this way. Not only is God worshipped; the individual character also is built up and refined through frequent contacts with the eternal world.

We may now return to the consideration of corporate worship. We thought a few pages back that the quality of any Service offered to God by a congregation depends in the last resort on that which each person present brings to the combined offering. Here we are helped by the conception of a group or crowd consciousness possessed by a number of human beings met together for any purpose. For good or for evil such a body of men and women is more than the mere adding together of so many personalities met in one place. Each has his own past life, his experiences, his achievements and failures, his conscious and unconscious memories; they are physically joined for a longer or shorter time as a group.

Two salient points are to be noticed. This large or small group of ordinary people is, as we have seen, much more than the sum of their personalities. The group itself has a corporate character, different from and transcending that of each individual. Each brings himself and adds himself to the group. And each also gains something intangible but real from the others.

There is here no doubt much possibility of evil. A crowd in an angry mood does damage or commits cruelties which each individual member of it may shortly after bitterly repent, and of which he would have thought himself incapable. History is full of instances of such ill doings caused by herd psychology.

But the bearing of these facts for good upon worship is less realized than it should be. Here is a group of worshippers of God. Each has experience of Him, greater or less, long or brief. The experience has been gained by

different persons in many different ways : by the theologian
in his study and at his prayers; by the scientist in the course
of his research; by the mystic in his intimate converse with
the eternal; by the simplest soul on his knees before God;
by the friend through talk with the person on whom his
affection is set; by the lover of nature in the countryside,
on the hills, or by the sea; many of them in more ways
than one.

But for what purpose have these gifts been bestowed on
each man? That they may be his own treasured possession,
no doubt. But also that they may be shared as generously
as possible with others. No one probably will be able to
put into satisfactory words all that God has done for him.
But he brings what he has into the worshipping group by
going into it himself. The words used by all in the Service
are the same, but each means something different by them.
By a kind of sacred infection each shares something of the
experience of the others. Here, again, each gives and each
receives; so that the group together offers a far richer and
more varied offering to God than any member of it could
give by himself.

This is the real strength of liturgical services. Only a
few are able to throw their whole selves into the magnificent words; but each may rightly take them upon his
lips and into his heart as a member of the Church whose
own the Service is. Here is part of the meaning of the
communion of saints. The worship of the Christian
Church is not a matter of this world only. At the height
of her vision she calls upon her children to join in the
adoration of heaven itself. " Therefore with Angels and
Archangels, and with all the company of heaven, we laud
and magnify thy glorious Name; evermore praising thee,
and saying, Holy, holy, holy, Lord God of hosts; heaven
and earth are full of thy glory; Glory be to thee, O Lord
most High."

But again the balance must be redressed. It is not enough to perform traditional rites, however august, to observe the dignified ceremonial, to recite the sacred formulas. It has been well observed that " free prayer can never die because the primal religious feelings can never die. Deep necessities and vehement desires ever give to the individual . . . the power by one passionate cry to make a direct path to God " (Heiler, *Prayer*, p. 73). Both modes of worship are necessary for the welfare of the human spirit, and neither can be neglected. The more splendid are the revelations of God to the individual soul, the greater is his responsibility for sharing them as widely as he can. This is the answer to those many men and women today whose religion is individualistic; who do not give to or receive anything from the whole company of Christian people, because they refuse to share with the worshipping congregation. The mind of the Church has always been against the claim that solitude is the highest means of finding God. She may for a time smile on the hermit in his desert cell, but not for long. Soon she says to him, " Come back; if you are called to a life of prayer apart from the general ways of the world, you must join a Religious Community. You must offer your prayers and praises, you must meditate on God, in company with your brothers and sisters. So you will have spiritual health. It is not good for you to be alone. You lose by it and the Church loses also."

So to the mystic, whose vision soars far beyond the insight of the ordinary man and who longs to dwell apart in the heavenly places, the Church says, " Solitary religion is not all. Come back to us; share your blessed experience with us all or with as many as can understand. Tell us as far as you are able the secret you have learned of God that we too may have part in your joy."

And today the Church must say again to the intellectual

Christian that to read and write books is good, but that the mind is not all. Many find congregational worship dull, sermons too simple or too pretentious, and therefore stay away from church. It will not do. Not only have such persons much to give, they may also have more than they think to learn from the "babes in Christ" who stand, kneel, and sit around them. Neither life nor worship is complete without the sharing of experience between men and women of widely diverse temperaments and attainments.

WORSHIP IN GENERAL LIFE

We must now return to the first sentence of this essay. It was there asserted that the aim and end of religion is worship. This is, above all, true of Christianity; but it is, in fact, little understood in our day, when almost everything else is exalted as the heart of religion except the obligation of worship. Let us leave out of account the accusation that Christianity is "dope for the people," or that it is an attempt to achieve personal comfort and happiness only; or that its true motive is a desire to stand well with the eternal powers, as a kind of insurance, or with persons who may be useful to us. These are accusations with which we need not deal here.

More dangerous, because it is on altogether a higher level, is the view which considers the chief aim of religion to be the service of mankind. No one can think unmoved of the immense volume of unselfish work which is now being done in the spirit of Christ for the poor, the sick, the unhappy. Settlements in the slums of great cities, visiting in the homes of the unhappy or the oppressed, housing schemes, and a thousand other works of charity are done in the name of Christ Jesus.

All this is excellent, and such activities must be the natural outcome of robust faith in our Lord and in the

Godhead of the Father. The Bible and the Church are full of calls to such works of mercy, and we cannot conceive of a world from which all the activities which flow from the Christian religion had disappeared.

So, too, in regard to morals. It is commonly supposed that the primary effect of belief in God should be to make people good; and no one can read the Old Testament or the New without being deeply impressed with the noble ethical code there set forth. The ideals of personal purity, of struggle against the lower impulses, have never in human history been so strongly inculcated as by the teachers of Israel and the followers of Jesus Christ. So high indeed is the claim on man's soul and body that it has always met with rebellion, and never more so than in our time. Yet it has been, and still is, accepted by the wisest, by strong men and women, by the thinkers and seers who look deepest into the heart of humankind.

So, too, a sound faith gives men peace and poise of mind, a sense of settlement and quiet which are otherwise far to seek. Christian belief reconciles the intellect and the heart, integrates the character and brings its various elements into harmony.

But none of these, not even love of man, goodness, peace, are complete in themselves. The first object of religion is to bring human beings into a closer relation with God, their Creator, their Redeemer, their Sanctifier. No this-world faith is enough. It may carry us a certain distance, but it breaks down in the end. The chief concern of faith is the other world, and it therefore seeks first to adore God. In comparison with thus, all else is secondary.

To make such a claim is not for a moment to disparage the ideals of service, or morality, or peace of mind. There are no doubt regular worshippers who do not display in their actual lives such fruits as these. But that can only mean that there is something wrong about their attitude towards God. The really sincere man or woman of prayer is necessarily active in good works; unselfish, self-sacrificing, loving, peaceable. Their attitude towards the eternal world, towards the God they serve, produces just these effects. But that is because they know that their first duty is adoration.

THE SENSE OF OBLIGATION IN WORSHIP

If all that has been written so far is true, then worship must be not merely a matter of choice or inclination, but a duty. Indeed, until quite recently all Christians regarded Sunday worship, at any rate, as a binding obligation. It may be that this sense was partly derived from the observance of the Jewish Sabbath, though cessation from work rather than worship would seem to have been the primary thought in the Old Testament. Yet in the time of our Lord attendance at the Synagogue on the Sabbath seems to have been a duty generally observed. The early Christian Church, as we have seen, transferred the observance from the last day of the week to the first.

It is true that in the New Testament the references to public worship are surprisingly few. Where they do not occur, however, it looks as if the reason for so little being said was the general recognition of the obligation. In historical and religious writings the common facts and duties of life are often unmentioned because they are so obvious to the writer. So soon as the Church emerges into the full light the practice of Sunday worship is seen as fully established.

Before long the obligation is recognized as binding under the penalty of sin; and in the great part of the Christian Church today it still remains so. Whether any religious body does wisely to threaten its members with punishment if they neglect their duties is a matter into which we need not enter here. The point is that regular worship has always been regarded as an elementary part of the Christian life. No doubt the reformers of the English Prayer Book intended that public worship on Sunday should be of obligation for the English people. But they took it for granted, since it was a duty unquestioned in the sixteenth century. Even the wildest and most turbulent persons kept at least to that part of their professed religion.

The rule has manifestly decayed in this country. Comparatively few members of the Church of England, or of the Churches in communion with her, today regard worship as an obligation in the older sense. A strange notion has grown up that there is even something wrong or hypocritical in going to church if one feels out of the mood, or disinclined for prayer. As some of us seldom feel any very strong inclination towards public worship, the habit has declined fast in recent times. The matter is of urgent importance, since it goes to the root of our Christianity. It is a question which all eagerly discuss. It is claimed, rather superficially, that those who do not go to church are just as good as those who do. Let that pass. But another argument often used is that it does not really matter whether any particular person goes to church or stays away. If, however, our argument holds good that the praise of God by the congregation is of much greater value than the worship of each individual separately, this matter needs further careful thought by those who dismiss it rather lightly.

We may supplement that point now that we are dealing with the obligation of Christian worship. Regular prayer and praise are very good for ourselves. Atmosphere is a strong force, and we are meant by God, as reasonable human beings, to live as in the presence of the eternal world. But such an atmosphere is elusive and difficult to retain. For the simple of spirit, as well as for the wiser folk, the atmosphere of a building dedicated to God's worship is more necessary than we sometimes think.

Moreover, the Englishman is as a rule humble, and thinks that his personal attitude about any particular question matters little. But it is of much more importance than he thinks; and the fact that a man or woman is seen taking part faithfully and regularly in the worship of his parish church is a great help to all those who live around him. The chief need of the world today is a revival of worship. The intellect has had its say; the determination to justify Christianity at the bar of modern thought is a high duty and is being well carried out. But if it is to be successful in bringing men back to the Church of Christ it must be supported by the practice of disciplined worship.

SACRAMENTAL WORSHIP

It would be impossible to conclude an essay on Christian worship without writing something on the Sacraments. It may be thought this is an extension which goes somewhat beyond the wide connotation of prayer claimed at the beginning. But for the member of the Church the Sacraments are intimately connected with worship. The Holy Communion lies at the heart of it. A great part of our religious experience is sacramental.

So it must be in the earthly life of a being strangely compounded of body and spirit. Living in a tangible world of beauty and interest, and communicating with his fellows by means of the members of his body, he is conscious all the while, if he is an intelligent human being, of another and a greater world, invisible yet real, the city of God eternal in the heavens. Yet the things of the here and now are real also, and the greater part of man's knowledge of eternity itself is gained by means of that which is seen and heard. The mute and material things by which man's life is surrounded are in the end chiefly valuable because they make known to him, if dimly, a reality greater than themselves.

Chief among these outward things are those which by their beauty and fascination most clearly bring eternity into view. Our relationship with other men and women, parent and child, husband and wife, lover and beloved, brother and sister, the intimacy of the family—these are for many the closest reminders of the life and love of God. The beauty of the earth, sunrise and sunset, seed time and harvest, summer and winter—there are many who first found here that certainty of the divine beauty which they have later intellectualized into some kind of theology, and made vocal in prayer and worship. Art, music, literature, science, are for many open windows into eternity and can be brought into the direct service of adoration.

This is no modern phenomenon. It may be that we are more conscious of it than our fathers were, but philosophers, poets, theologians in all ages have discerned the sacramental approach to religion. It is, no doubt, true that such a consciousness can be traced back in some senses to primitive animism. But we believe that in those early times God was already educating His creatures towards pure worship. The sacramental theology of the Church is not emptied of truth because its roots go far down into man's past history.

THE CHRISTIAN SACRAMENTS

The sense which we have been considering, by which man seeks to find eternity in the things which are seen, has been satisfied by God at its highest point. The Incarnation of our Lord Jesus Christ is alike the fulfilment of man's longing for eternity and the chief of the Sacraments.

This is not the place to attempt a lengthy theological disquisition; it is enough to state the fundamental Christian belief that in the Person of Jesus Christ the eternal God is sufficiently made known to man, in order that man by following His example may be brought nearer to God. It is by the visible bodily Presence of Christ, by the words spoken through His lips and tongue, by the living of a human life perfectly conformed to the will of God that we "know the Father." Thus eternal truth is made accessible by means of outward signs.

As in the Person of Christ we learn the character of God, so in His example we see the worship God would have from us. We have already considered briefly the activities of our Lord in prayer and worship. But it is abundantly clear that the Christianity of the Gospel is a sacramental religion. Whatever may be the critical points raised in regard to the divine institution of Baptism and the Lord's Supper, the action of the Church from the very first makes it clear that she had received from the Master commandment to do these things.

The Sacraments are inseparable from the Church, and have been so from the beginning. Much rebellion against the discipline of the Church in these days is caused by misunderstanding of this point. The Sacraments belong to the fellowship of Christ, visible in the world; at every point the life and worship of the Church are carried on through them. They cannot properly be claimed by those who are not members of the Body from which they gain their meaning and their power.

THE SACRAMENTAL LIFE

But we must now get down to practical matters. What is the significance of the Sacraments in ordinary life and for the general body of members of the Church?

At what points do they specially touch man's experience of God?

There is a controversy as to the number of the Sacraments. In the Roman and Eastern Orthodox Churches, after a long period of uncertainty, they have crystallized into seven—Baptism, Communion, Penance, Confirmation, Orders, Matrimony, and Unction or Anointing. In the Church of England and other Christian bodies a distinction is made between the two " Sacraments of the Gospel " and " those other five commonly called Sacraments " (Article XXV.). Dispute has waxed hot on the subject; yet it is a controversy more of words than of experience.

For the fact remains that at certain critical moments in man's journey through this world the Christian Church, or the vastly greater part of it, provides through certain outward and visible signs the help required for the special emergency. The Church believes that whether or no an outward sign is specified in the Gospel narrative, each of these rites is used by God for the conferment of His vitalizing power on His creatures.

Thus Baptism is the symbolic act by which a human soul, whether in infancy or in later life, is " grafted into the body of Christ's Church." The outward sign here is one of cleansing. By the washing with water the person baptized is freed from the stain of sin and set upon the highway of the Christian life. At the same time that he is admitted into the fellowship of Christ's religion certain solemn obligations are laid upon him. These Baptismal vows are nothing of an extraordinary nature; they are the kind of rule by which any wise and thinking man would wish to be bound.

But the human being needs also some power from outside himself by which he may be enabled to keep the promises made at Baptism. For these, though simple enough, cut across many natural impulses, and most people suffer at times from strong temptation. Here is the need for the sanctifying Presence of the Holy Spirit. Confirmation, according to the theology of the Church in general, is not merely the acceptance by the individual of personal responsibility for the promises made at Baptism; it is a positive and strengthening (confirming) gift of God conferred by the outward sign of the laying on of hands by the Bishop.

Moreover, the central significance of the Gospel of Christ is His dwelling in the heart of every member of His Church. Union with Christ is achieved at Baptism and fortified at Confirmation; but the Presence of the Lord is assured much oftener by the faithful receiving of the Holy Communion. "This is my Body, This is my Blood." The Church believes that in this chief of Sacraments, through the outward symbols of the Bread and Wine, man receives " the strengthening and refreshing of his soul." By this means his sinful body is made clean by Christ's Body and his soul washed through Christ's most precious blood; Jesus evermore dwells in him and he in Jesus.

There is, however, another need deeply involved here. We have no doubt the " once-born " among us—those who know little or nothing of the experience of fall and renewal, of serious sin and the need for forgiveness. But these are few, and at some time or other in most men's lives, generally many times, there is urgent need for deliverance from evil. For many an assurance of pardon from God is a psychological necessity. They cannot be at peace until they have it. The way in which Absolution is given, or how often it is sought, are secondary matters. The primary fact is that the great majority of Christians today, as in all ages of the Church, make confession of their sins and receive sacramentally the gift of pardon.

The world has at last been discovering that the Church in this vital matter has been right all the time.

We need not go farther into detail regarding special Sacraments. There are other occasions, such as Marriage and Ordination, on which the Church sets the seal of a sacramental act. Again the word matters little; the fact is that at these times the power of God reaches men and women through a symbolic sacramental experience. The Sacraments depend on no hard dogmatic theology; they are the gift of God's generosity, meeting the primary needs of His creatures.

EUCHARISTIC WORSHIP

We have considered very briefly the main modes by which man has always sought and found God. Let us now return to the more specific subject of worship, linking it on to our thought of the Sacraments. These symbolize a permanent attitude of the human spirit to God, at all times and in all places. But at certain moments all is gathered up in a special offering. This act finds its highest point at the Holy Communion. Other Services contain praise, prayer, intercession, reading of Scriptures, instruction; but we have seen that from the first the worship of the Church centred on the Lord's Supper.

Today, as always, the overwhelming majority of Christian people in this world regard the Sunday Eucharist as their chief moment of worship. The tradition of non-communicating attendance is a falling away from the primitive model and theologically difficult to justify. The highest point of adoration should be the receiving of Christ in Communion. Doctrines which would define the mode of His Presence differ, but even this, strongly as many people feel about it, is really a secondary matter. The essential thing is that all believe in the coming of the

Lord Jesus to them at this supreme moment for two purposes. First, that they may be filled with His divine life, and being made one with Him may be one also with their fellow communicants. And secondly that they may offer to God once again " the continual remembrance of the sacrifice of the death of Christ and of the benefits which we receive thereby."

" Glory be to God on high, and on earth peace, goodwill towards men." Such is the true meaning of Christian worship.

THE CHRISTIAN WAY OF LIFE

By F. R. BARRY, D.S.O., CANON OF WESTMINSTER

XI

THE CHRISTIAN WAY OF LIFE

I

It is not the business of the Christian teacher to apologize for Christianity, but to try to tell people what it is. A religion that stands on the defensive is one that has ceased to believe in its own truth. And Christianity does not need defending: what it requires is to be proclaimed and to be made manifest in life. Least of all in the sphere of ethics does the Christian religion need apology. It offers the world what alone can save it; and far and away the most convincing argument for the truth of Christianity, in all ages, has been the appeal to the Christian way of life and the demonstration of Christian character. For twenty centuries that has been accepted, and even those who have not themselves embraced it have regarded it as the ideal way of living.

But that assumption no longer holds. In vast areas of the world today a determined attempt is being made to eradicate the Christian tradition and demonetize its moral currency. The ethical ideals of Christendom which have been the basis of Western civilization are now being vehemently repudiated, and indeed in some States proscribed and persecuted, as not merely impracticable but false, and as not merely false but treasonable. We are back again in the age of Diocletian. The Christian ethic is fighting for its life against the tremendous strength of the Power States. We cannot forecast the issue of that conflict. For those who believe in its divine origin the ultimate triumph of truth is secure; yet we cannot disguise from ourselves that Christianity has before now been blotted out in its most vigorous centres—across the whole of North Africa, for instance, to say nothing of Anatolia and the Near East, leaving apparently not a wrack behind. It has happened before, and it might happen again. It is not by any means inconceivable that we may yet see a great pagan belt stretching from the Rhine to the Pacific with small Christian minorities enisled in it. We cannot predict what God will do with history. There may yet be a " remnant " that saves out of the ruin and wreckage of great cultures. The one thing we can predict with certainty is that if the Christian ethic goes under Western civilization falls with it. In returning to it is our one hope.

The world, then, stands at the parting of the ways—at one of those crises of choice which are the judgments of God in history. Either it must recover Christianity and establish its foundations in righteousness, or reel back into chaos and barbarism. " Choose ye this day whom ye will serve." The momentous decisions which are being worked out, in politics, in economics and in international relationships, are but outward expressions of a conflict which is being waged in the soul of the modern man. In this conflict there is no neutrality; it is life or death, conquest or defeat. Suspense of judgment is no longer possible; the state of the world today precludes that. The hour has struck when we must take sides. For it lies deep in Christian experience that ages of crisis and desperation are the times most pregnant with opportunity. " When these things begin to come to pass, then look up, lift up your heads, for your redemption draweth nigh." Its faith was forged in just such a situation, and it is when all adventitious help fails that its redemptive power is most manifested. So, we believe, it will be proved in our time. Beneath all that appears on the surface, a world panic-stricken with despair and demoralized for lack of a faith to live by is more urgently conscious every day of its need for a new life to redeem it and a truth which can lead it back to sanity and the things which belong to its peace. Never before in the history of mankind has the Christian Church been confronted with an opportunity so vast and searching.

In our own country the prospects are brightening. The wild reactions of the post-war years have brought their inevitable disillusionment. The fierce anti-Christian propaganda which was being conducted by the intellectuals is now being increasingly discredited as its consequences begin to become plain. Everywhere thoughtful men and women are turning back with an intense anxiety to seek for a faith which will stand the test. And for practical purposes there is no other, for the men and women of our own tradition, than the Christianity we had half-forgotten. Further than this, there is no room for doubt, despite all the evidence to the contrary and all that may be said on the other side, that the Christian ethic is winning in England. Ours is indeed a far more Christian nation as regards its general outlook on life than it was ten or fifteen years ago. Recent events have demonstrated signally how sound and fundamentally how Christian is our public opinion on a moral issue. This was shown on two important occasions—in the sudden wave of moral indignation in regard to the betrayal of Abyssinia, and in the clear popular verdict supporting the miners' claim for increased wages.

Moreover, the death of King George V. has revealed pregnantly and unforgettably unsuspected depths in the soul of England. The reverence and gratitude he evoked were due to the recognition by our whole people that he stood for what is best in the nation and had kept us true, through anxious years of peril, to the Christian values in

our national life. The emotions called forth by his passing have been a solemn and haunting reminder that in
loyalty to them is our only salvation. The Christian ideal
is being reborn among us. Whatever may be the truth
about " the Churches "—and it may be questioned whether
the situation is nearly as bad as is commonly represented
—the diffused influence of the Spirit of Christ is gaining
strength in our nation every day. Yet as Sir Richard
Livingstone has warned us, no moral tradition can long
survive the destruction of its intellectual basis. We cannot have the fruit apart from the Tree. If we want a
world of peace and good neighbourhood, if we want a
world where the common man is honoured and things
are the servants of men, not their masters, it means a
return to the Christian religion.

And, after all, what else is there left? All the suggested alternatives have failed us. In a world half desperate
with the fear of war, half starved by the economics of
bedlam, where man is becoming the victim of circumstances and persons the helots of blind forces, the supreme
task of the next generation is to get Man back into the
centre and mould mere process again to human ends.
But what is Man? The modern world does not know the
answer to that question; and hence all its misery and confusion. The most unhappy and ineffective people in the
contemporary world are those who, distressed and
wounded at heart by the trend towards reaction and
cruelty, are trying to stand out still for human values but
without any more ultimate conviction. The attempt to
recover spiritual values but without readmitting Christ's
religion is in truth a forlorn experiment which is being
compelled to acknowledge bankruptcy. We have tried to
organize peace and freedom by the appeal to Common
Humanity. But Common Humanity is not enough. The
appeal to Common Humanity has failed. Every day makes

it more certain that in order to believe in Man it is not enough to disbelieve in God. An anthropocentric attitude to life has led to the dominion of mechanism in which personal and human values are at the mercy of non-moral forces. As *laissez-faire* in the sphere of economics has been found in practice to lead not to freedom but economic servitude, so a non-theistic enlightenment circles back to primitive superstition and the dark gods of blood and race and violence. The ferocious collectives of our own time are substitutes for a lost religious faith.

What *is* Man? The Christian answer rests securely upon its faith in God and the philosophy which follows from it. Christians are not primarily people who " believe " the doctrines and creeds of Christendom, though these are implicit in their affirmations. They are primarily people who believe in God and Man through Jesus Christ. And there is but one sure basis of freedom—the fundamental Christian conviction that men are made for God and eternity, and that therefore States exist for men, not men to be instruments of collectives, as economic systems exist for the real wealth of spiritual persons. In this are contained the two great commandments.

This conviction is now face to face with the rival philosophy of the absolute State. For it Man is a function of the State, as in much contemporary fiction he is merely a function of the sex-instinct. " Thou shalt love the absolute State," it says, " with all thy heart and with all thy mind and with all thy soul and with all thy strength. This is the first and great commandment. There is no other commandment greater than this. Blind obedience is the whole of goodness and strife is the fulfilling of the law." Between this and the Christian philosophy the modern world has now got to choose, for there can be no compromise between them. To accept the *de facto* State as ultimate is to surrender all moral standards. For then—as has been openly admitted in Moscow, in Rome, in Tokyo and Berlin —truth and justice are conceived starkly in terms of the self-interest of the State—that is, of the classes who happen to hold the power. " Justice is the interest of the stronger " —this is merely Thrasymachus streamlined. But it is the one fundamental atheism which denies the Sovereignty of God, and thereby the significance of Man, by deifying a temporary group.

The foundation of the Christian moral ideal rests upon the Sovereignty of God—the Father of our Lord Jesus Christ. The " other-worldliness " of the Christian ethic, which is often adduced as a ground for criticism by people who ask for something " more practical," is the secret of its relevance in practice to the concrete decisions of our own day. For without some ultimate spiritual conviction politics must always in the long run remain a naked struggle for power. But if God is King, then there is a law higher than that of the national sovereign State, and to that law it must conform or perish. There is no lasting hope of peace on earth except among " men of God's good pleasure "—men whose hearts are reconciled to God and whose minds are enlightened by His truth. Thus, as Christopher Dawson has observed, " the only specifically Christian politics are the politics of the world to come." This is implied in the phrase " the Kingdom of God," so cardinal in the Christian moral attitude. And when we ask what the Christian ethic *is*, this is the phrase which must be examined.

II. THE KINGDOM OF GOD

Christianity is a way of living. But it is not primarily a rule of conduct or even a scheme of ethical ideals. Christianity is a religion; God, not Man, is the centre of its interest, and its whole conception of life is through and through religious and supranatural. It starts out from the primary conviction that Man is made for God and Eternity and that therefore the purpose and meaning and goal of human life are not to be sought within Man himself but in obedience to the Will of God. Its way of life is essentially God-centred, and involves continual " conversion " by the operation of divine " Grace." It offers no complete scheme of ethics worked out in terms of human rights and duties like those of Aristotle or Confucius: it offers a way of fellowship with God. To live well is, for the Christian religion, to live in that relationship to God the Father of our Lord Jesus Christ which Jesus Christ Himself has made possible. It is a response to a revelation rather than a system of morality. " This is life eternal, to know Thee the only true God and Jesus Christ whom Thou hast sent." The Christian ethic is thus incompatible with any interpretation of human nature which is set wholly in a space-time context or conceived entirely in terms of evolution. The characteristic Christian scale of values, all that is unique and distinctive in the way of life which it inculcates, follow from its central affirmation. But because the God whom Christ reveals to us is in His own nature Love and Goodness, therefore the true way of life in God is verified in love for our neighbour and transformed human relationships. The second commandment grows out of the first. " Beloved, if God so loved us we ought also to love one another."

Thus the Christian ideal of conduct is from the first something far more than a principle of "rightness" and "wrongness." It concerns, rather, a quality of life, a revelation of new possibility and the acceptance of a divine vocation. It is to walk (as St. Paul said) in the Spirit—not being conformed to this world but transformed by the renewing of our minds. It is to be born into that realm of spiritual and moral reality in which Jesus of Nazareth is Sovereign, as the Revealer of the Father's Will, the Inaugurator of the New Age and the Mediator of God's redemptive purpose. "Grace and Reality are by Jesus Christ."

This revelation of life that is real (in the New Testament phrase, life eternal) comes to us both through our Lord's recorded teaching, as the expression of His thought and experience, and through the manifestation of His Spirit in His life and death and resurrection. Not less, and perhaps even still more, it comes through the qualities imparted to or evoked from the lives of His followers by the operation of God in the hearts in which Christ is enthroned. These are often described in the New Testament as the gift or fruit of the Holy Spirit. Passages such as Galatians v. 22 or the still more famous 1 Corinthians xiii. are the best known among many attempts at portraying these qualities in words. These are pictures of "the real thing"; and it is not much more than a verbal question whether we call them portraits of Christ or descriptions of the ideal Christian character. They are so true to the portrait in the Gospels, though with an added richness and depth, as to be in essentials identical. Indeed, we hardly exaggerate in saying that if the text of the Gospels had perished we should know from St. Paul's and St. John's letters, and from the classical Christian biographies, what manner of man the Master Himself had been.

To the man in the street, no doubt, the Christian ethic is based primarily on Christ's teaching. It is taken to mean putting into practice the moral precepts recorded in the Gospels and especially in the Sermon on the Mount. No one will wish to deny the truth in this; but as soon as we begin to ask questions we are faced at once with all kinds of difficulty. To begin with, the Gospels themselves make clear that His own primary preoccupation was not so much ethical as religious. A Teacher He was, and the Master of all teachers, but not chiefly a teacher of morality. He laid down no system of conduct; His concern was with the divine reality which He called the Kingdom or Reign of God. All that He had to say about conduct was essentially the result or even by-product of His religious and spiritual insight. Secondly, our Lord's moral teaching is strictly conditioned by His own circumstances and was given to the men of His own time, not to us in an age so unlike His and in circumstances which He could not foresee. How then can we find in the Sermon on the Mount or in other recorded fragments of teaching a rule of life for the twentieth-century man? Moreover, when we examine what He said, there are so many moral problems and perplexities—many of which press on us most heavily—of which He seems to have taken no cognizance, that the claim to possess in Christ's moral teaching a guide to conduct for our own times appears almost impossible to justify. And, indeed, a close examination precludes the idea that His own intention was to lay down rules for posterity. On every occasion He refused to legislate; and the eschatological colouring of His preaching makes it at least a debatable proposition whether He thought there would be any posterity or a future for the existing world-order. The modern idea of historical evolution was almost certainly alien from His mind.

Thus from more than one point of view it appears that the axiom of the plain man requires some measure of re-interpretation. If we equate the ethic of Christianity with the moral teaching contained in the Gospels we shall find ourselves driven into a tight corner. It will not be easy, then, to rebut the criticism that it is irrelevant or insufficient to the moral perplexities of the modern age.

But what is mistaken here is the premise. The teaching

of Jesus is supremely important for the guidance of life
now and at all times: but it was never intended to lay
down detailed prescriptions about conduct. The early
Church did not think of it in this light. There is,
admittedly, in St. Matthew's Gospel a tendency to represent Christ as the legislator of the new Israel and the
Author of an ideal Law (*cf.* also the "royal law" of
Jas. ii. 8). Once or twice it even attributes to Him certain
echoes of the Rabbinic casuistry. But in general it remains
true that the central interest of the first believers was not
the teaching of Jesus, but Himself. However it was that
they regarded Him—and that is beyond the scope of this
chapter—it was not as a teacher of morality. If they had
thought of Him chiefly in that light, it would surely have
been their first business to collect and tabulate His maxims
and hand them on for the guidance of converts. In fact,
as we know, they did no such thing. They proclaimed
that in Him is the way of life; but precisely in what form
of conduct the "noble path" of living consists they did
not attempt to define. What they said was that He is
Himself the Way and the Truth and the Life. The implication is that the Christian ethic means not so much
"carrying out His teaching" as the appropriation of His
Spirit.

The eternal value of His recorded sayings is that
through them He is Himself revealed to us. The words
live, and He lives on in them; as the artist lives in his art
and through it communicates his mind to us. They are
the utterance of His own being, just as He is described in
the fourth Gospel as the Word or utterance of the divine
Goodness. Thus through the words Jesus Himself draws
near in the plenitude of His might and authority. When-
ever in times of corruption or forgetfulness men have
found their way back to the Gospels and heard again the
accents of Galilee, there has always followed a moral revo-

lution and a rebirth of Christian moral standards. The words that He spoke are spirit and are life.

This is the truth in the plain man's assumption; it is a truth ever so much more pregnant than that of the first, unexamined statement of it, and opens the way to a more creative living. It puts us in touch with the vital principle of Christian moral and spiritual growth, which, in each generation as it passes, can bring forth richer and more abundant fruit.

The whole method of our Lord's teaching excludes the slick, cut-and-dried assertion which could become a paragraph in a textbook. He knew that no teaching is fruitful until it is possessed by the hearers and worked into the substance of their own lives. (The parable of the Sower states His theory of it as perfectly as it illustrates His practice.) A question was seldom directly answered; sometimes He replied with another question, sometimes with one of His packed, pregnant epigrams, sometimes by telling one of His stories. The aim of His method was, in all cases, to put them in touch with creative principles which would gradually unfold their content as men grew into appreciation of them and so work their inward transformation. It was thus, too, with His teaching about conduct. He sought to expose the hidden springs of motive, to reveal the interior laws of human character, and to open the eyes of men's understanding to the self-imparting source of all goodness in the loving Will of the holy and living God. For Him, the ultimate principle of morality is that men should treat one another as the Heavenly Father treats them. The consistent purpose of His whole ministry was to reveal, both in word and life, the essential quality of the Father's Will in its outgoing action towards the world of men. This is for Him the supreme reality, the one master light of all His seeing: it was what He called the Kingdom of God on earth: and in everything that He said and did—in the craftsmanship of the shop at Nazareth, in the preaching and healing of the public ministry, in His relationships with men and women, and in the supreme act at Calvary—He was manifesting forth its power and beauty. The Kingdom of God is life in its true quality. It is God's love sovereign in the hearts of men, and life eternal in fellowship with Him.

But the highest, as Goethe said, cannot be spoken. All that could be done, in the nature of things, was to illustrate by analogy and picture something of what He Himself possessed in this central certainty of His own experience. Thus He sought, by poetry and parable, to indicate to the mind of His contemporaries such aspects of the "many-splendoured thing" and the revaluations involved in it as it was possible to convey to others. The paradoxes of the great Sermon are meant to suggest the radical transformation in men's approach to the world and one another which are characteristic of the realm of God. For to accept the good news of the Kingdom is to be reborn into a new order of spiritual experience and insight and to live one's life from a new centre. It meant the "transvaluation of all values" and a reversal of all accepted standards, so that the last are first and the first last. Thus its first demand was "repentance"; and there is no entrance into the Kingdom of God except by way of spiritual rebirth. Unless men receive it as children they shall, He said, nowise enter into it.

The idea of the Kingdom is, from this standpoint, exclusively religious and other-worldly. It is not in Man's power to create; it is God's gift and the act of His initiative. Hence an intense faith in its nearness might have been expected to lead to Quietism, as it did, in fact, in those circles which seem to have been most closely related to Him—the people who are described in the Gospels as "looking for the redemption of Israel." But His sense of moral and spiritual realities was far too keen to rest in any solution which would evade the imperative of facts or the concrete tasks of the world He lived in. The parables show how vivid was His interest in the actual business of living. They reveal, moreover, the strength of His conviction that the world of men and things is God's world, and that in it, through its daily processes of family life, industry and government, the Heavenly Father is working out His Will. He who lived in communion with Reality was a realist in His outlook on life and would never take refuge in a vague idealism. He knew that the Father's Kingdom must come "on earth as it is in heaven." He must come to grips with the facts, knowing full well that the price of it was the Cross. The Kingdom is to redeem the present world order.

In other circles amongst His contemporaries, and especially amongst Galilæans, the Kingdom of God was almost identified with the rising tide of Jewish nationalism and the hope of autonomy from the Roman *Raj*. We have made the Kingdom of God a pious phrase; when the Galilæan crowds heard Him use it instinctively they were fingering their daggers. They found Him profoundly disappointing because He refused to equate the New Age with the programme of nationalist leaders. (This may be the real point of the Baptist's question—Matt. xi. 2; Luke vii. 18.) But He had in truth far more affinity with them than ever He had with the Pietists. He did look for the coming of a Kingdom which was to be realized on earth. And it implied a social revolution. The detachment which He preserved all His life from political and social programmes was due to His sense that such rearrangements would leave the heart of the problem untouched. They might shift wealth or power or privilege from one set of men to another—on the same fundamentally false assumptions. He stood for a radical revolution. And it is perhaps not insignificant that He seems to have distrusted "reforms." The Marxians, too, stand for revolution; and they display distrust and contempt for the Fabian reforms of the Social Democrats, which would merely amend the existing system. Like them, He believed it must be revolutionized. His thought moved in an atmosphere of crisis —the end of our age and the coming of another. Like them, He lived on the threshold of a new day which should invade the existing world-order and establish a new epoch in history. Like them, He demanded absolute allegiances, a willingness to hate father and mother, an uncompromising self-committal to a conviction which would change the world. He called men to take part in this adventure, but only if they were prepared to lose their lives in it. It might even be said that the Communist Manifesto reads very much like parts of the Synoptics with Jesus Himself eliminated out of them. But in this reservation is the vital difference. For the Marxian programme proceeds from economic and social revolution to the transformation of human life. The Christian revolution proceeds from changed human lives to a changed order, and flows out of character redeemed by God. It involves far-reaching economic changes, and those who have felt the pressure of Christ's spirit on them are as sensitive to the need for these as any Dialectical Materialists. But they know that even more radical is the necessity for changed men. Which revolution is coming to the world now?

We fail to understand our Lord's teaching if we tone down its "apocalyptic" colouring. But because the Kingdom of God which He proclaimed is the Kingdom of God's love and righteousness, His conception of it is through and through ethical. Those "principles of right relationships" which shine out of the fragments of His teaching are based on the ways in which God treats His children in the grand impartiality of His love. We must be merciful as He is merciful; like Him, we must be "kind to the ungrateful"; like Him, we must forgive to infinity. He is the God to whom persons are dear, who seeks for the one that is lost till He finds it. Therefore the cardinal principle of action is that we should will for all persons that fulness of life and joy in God which He wills for us and for all His family.

III. THE FELLOWSHIP OF THE KINGDOM

But the teaching of Jesus is not all. What He taught, He lived, and for what He lived for died. It was at least one aim of His public ministry to gather men and women about Him who should form, as it were, the nucleus of an "Order" of the Kingdom of God. To them He sought to reveal His inmost mind and impart the "mystery" of the Kingdom, training them to appropriate its principles. He bound them together in loyalty to Himself, and taught them, within the school of their common life, the true secrets of greatness in the new age. He exhibited to them the way of service. He would have them live as a community detached from the values of the world, unmoved by its censure or rewards, unseduced and unfrightened by majorities, ruling their lives by the laws of the Coming Kingdom and in act finding those laws verified. In sacramental meals meant to symbolize the "divine banquet" of the new day of God, He taught them to live in anticipation of it and incorporated them into its promises. And "in the same night that He was betrayed" He made them, for the last time on earth, communicants in the assurance of its victory through His own death and resurrection.

Out of this Order of "friends of the Kingdom of God" there emerged the Christian Society alive with His life and ruled by His spirit. It was at once the foretaste and the instrument of the Kingdom which is to be fulfilled on

307

earth. Within the common experience of the Church as, under the inspiration of His presence, insight and understanding deepened, the values of the Kingdom grow clearer. "The Way" becomes a name for Christ's followers. New standards begin to be accepted; conversion is seen to involve a transformation of personal and social relationships; the acceptance of mutual responsibility as between fellow-members of Christ's Body clothes itself in an economic system which, with its centre in the common worship, provides support for the helpless and necessitous. Honest work is related to God's Fatherhood; family life is raised to a new glory by the redeeming touch of Christ's spirit; the official contacts of man with man—master and servant, subject and ruler—are reborn into spiritual relationships. There begins to take shape a new social order, sustaining all that was vital and worth preserving in "the system" under which they lived, redeeming all that was morbid and degenerate; and it lived on when the imperial system crashed.

Through all these formative years of the early Church—as they are reflected in the New Testament—there is at work a life-giving Spirit, a new source of moral creativity, leading men on to an ever fuller response, a growing insight and appreciation, and an ever wider recognition of the range of human possibility as the spirit of Christ possesses the hearts of men. The Kingdom of God is beginning to come true in the common tasks of earth's works and days, redeeming the social order which surrounds it by its own inward dynamic. As to the content of the Christian "Way," there is, from the first, constant development. There is no ready-made "Christian Sociology." There is the essential loyalty of disciples, and the characteristic Christian scale of values. And in all ages it is "the same Spirit" manifest in "diversities of administration."

For any living ethical inspiration must embody itself in changed forms of conduct as circumstances vary and develop. Thus to take a most obvious example, at a time when increased production was the primary need of society, thrift was one of the obvious social virtues. In the changed conditions of the twentieth century it is doubtful, at least, whether it is so still. The actual conduct which is required of Christians must, obviously, take its shape in immediate relation to actual conditions—else our ethic becomes a social anachronism. What is constant in all Christian generations is the " Charity " which draws from Christ—the fixed will to treat all our neighbours as persons made for communion with the Father and to master the economic system for the spiritual ends of God's Kingdom.

The Christian life does not mean " copying Jesus "—for the great majority of His modern followers there can be no literal " imitation of Christ." It means to live in the power of His spirit and thus by His Grace to be admitted to participation in His redemptive work.

IV. IS THE CHRISTIAN ETHIC " FINAL "?

This, in conclusion, is the answer to an objection about the Christian ethic which seems now to be widely entertained. The modern mind is obsessed by " evolution." It is prone to assume that what comes later must be better than what has preceded it. Even if it avoids this crude fallacy, it tends to regard all truth as relative; it must soon be merged in a subsequent discovery or displaced by a better informed theory. The idea of a final revelation, whether in religion or morality, cuts across many of our assumptions. Thus the claim that the Christian ethic is permanent, for all times or circumstances, is met today by a great misgiving. The revelation given in Christ, men say, was after all two thousand years ago and in an age so unlike our own : has it still promise and authority for the complex world of the twentieth century? It has helped mankind nobly along its way; but is it not destined to be superseded by another ideal and a changed standard? Is Christ Himself a " final " authority, who must dominate all future history, or is He one among many torchbearers who must now hand the torch to another? Many people are asking that question, and it is necessary to come to terms with it. But it rests on a fundamental confusion. In the natural sciences, as has been pointed out,[1] the latest theory does displace the earlier. But where we are con-cerned, not with theory or inductive reasoning from observed facts—where the evidence is constantly being changed—but with moral and spiritual qualities, succession in time is wholly irrelevant. If a statement is true it is just true; and the fact that three hours or three centuries have elapsed since the statement was first made does not change its truth into falsehood. A thing of beauty remains a thing of beauty. No subsequent revelations of beauty can make it obsolete or anachronistic. Every great work of art is " final." " Beyond Pheidias art cannot go." Shake-speare and Milton and Beethoven can never be dispos-sessed of their sovereignty, though many subsequent artists and dramatists may apprehend and express different aspects of the truth and beauty which is revealed by them. All education in the humanities is based on a study of " the classics " in literature and art and conduct, because there flows from them an influence which inspires and directs the insight of others. The nearer the pupil draws to the " master," the more will there be released in him some new creative appreciation which he will seek to express in his own fashion.

This illustration is highly illuminating. For that is the

[1] Roger Lloyd, *Christianity, History and Civilization*, p. 233, n. i.

best possible analogy to the "finality" of the Christian way. The objection rests on the tacit assumption that the Christian ethic is a code, once for all laid down and defined. And codes must be always out of date. If Jesus had consented to legislate, His teaching must have been superseded by the changing circumstances of human life. An ethic which claims to be final in that sense—to prescribe exactly how men must behave, irrespective of changing needs and situations—is out of the running from the word Go. The Koran claims to be final in this sense, and it is a moral and social anachronism. The religious legislation of Hinduism is an actual obstacle to moral progress.

But, as we have sufficiently insisted, the Christian ethic is not of this kind. It is not a code but a living Person. It is not a set of copybook maxims but communion with the eternal Christ, who is ever active and redeeming and ever evoking from human nature new possibilities of goodness. He is "final," therefore, in this sense, that the more we learn and the nearer we get to Him, the more truth and reality we find in His inexhaustible resources. The Christian ethic is yet to be fulfilled as mankind "grows up into Him," to the measure of the stature of the fulness of Christ. It is, therefore, always "dynamic" and it is inherent in its very genius that it must be continually developing—not away from Christ but towards Him. We are still but just beginning to understand.

The world of our day is temporarily demoralized. Men's hearts are failing them for fear, and there seems to be no power left on earth to stay the rot and revive faith and love. "The nobler elements in our civilization seem to be at the mercy of the lower"; something seems to have gone dead at the heart of it, and it seems to have no such inward resources as can revitalize and restore it and bring its social and economic mechanism under moral and spiritual control. There is today no other leadership but that of Christ which can avail to save us. And it is the vocation of Christ's people to call men back from their feverish fears, their nightmare illusions and false values, into an order of peace and reality, a world which is ruled by God our Father and in which Christ is mighty in redemption—the Pioneer of the Divine Kingdom and the Perfecter of Faith, Hope and Love. " The Kingdom of God is righteousness and peace and joy in the Holy Spirit."

CHRISTIANITY AND CIVILIZATION

By PERCY DEARMER, late Canon of Westminster

XII

CHRISTIANITY AND CIVILIZATION

THERE is such a thing as European civilization on both sides of the Atlantic: it is now predominant and pervasive throughout the world; and, like all civilizations, is due not to climate, geography, diet, race or skin-pigment, but to religion.

Those who have lived in non-Christian countries know something of their tragic imperfections: they know also that few parts of the world can now be called entirely non-Christian: women and children, the sick, the weak, the poor—and others—still suffer in their millions, but almost everywhere an influence is at work dissolving the evils. There is, however, little good in dwelling on others' defects. It will suffice to say in the words of James Russell Lowell:

> "You cannot point to a single square mile in the world where sick people are cured, children protected, womanhood honoured, and the sacredness of human life regarded which does not owe all this to Christianity."

There is then a Christian civilization. It did not spring fully equipped in the first century, nor indeed had the whole of Europe become even nominally Christian by the tenth; but it was slowly built up amid the ruins of the old pagan world which had been conquered by the barbarians. Gradually and painfully certain battles were won for the new spirit; but much of what we can boast at the present day has been achieved during the last two or three centuries, and some of it only in certain countries.

SCIENCE

But let us leave aside those things which are generally recognized and consider for a moment the great outstanding feature of the modern world, Science, that unprecedented mastery of exact knowledge which has made the material fabric of civilization. In this the nations are at unity; this the non-Christian peoples have accepted with unanimous enthusiasm, through this they are emerging into a universal culture. Most strangely it is this tremendous feature that is ignored when men discuss the gifts of Christianity to the world. Yet modern science has arisen entirely within the borders of Christendom; all other religions have lacked the sensitiveness and curiosity, the daring and love of truth, the sense of order and the unity of spirit which have combined to produce it. Five centuries before Christ the new idea of scientific enquiry dawned in Ionia, and philosophers began to seek for truth and order in Athens; but the Greeks were too factious and unpractical to carry out the task so wonderfully begun. The incurious Romans were content to be practical and to establish the idea of law and order. Persia, China, India showed no desire to carry the torch that had been lit, though they produced great literature and art, pondered deep philosophies, and showed in Zarathustra, Confucius, Buddha that they had as much to give in the finest elements as any peoples that have ever been.

Then there arose on the edge of Asia, on the edge, too, of the Mediterranean Empire, a little brotherhood which had a new idea of human possibilities because it was believed that God had revealed Himself in a man. They grew from a Hebrew root, and could not have existed without the passionate Jewish conviction that there is one God, and He good. This their Founder had deepened, extended, refined, basing their faith upon a profound quadrilateral—the Fatherhood of God; the consequent Brotherhood of Man; Salvation to Eternal Life, possible for all because of the infinite and therefore equal value of all human souls; the Kingdom of Heaven, proclaiming the hope that God would reign on earth and that His excellencies would prevail.

Obscure for the most part and provincial, this group of men could have but a partial understanding of what they called the Way; but at the outset they absorbed the spirit of Hellenism and added it to their basic Hebrew tradition, so that their earliest extant writings, the letters of St. Paul, blend Greek with Jewish ideas, as do the later reflections of John. They wrote in Greek, and their popular art, of which much has survived, was Hellenistic. They did not realize for some generations their affinity with Plato; they never understood the fullness of their own Master, tending to interpret Him mythologically, and to overshadow His Gospel of the Kingdom with the overstrained ideas of sin and ransom which they had inherited from Judaism; but they knew that they knew but in part and prophesied in part, as St. Paul had confessed, and at the end of the century it could be written that they had many things to learn, "but ye cannot bear them now." They had, in fact, the new virtue of humility; and perhaps it was that virtue more than all else which made it possible, after fifteen centuries of travail, for science to be born.

Nothing, indeed, was further from the mind of the early Christians than a school of natural science; but they had already laid the foundations. They had levelled the myriad restrictions which limited the Jew; their Master's very being had been bound up with freedom of enquiry; they discussed high matters at their weekly common meals; like the Greeks, and unlike most nations, they were free from priestly rule when their sacred books were laid down; they had more of the democratic spirit, since, though slavery could not be abolished, it could be and was ignored. And they had the new humanism of universal Charity. In many ways their ideas were rudimentary, and their imperfections no doubt were deplorable. During the centuries that followed, the now dominant Church was guilty of superstition, bigotry, oppression, cruelty. But something persisted which was Christianity, a little flock of Christians went on, sometimes reduced as to a tiny stream, sometimes almost disappearing. The Kingdom of Heaven is not the Church. It is the Leaven.

Christianity has indeed been but one of three forces in Church history: the spirit of Jesus, or " Holy Spirit," as it is called in the New Testament, has always had to struggle with two vices that are parasitic upon all religions—clericalism and credalism. Clericalism, the spirit of the Sadducean priests, Pharisees, and scribes, caused the death of Jesus. Credalism or systemization, the creation of static confessions and compulsory theologies, which have been generally lengthy and elaborate, and sometimes quite remote from the Gospel (old bottles for new wine), has often been near to crucifying Him afresh.

But Christianity persisted during both medieval and modern times. In the long period—hostile critics have called it the glacial epoch—of the Dark and Middle Ages, innumerable men and women lived faithfully in the primitive Christian virtues: even among half-tamed barbarians, every generation produced examples of gentleness, kindness, self-regardless devotion to the weak, which paganism had hardly known;[1] and the world, for all its wickedness, called them saints and esteemed them far above its knights and princes. The Dark Ages were an era of heroic missionary adventure; the Middle Ages achieved a marvellous art, brought education within reach

[1] See, e.g., S. Dill, *Roman Society in Gaul in the Merovingian Age*, pp. 409, 424.

318

of the poor, organized it systematically in a curriculum, generally without fee, and finally invented the university.[1]
And here we return to the subject of science.

Briefly, and to sum up a chapter on " The Origins of Modern Science," by Dr. Whitehead,[2] " The Middle Ages formed one long training of the intellect of Western Europe in the sense of order." Learning came to it from Byzantium, where also Justinian had codified the Roman law. There was something in Christianity that made it hospitable to human discoveries : the Church created the idea of law as the expression of a collective will;[3] the practical orderly spirit was a heritage from Rome; something of Plato had been transmitted through the Fathers, and the Stoic sense of moral order; such of Aristotle as was then recovered enjoyed an almost scriptural veneration. But behind all was the intense rationalism of the Schoolmen : everything had to be articulated and defined; and this because, instead of the arbitrary deities of Egypt, Asia and Greece, the only wise God of Christian experience was worshipped. " The inexpugnable belief that every detailed occurrence can be correlated with its antecedents," and therefore exemplifies general principles, can be found in no other civilization; and " It must come from the medieval insistence on the rationality of God."[4] Thence comes the faith in an Order of Nature which can be traced in the smallest occurrences; and it was this faith that alone made modern science possible. But the medieval era was also one of cruel oppression and persecution, clericalist and credalist rule prevented the free expression

[1] Professor J. W. Adamson in Hearnshaw's *Medieval Contributions to Modern Civilisation*, pp. 199-202.

[2] In *Science and the Modern World*, Cap. I., pp. 14, 15.

[3] E. Troeltsch, *The Social Teaching of the Christian Churches*, I., 325. See further, Gierke, *Genossenschaftsrecht*, Vol. III., and Figgis, *From Gerson to Grotius*.

[4] Whitehead, as above.

of new thought, and without freedom of enquiry and of statement truth cannot be discovered.

Thus science was formed in the womb of the Middle Ages, clericalist and credalist notwithstanding. It stirred in the Renaissance: its birth-pangs were the Protestant revolt, when observation began to replace authority. Science is the enduring product of the Reformation.[1]

ART

To leave ourselves room for the more difficult aspects of our subject, I will take for granted the evidence I have stated elsewhere about Art, that necessary fundamental element which Christianity shares with all other civilizations, and I will quote only the summary in two short extracts.[2] Christianity had its birth in the poetry of Jesus: from the beginning the other arts were used in the contemporary classical tradition; they were continued, extended, and enriched throughout the Christian era, what is called the Renaissance being not a break in the plastic and pictorial arts, but a continuation. And the general art of Christendom is far larger, broader, richer, more vital and ever growing than any other in human history: "There is no parallel to the painting of Christendom, except in the exquisite but comparatively limited art of China; little to its sculpture outside the Greece of a short period; little among all the beautiful buildings of the world to the breadth and richness, the content, of its architecture; and no parallel of any kind to its music. . . .

[1] I am glad to find support for this conclusion in Professor John Macmurray: "The one creative achievement of the Reformation was science and the scientific spirit. Science is thus the legitimate child of a great religious movement, and its genealogy goes back to Jesus" (*Reason and Emotion*, p. 172).

[2] From *The Necessity of Art*, pp. 65, 71. Also, for the medieval period, "Art," in Professor Hearnshaw's *Contributions*, already referred to.

" This Christian art has some characteristics which most people recognize, the free and exuberant variety of its ornament, for instance, its naturalism, inventiveness, delicacy, romance, its aspiring intellect, and genius for progress and invention. The art of Christendom, indeed, teems with beautiful inventions, like interior space composition in architecture, or the great spandrelled domes, or the spire, or stained glass, or oil painting as we have it. Every one of its styles of architecture is a marvel of originality, and they owe their very existence to the new religion which first admitted the slave into fellowship and then knocked off his fetters. . . . It introduced both tenderness and laughter. It made the very stones to chuckle, and if its great cathedrals seem the embodiment of prayer, they are also like homes where the laughter of children is never far away. In its statuary and painting there is a depth of humanity which the pagan art of Europe had not known. . . ."

<h2>MORALS</h2>

Wise men have everywhere proclaimed certain moral standards, and the human race has always recognized some actions at least to be right and some wrong. It would be difficult to believe in God at all if this were not so. The grosser crimes condemned in the second table of the Decalogue were condemned also by pagan antiquity, and the higher virtues had been in great part discovered not only by the Hebrew prophets, by Plato and the philosophers, but by the great teachers of Asia as well. God had not left Himself without witness. Christ came to fulfil. The Stoics, if they did not rise beyond the cold hopelessness of Marcus Aurelius, had established a lofty morality; and when they believed in God they reached to the conception that all men have rights as His children. Augustine was content to claim for the Christian religion that the higher standard, once thought attainable by a few philosophers, had been made the common practice of ordinary Christians.[1]

What Christianity did was to make a new basis and a new building, as St. Paul saw, in the virtues of Faith, Hope, and Charity. Of the first, Faith in God and in Christ, this is not the place to speak. Hope was a dominant note in the teaching of Jesus; soon perverted into a crude eschatology, it was then almost lost during the greater part of the Christian era, until it became a basic principle of human effort in modern times. The meaning of Charity is confused if we alter the word to " love," which was no new thing, and is both narrower and normally more intense; Charity is a devotion and affection which is disinterested and universal; furthermore, it is unqualified— " Love your enemies." This was so new that a new word had to be adapted for it in both Latin and Greek, and so difficult that it never acquired a verb, and was debased into a synonym for almsgiving. Let us therefore use a capital initial to indicate that we are using the word in its full meaning : Charity was the distinctive virtue of the first Christians, and the spirit of it in all the struggles and losses of a long growing period has never been lost. Christ has often been overlooked, His message abundantly distorted; but He has remained the pattern of Charity.

Much has been written about the Charity of the early Church.[2] *Vide, ut invicem se diligant!* Exhibited indeed in almsgiving, elaborately organized, and in the care of the sick, of slaves, prisoners, widows, and orphans, it certainly was;[3] but it was also a sense of brotherhood, a

---

[1] *De vera Religione*, III., 51.

[2] Well summarized by Dr. Glover, *Conflict of Religions*, Cap. V., and later books.

[3] Harnack, *Mission and Expansion*, I., pp. 152-198.

respect for personality, a universalism that ignored race and class, and gave a new position to woman, that sought for unity and rejoiced in freedom. Marriage was consecrated, the family secured; labour was honoured—no longer a mean thing, it was required as a duty. Men were quite changed; they showed a passion for doing good, a burning desire to save others; they formed intensive groups which bore health into the world. They were happy; and their common virtues of honesty, chastity, uprightness, gentleness, humility, were themselves due to the Charity and faith that were in them. All this is well documented, and is familiar to historians. To state it—and I have understated it—is only to say that the teaching of Jesus, overwhelmingly clear in the Gospels, was taken seriously. Christians really believed that they were brothers and sisters.

That Charity still lies at the heart of Christian civilization; and we can see it struggling for recognition in our international problems of today, especially in those places where it has not been obscured by clericalism and credalism. At first it was rudimentary and a minority ethic; but it was the germ of that social and political development without which the world cannot be transformed to Christ. The first stage was necessarily a set-back: as the world pressed in the pace slackened, till nominal Christianity became the religion of Europe. This meant that when power came it was seized by courts and hierarchies, and took the old form of force, tyranny, war, which had been unknown within the original community of fellowship and freedom. It also meant that the old Mediterranean religion came quietly back—mythology and magic, as well as violence.

All this the historian recognizes as part of an inevitable process. Other movements have died as the first impulse was lost, other civilizations have perished. But there was something in the world now that could not die. Christianity was not based upon a myth, but upon a dynamic historic Person; His teaching, though hidden and greatly misunderstood, was not consciously disobeyed. The original transformation of values was not reversed; nor could the ultimate vision of human solidarity disappear; for the faith of the Church was that what Christ had done He had done for all the inhabitants of the earth.

The Nordic barbarians destroyed all civilization outside the Eastern Empire, and, when they had been marvellously reclaimed by the Church and men were laboriously building up a new world in the Middle Ages, fresh invaders, Tatars and Turks from the remote steppes of Asia, poured in over the vast domains of Eastern Christendom, replacing the civilization of Constantinople by the Ottoman Empire, just as Russia was recovering from the Tatars and Spain was emerging from seven centuries of Moorish rule.

Europe was not a quiet area for progress during those twelve centuries; but civilization was enriched by much ardent Charity, as well as by art and the preparation for science which we have mentioned. If moral ideals were little realized, they were strenuously asserted; if monasticism failed in the end because it was sub-human, it had at least maintained an ideal of meekness and peace in a cruel and turbulent world.

Ethics, indeed, cannot be strong or complete without social and political development; and the idea of social reform is absent from St. Thomas Aquinas and the medieval Church,[1] though not that of economic theory. Politically the great churchmen believed (in strange contradiction to the words of Jesus) that the world could only be saved by the domination of the Church : hence the grave moral stain of authoritarianism and persecution.

[1] Troeltsch, *op. cit.*, I., p. 303.

Against this many had protested before Wyclif's theory of Dominion, Dante in particular setting forth the dream of a universal empire in the *De Monarchiâ*.

When Dante said that ruling was not the Church's business—*Virtus authorizandi est contra naturam ecclesiæ*[1] —he was laying the foundations of the modern era. But both reformers and ecclesiastics were agreed about something even more fundamental. The idea had become established of an objective fellowship holding absolute values.

That on the political side; and on the social side a new conception of industry.[2] Trade was no longer thought of in terms of slave plantations but of free labour. The ineradicable Christian respect for human personality is now changing the texture of social life : individualism grows and with it a social organization of skilled industries in guilds, which spreads from Constantinople over Western Europe. Above all — and the modern reaction of the economists makes it the more salient—the "just price" was central; ethics was held to govern economics.

What the early Church had done was to create a social impulse, a new "élan," and to give it *direction*. The ship was set upon its course; and through many tempests and contrary winds that course has been in view.

THE TWO STRAINS : CHRIST AND ANTICHRIST

The Soviet government in Russia persecutes the Orthodox Church on the ground that it has retarded and not helped civilization, being not only a general opiate, but in its very essence "pessimistic" and "life-hating." If this is indeed true of the East, it must be also true of the West, of many aspects of Protestantism, as well as of

[1] *De Mon.*, III., Cap. XV.
[2] Troeltsch, *op. cit.*, I., pp. 326 *ff.*

Catholicism in its various forms. It is only true in the same way that communism may be described as a system of murder and slavery. That is to say, side by side with real Christianity, there has existed a perversion, a parody —the web " is of a mingled yarn, good and ill together "; and if we may call that which is contrary to the life and teaching of Jesus anti-Christian, then this must come from that spirit of anti-Christ which St. John deplored. The spirit has been well described in a recent history of Europe : [1]

> " A world which had come to believe with St. Augustine that Time was a brief course of passing moments created by God and destined at God's pleasure in the twinkling of an eye to pass away and to give place to eternity. In this frail, uncertain, and crumbling dispensation, so full of wickedness and misery, the Christian held that all mundane interests paled before the awful problem of the soul's salvation. The reward of the righteous was everlasting blessedness. Sinners (including unbaptized infants) would burn for ever in the fires of hell. Sacred books, interpreted by a Providential Church, illumined the path to heaven. Following those lamps, and those alone, and constraining others to pursue the same course, the believer would be saved. False opinion would mean ruin."

This, which is called " Augustinianism " (though in Augustine, as in the Church at large, there was another side which was devotedly Christian), lasted on, not only in Catholic but also in Protestant forms; and indeed when a man at the present day says, " I am not a Christian," he generally means that he is not an Augustinian or a Calvinist. Yet " St. Augustine's teaching was never wholly accepted even by the Western Church," and " the whole

---

[1] H. A. L. Fisher, *A History of Europe,* I., p. 104.

history of Western theology from that day to the present may be described as one long effort—with many checks and reactions no doubt—to escape from the influence of St. Augustine."[1] But it did not escape till modern times from the spirit of authority or domination, which had been attacked by Christ, the spirit indeed of clerical tyranny and of persecution.

The only honest and wise course is to admit without any attempt at condonation the continued existence of anti-Christ in the Church, confessing, as did an apologist of fifty years ago: "In the course of history the sceptics, in matters of mercy and justice, have often been nearer Christ than professed believers; and the Christian Church has favoured practices and encouraged institutions, which have been a travesty on the teachings of Christ, and an offence to every feeling of humanity."[2]

Other-worldliness is not the error, as is sometimes urged. It is on the contrary the supreme and final message of the Christian religion, and the only ground of that optimism, that Hope, which is at its heart. For if there is a life transcending this animal existence and not ended by death, then there can be restitution and fulfilment. Otherwise all civilization, with all schemes for human advancement, is but "a striving and striving and an ending in nothing." The eschatology of Jesus, whatever accretions may have gathered on it, was at least the indomitable certainty of a dazzling future. But the anti-Christian spirit destroyed even this; for there is no optimism, except for the rounded selfishness of a criminal, in a world view that consigns the vast majority of mankind (99 per cent. or more, according to many authorities) to unending torture in hell.

The spirit of anti-Christ as it has manifested itself in

[1] H. Rashdall, *The Idea of Atonement*, pp. 348-349.
[2] C. L. Brace, *Gesta Christi*, p. 2.

history may be described as the sin obsession embodied in the legend of hell, and moulded to its own ends by clerical dictatorship. Many great writers have used much stronger language. In no Church has it been more than a part of its actual religion: from few Churches has it been absent. It is really anti-Christian because it is in direct contradiction to the good news that Christ proclaimed—not the gross opposition of the wicked world, which could be met and repulsed, but a subtle perversion which seeped in through the well-intentioned efforts of clericalism.

" The Kingdom which the Early Church had expected was indeed an ideal state of life upon earth, not an eschatology of heaven and hell." That central message of Jesus, the Kingdom of God, was, in fact, dropped quite early, the idea of the Kingdom being replaced by that of a static, authoritative Church, and its promise by a system of rewards and punishments.[1] This led to a concentration on personal salvation, a Buddhistic search for " merit," and in wide circles to a world-hating asceticism by which we mean, not discipline, nor drastic renunciation of evil, not courage, nor self-sacrifice for others, but asceticism in its strict sense.

It is now known to historians that this spirit, which still exists in many minds side by side with the Gospel, came into the Church from the outside, the sin obsession and the legend of hell from a debased Judaism, and asceticism from the pagan world. The source of the guilt-complex is coming to be generally realized, now that Bible commentaries are spreading the information that such sentences as those about " weeping and gnashing" are editorial additions rather clumsily tacked on to the tolerant hopefulness of certain parables. It is not less true of asceticism, " a subtler enemy of the Christian life than pietism or worldliness," that " the early Christians found

[1] Troeltsch, *op. cit.*, I., pp. 113-115.

328

it in the air around them; and their long resistance to it is one more proof of its essential heathenism."[1] Indeed, it has been found from the papyri that large monasteries of Serapis existed in Egypt before the Christian era; and it was in Egypt that Christian monasteries began, taking at first violently ascetic forms.

The condemnation of sex relationship is the most conspicuous example of asceticism; and by far the most important, because it caused much of the thought and action of the Church to be directed by abnormal persons—the frustrated, the solitary, the sub-sexed, the unsexed, the homosexually minded, or the sadistic. (There is no defence for the gross horrors of religious persecution after the eleventh century, but there is a psychological explanation.) Judaism had always been wholesome and indeed enthusiastic about the family, and Jesus had treated marriage as a holy thing; but paganism, as Dr. Edwyn Bevan has shown,[2] regarded sex relations not as our neo-pagans have imagined, but as something " almost wholly evil," and at best undignified and utilitarian. Christianity had invested the physical as well as the spiritual relations of man and wife with divine significance, as "a great mystery." The Gospel exalted human love, as well as human charity. It was the heretics, Marcion in the second century, Montanus after him, who brought in the idea of uncleanness from heathenism. And here we have a clear instance of the anti-Christian perversion running side by side with true Christianity. The Church, as Troeltsch said,[3] never ceased to regard marriage as belonging " to the divine order of creation," and yet it encouraged an illogical dualism which split sex ethic in two parts, and soon led to "a grotesque exaltation of sexual restraint, which led to a low estimate of woman as a danger and as evil." " These

[1] H. M. Gwatkin, *Early Church History*, I., p. 239.
[2] *Christianity*, pp. 53-58, 126.   [3] *Op. cit.*, I., pp. 131-132.

ideas," he says, "certainly arose out of the overstrained imagination of monasticism, and not out of the thought of Christianity."

Thus, although Jesus had been attacked because He was not ascetic and had even refused to let His disciples fast, the Church was overshadowed by life-hating ideas; and this asceticism destroyed, as Troeltsch also points out, the original charity.[1] It was, in fact, the sin obsession which caused the now powerful Church to accept slavery, war, cruelty, as a judgment and punishment from God. Man should give alms, since thus he can reduce the years of his future torment (hell—that is, *eternal* torment—he hoped was only for others); but why should he not be cruel, since God Himself was cruel? As a matter of fact cruelty was not condemned until modern times, and is absent from the codes of antiquity and from the elaborate medieval analyses of the Seven Deadly Sins.

Slavery affords a striking example of the dualism we are discussing.[2] Slaves (who were the great majority of the population) were treated in the Church at first as brothers and sisters; kindness to them was encouraged, and it was a good deed to set them free; under Stoic influence pagan emperors, like Hadrian, also improved their lot, and further mitigations were enacted by the Christian emperors. But the institution was not condemned; and its condonation really strengthened it, helping its survival right into the Middle Ages. It slowly weakened, however, under Christian influence, and changed into serfdom during the Medieval period. Serfdom in turn disappeared among the more advanced Christian communities west of Prussia; but soon afterwards, in 1442, the Portuguese began the trade in negro slaves; in

[1] Pp. 59, 136.
[2] Overbeck, *Studien zur Geschichte der alten Kirche*, gave a very clear analysis, since condensed in many histories.

1502 Spain brought negro slaves to Haiti; by the end of the century the English slave trade was at work, and in 1620 the English began to employ slaves in Virginia.

We may close this melancholy section by the thought that if the Gospel had been, like Islam, nearer to the level of the average man it would have been more readily accepted and practised with less distortion. And we may remind ourselves that at the best there are always two strains: what a Professor of Medieval History has said about his own subject is not untrue of other eras, before and since:

> " The Middle Ages were not dark, but were illumined by a light which enabled those who walked by it to attain heights of holiness rarely reached by men . . . not dark, or fruitless, or unprogressive, it is also true, on the other hand, that they were far removed from the ideal."

And then, after a brief summary of the evils that men then inflicted and endured, he claims that they were able " to purge themselves of their more enormous faults, and prepare the world for the higher and more widespread civilization of the modern day."[1]

THE MODERN WORLD

In the eighth century human sacrifices were still being offered to Thor at Upsala. In the eighteenth, certain things happened which had never come into the world before; and of this century we are the offspring.

Bewigged, complacent, a little enigmatic, the statesmen and prelates of that age look down upon us from the walls of many a historic room. We are seldom thrilled. They

[1] F. J. C. Hearnshaw, *Medieval Contributions to Modern Civilisation*, p. 16.

cannot plead their cause: but they give us things undreamt of before; and we live in a civilization of their enlightenment. During the eighteenth century the whole of our country was provided with hospitals; and mothers were sheltered in child-birth for the first time. The conscience of Englishmen discovered that slavery was wrong: no people and no age had thought of that before; but now the rest of Europe followed the lead of Clarkson and Wilberforce (in Upsala the slave trade ceased in 1813). Tolerance, not hitherto regarded as a virtue, was established in the more advanced nations, and one of the chief scandals of Christianity was thus removed. Federation, which is destined to be the key to the ancient problem of human relationships, between Churches as well as between nations, and is already effectual in the British Commonwealth and the United States, was launched upon the world before the close of the eighteenth century. Education was increasingly spread among the working classes as the century went on; and in our country Sunday schools for reading and writing as well as religion were everywhere established at its close.

In fact the modern civilized world came to its birth in the Age of Reason. And was it not a high achievement, after all the bitter past of conflict and superstition, to work consciously and deliberately for enlightenment and to inaugurate the liberty of that age? Yet it may well be that the historian of the future will record, as the achievement which above all changed the course of the world and made it inconceivably better, that outburst of missionary enthusiasm in its modern form, which in England began with the two great societies of the century's opening years, and spread again when the Church Missionary Society was founded at its close. If the abolition of slavery saved the modern world from the corruption and death which would have followed on the opening of Africa, the universalism of the missionary has come, perhaps only just in time, as distance is annihilated, to save that modern civilization from being overwhelmed. The vast work oversea has been a venture disinterested and heroic, successful already beyond men's dreams, and marvellously beneficent.

Progress indeed had been slow. There was, for instance, a not inconsiderable lag between the abolition of polygamy by the early Church and the recognition of women as intelligent citizens in the twentieth century. Hospitals, again (as distinct from hostels for pilgrims), had been rare before the eighteenth century. We hear of some in Constantinople under the Christian emperors; but London had only St. Bartholomew's (founded in 1123) and St. Thomas's (*circa* 1106) until 1710, and until that date twenty-three of the largest English counties seem to have had none: it was only in the eighteenth century that hospitals and the new maternity institutions and dispensaries were adequately supplied for London and the rest of the country. Slow indeed! Yet in earlier ages two thousand years would have been well spent over a slight improvement in the technique of chipping flints. And today the pace is further accelerated, as is strikingly shown by a comparison between the recent survey of London and that of Charles Booth thirty years before.

Huge arrears were still to be made up a century and a half ago. Although the poor were learning to read, the grammar schools had lost the vigour of Tudor times, university education was in a backwater, and dame schools were normal in the villages. Although the Methodists and Evangelicals had effected a moral reformation, drunkenness and vice were still abundant. Although Quaker efforts had improved the prisons since Howard had brought about the Act of 1778, the work of Elizabeth Fry had yet to be done. The industrial revolution at first in-

333

creased the oppression of working folk; freedom of speech and of combination were denied; festering slums abounded over Europe.

By 1836—a century ago—much had been done in this country: freedom had been secured, religious disabilities removed. In 1829 Peel had inaugurated the method of security which alone can make civilization possible for all, the police system—a new thing—for, though there had been from antiquity soldiers, officials, spies, jailers, executioners, and occasional watchmen, there had never been an organized system of protection.[1] In 1832 the Reform Act had taken the first step towards that political brotherhood, the recognition of equal human rights, which was completed by the admission of women to citizenship, almost everywhere outside the Latin countries by 1928.[2] In 1833 Wilberforce lived to see Parliament making all slavery unlawful under the British flag, and other countries soon followed the example; in 1833 another religious leader, Lord Shaftesbury, passed the chief of his Factory Acts, which were a new and all-important advance in civilization. In that remarkable year also the first government grant was made to education, the first step to national responsibility and control. Reform was now a general concern, though still it existed in Christian countries alone.

CHARITY

To describe what has been accomplished during the last hundred years in Christendom would require several volumes; but we can all call to mind enough to realize that this vast amelioration is due to a new spirit of com-

[1] Two attempts in France under Charles V. and Louis XIV. had quickly ended in tyranny. Basil Thompson, *Scotland Yard*.
[2] 1893 in New Zealand, followed by Australia and other countries; England, 1917 and 1928.

punction—the general desire to make the lives of others happier and better. This is Christian Charity, at work now on a vast scale. Popular education, the common cause today of the civilized world, is an attempt in some measure to love one's neighbour's children as one's own. Old-age pensions may sound prosaic and political; but it is an application of the Golden Rule which has rescued many millions from sorrow and dishonour. As far as history can tell us, the poor have lived in huts, hovels, tenements, and slums; and now, throughout Christendom we are systematically building for others decent homes such as we should desire for ourselves.

Yet, even in this brief epitome, we must not overlook the innumerable voluntary councils and societies in which men and women are seeking the good of others as if it were their own. It was Wilberforce and his friends who invented this way of doing good[1]; such leagues and committees are also the storage batteries of our modern social activity—our *Charity*, let us repeat it, since the way of Christian civilization can never be made plain so long as we misuse that central Christian term. No one can count all the activities. Just as I am trying to do so comes a reminder of one which I was forgetting—a lifeboat went out into the storm at Lowestoft and was sixteen hours on the waves before the men—just ordinary men—had rescued a crew of unknown foreigners. It is not only comfortable committees and well-supported institutions that serve Christ in the world!

Why is all this Charity, this social activity, so universally accepted as a matter of course today? Because it has sunk into the general conscience that we should do to others as we would be done by.

The first Christians had not aimed at removing social wrongs or abolishing poverty: that was beyond their

[1] G. M. Trevelyan, *History of England*, p. 599.

power, and probably beyond their imagination. But they did aim at showing Charity with all their might. They did realize with intense conviction that they were, as they said, "a new people"; and this gave them, as Harnack notes, a political and historical self-consciousness, impressive and complete.[1] They did perceive the possibility of a social order based on the infinite duty of men to one another. That idea was new, and it came from Jesus Christ. It is spreading today to non-Christian countries——from Christendom. The first battle of the Sermon on the Mount is won. Charity has become a part of "Leviathan" and is intimate in the very structure of society.

Thus have we discarded the old orthodox heresy of a separation between sacred and secular things. From Siberia to San Francisco men are agreed about one central principle of Jesus. He believed in men, loved them, saw their infinite value and the possibilities of each for good. Those possibilities could only be realized in a right environment, and He therefore taught the Kingdom or Commonwealth of God. Environment depends on structure—that is, on what we now call politics and economics, and have found to be so infinitely intricate: gradually, through medieval and modern times, Christendom has learnt the importance of this social structure for the goodness of the people, their salvation in eternal life.

TO-DAY

Christianity brought the idea of progress into the world.[2] In the words of Professor Bury, "Christian theology constructed a synthesis which represents the past as leading

[1] *Mission and Expansion*, I., p. 240.
[2] This is well worked out in the chapter on "Christianity and Progress" in the recent Hulsean lectures of H. G. Wood, *Christianity and the Nature of History.*

up to a definite and desirable goal in the future," because the history of the world is recognized as a unique phenomenon in time.[1] Instead of the Greek idea of recurring cycles (which is also the idea at the root of Asiatic pessimism)—time, like a machine, eternally repeating the same disheartening rhythm — Christianity brought an eschatology, a belief in Providence, and prayed continually that the Kingdom would come on earth. Its own history is a long story of self-transformation, quickened in modern times by the popularization of the Bible—for the Old Testament as well as the New is rooted in the idea of a time process. When men believe that God has a purpose in the world, they cannot but co-operate according to their lights: by organization they improve the structure of society, they develop the cultural tradition, they promote education; knowledge accumulates with each generation; psychology, now becoming scientific, affords further ways of extending the power of the Spirit.

In this year of grace we must therefore expect to find ourselves as usual in the midst of the Process. Freedom and the sense of equality in God's sight are due to the Christian valuation of personality, the Christian conviction of brotherhood; they are attacked today, on avowedly pagan grounds, in the reactions of war-worn Europe, but they have the stronger part of the world behind them. Even the dictators, discarding the basic principles of inviolability of the person and equality before the law—in their fumbling for short cuts—do claim to represent the will of the people whom they have silenced, and repudiate the despotism of hereditary right; even their crimes have been committed for ideals which we can recognize, in part or in some forms, as derived from Christianity. Since the word Charity has been reduced in meaning, we must not be surprised if some call their principles humanism,

[1] *The Idea of Progress*, p. 22.

337

or communism, and some cannot see beyond their own frontiers.

We began by saying that when an element of civilization is found only in Christian countries it must in some way be due to Christianity, and we suggested science as a less obvious instance of this. All our Christian civilization in process of achievement can be summed up under three heads: (1) Individualism, the infinite value of the human soul, the importance of personal liberty and personal wholeness or salvation; (2) Socialism, in the sense of applied Charity, or brotherhood in action; (3) Universalism, or the solidarity of the human race, which is more difficult to bring about, and includes the other two as it extends.

Universalism was made practicable by the discovery of Federation, for lack of which Great Britain and the American Colonies had failed to live in unity; and this principle of autonomy with unity would have prevented the disruption of the Christian Church, had it been earlier discovered—Catholicism without it is a mere will-o'-the-wisp. Federation! again a dull, political-sounding word, but it means the discovery at last of the way to universal Charity. The principle of universalism has been in the world since Christ: by the end of the eighteenth century a way was discovered of carrying it out.

This universalism, the freedom and value of each human soul, brotherhood within each group or nation, and complete active Charity between all nations, we owe, as Bergson has pointed out, to Christianity: philosophers in Greece, Chinese sages, came within a step of it—" mais le pas ne fut pas franchi." It may be said, he continues, " that progress was slow; eighteen centuries elapsed, in fact, before the rights of man were proclaimed by the Puritans of America, to be soon followed by the men of the French Revolution. None the less, it began with the preaching of the Gospel." Not as a maxim, but a message of love.[1]

A universal society will be upon us when each person everywhere is free to lead the good life in a world-community of equal men and women. That may be far off; but we are in the Process. Much has been done, though there are many evils—oppression and war; the exploitation of men and women; brutality to other races; the misuse of private ownership; the unjust distribution of goods, education and leisure. And today men are full of fear for the horrors that have already befallen us and the confusion that reigns in their minds. Advances that had been gained, and religious sanctions long established, have been set back at the bidding of violent and half-educated men; and when democracy is abolished the naked truth emerges that in the modern state its place must be taken by censorship, the silencing of a free press and of free speech, lies, espionage, political prisons, camps and settlements, terror, torture, and murder.

There is much to affright; but we need not be afraid. If Christianity has been imperfectly realized, the alternatives are shown to be so frightful that a religious revival is certain. The Churches are themselves moving towards federation, perhaps just in time; and if the recent failures have not taught us our lesson, we shall be blind indeed. Too slowly had we shed the impurities of traditional religion; and now the convulsion of a world is warning us to be faithful to the message of Christ, to repent indeed and be saved.

The danger of war need give us no cause for despair. Touched by a new conviction, and embarked in a new era, we are attacking what a hundred years ago no one, except the Society of Friends, had troubled to condemn. During that period, private war, the duel, has been

[1] *Les Deux Sources de la Morale et de la Religion*, pp. 76-78.

abolished, at least in the English-speaking world, and the new idea has arisen that war is not a thing to be accepted complacently as a matter of course—new indeed the idea since Constantine, before whose partial conversion to Christianity the fact that Christ condemned war was as consistently maintained by the Church fathers as the fact that He condemned lust.

The clouds are heavy. If they broke, there might well be an end of that civilization which is already at heart Christian. But there is no cause for fear or despair. We can accept the estimate of one who represents Geneva, Oxford, and Spain—Professor Salvador de Madariaga—when he says: "The obvious progress achieved in the last ten years by the forces working towards the World Common-wealth, in spite of terribly unfavourable circumstances, proves that such forces are in harmony with the historical spirit of our times."[1]

A few prophets had dreamt of a world which might one day be organized for peace and for some universal Com-monwealth of Man; but the world would not follow them, and nothing was ever practicable. And now sixty nations are banded together in a great organization, not only to avert war but to better the general lot of man-kind, and to establish a working comity of the nations. Much has been already done, while at the same time the foundations have been laid for more arduous accomplish-ment; and we should be faithless indeed if we failed; for we should be taking our hands from the plough at the very moment when the greater part of the world is seriously organizing itself to carry out just those principles of Christ which have seemed the most impracticable.

[1] *The Times*, January 15, 1936.